I0812775

IMAGES
of America

SHELBY COUNTY

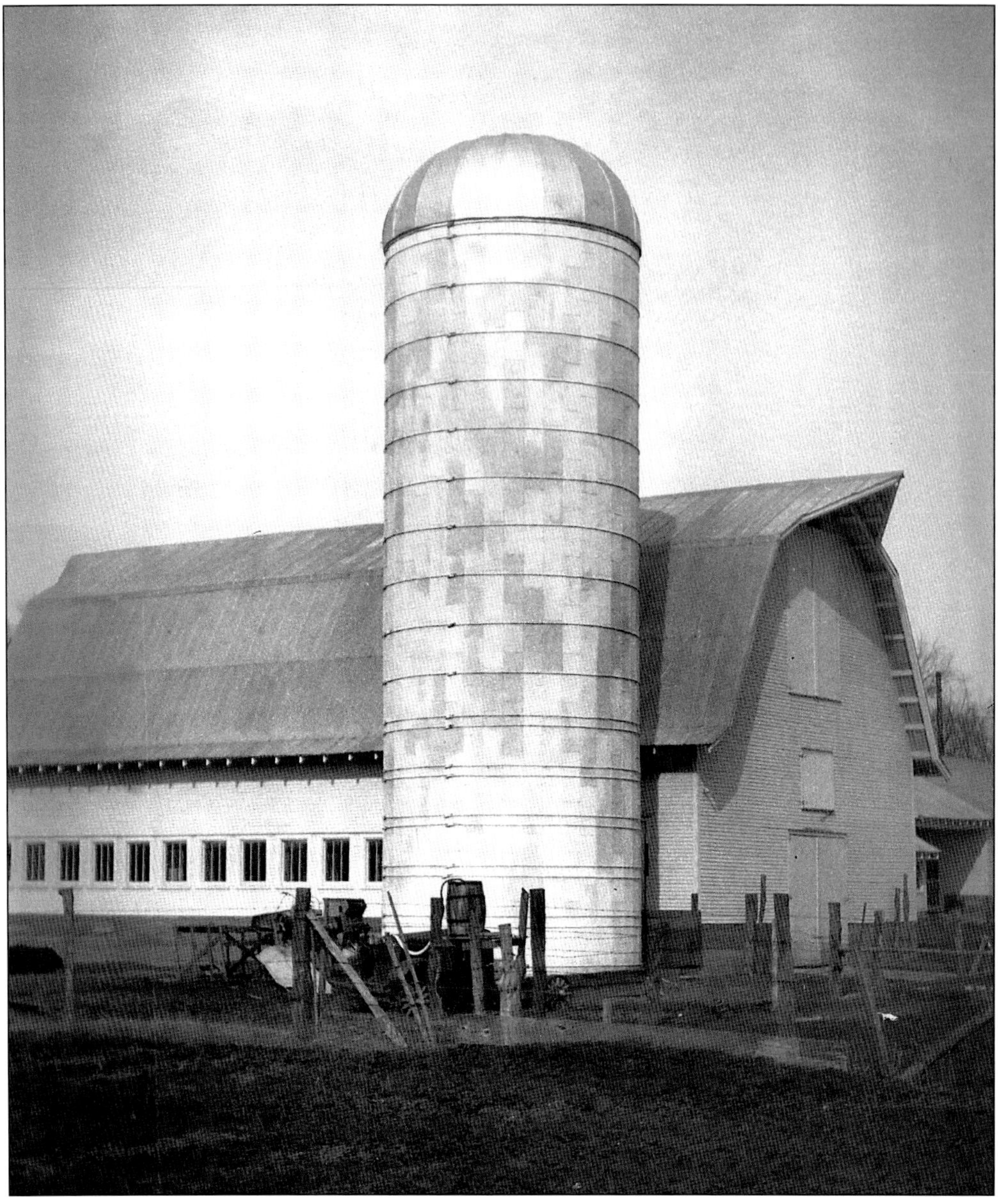

Shelby County was dotted with small farms, many dating back to the early 1800s when farmers came over the Cumberland Mountains from North Carolina and Virginia. During the 1920s, dairies grew in number, and white grain silos began to appear. On many farmsteads, all that is left today is the lone silo, a remnant of the county's agricultural past.

On the Cover:
Nina Cole, shown here around 1915, poses in front of a rural church. One of the first churches organized in Shelby County was the Big Creek Baptist Church near Millington. Established in 1812 with 24 members, the church is still active and located near the same site as the original meeting place. The oldest church building in Shelby County is Calvary Episcopal, built in 1838 and located at the corner of Adams and Second Avenue. The sanctuary is also the oldest public building in Memphis.

IMAGES
of America

SHELBY COUNTY

Robert W. Dye

ARCADIA
PUBLISHING

ISBN 978-0-7385-4192-1

Published by Arcadia Publishing
Charleston, South Carolina

Printed in the United States of America

Library of Congress Catalog Card Number: 2005930509

For all general information contact Arcadia Publishing at:
Telephone 843-853-2070
Fax 843-853-0044
E-mail sales@arcadiapublishing.com
For customer service and orders:
Toll-Free 1-888-313-2665

Visit us on the Internet at www.arcadiapublishing.com

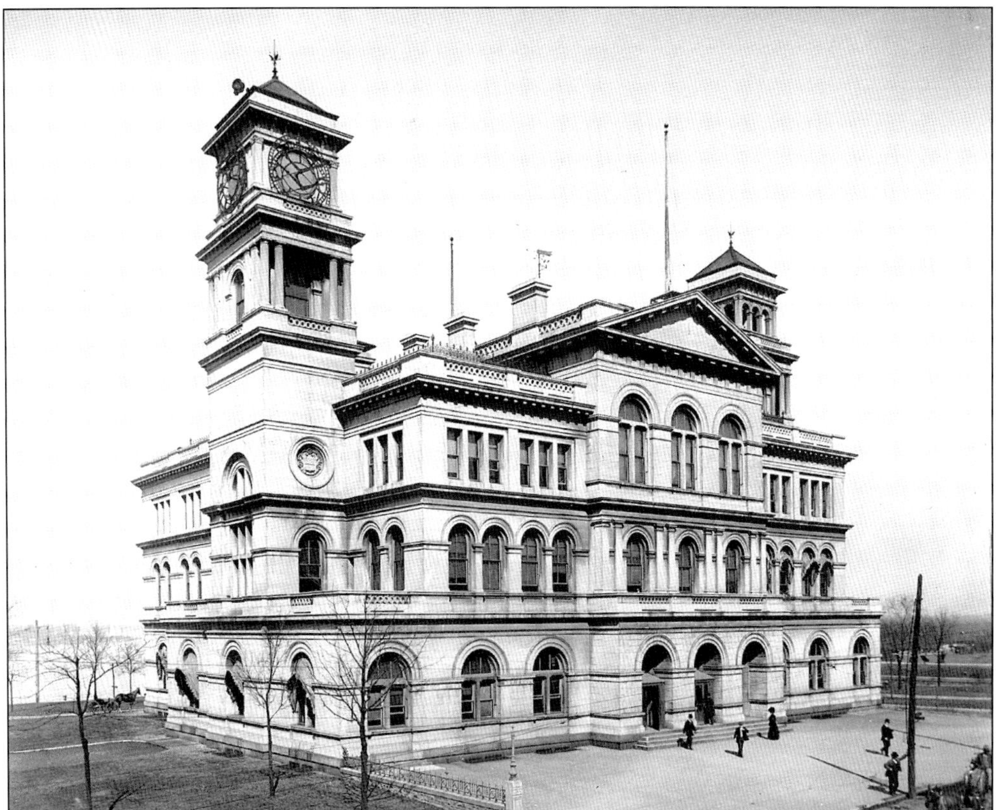

Built in 1876 by architect James G. Hill, the Custom House with its two large towers sat high upon the bluff, easily visible to riverboats on the Mississippi. The building has seen additions in 1903 and 1923. The 1923 addition included paired columns on the east front side based on those of the Louvre in Paris.

Contents

ACKNOWLEDGMENTS

The photographs included in this work come from various collections, each one a unique glimpse into the history of Shelby County. The Mississippi Valley Collection at the University of Memphis is one of the best photographic archives in the city. I'd like to thank Ed Frank and his staff for their tremendous help. The Shelby County Archives is a most valuable source for information, and their help was greatly appreciated. Photographs were also obtained from the Memphis Room of the Memphis and Shelby County Public Library. Images were also generously loaned from the following individuals and businesses: Hessen Inc., Donne Walden, MemphisArchives.com, Mrs. Dorothy Ann Wilson, Clarene Pinkston Russell, *Millington Star*, Faye Osteen, Margaret Schwam, Dr. Nicholas Gotten, Bartlett Historical Society, Andrew Pouncey, Paul Madison Wilson archives, Pat Veach, Elmwood Cemetery, Detroit Publishing Company, Jo Ann Jones, Robert William Dye, U.S. Army Corps of Engineers, and the Library of Congress.

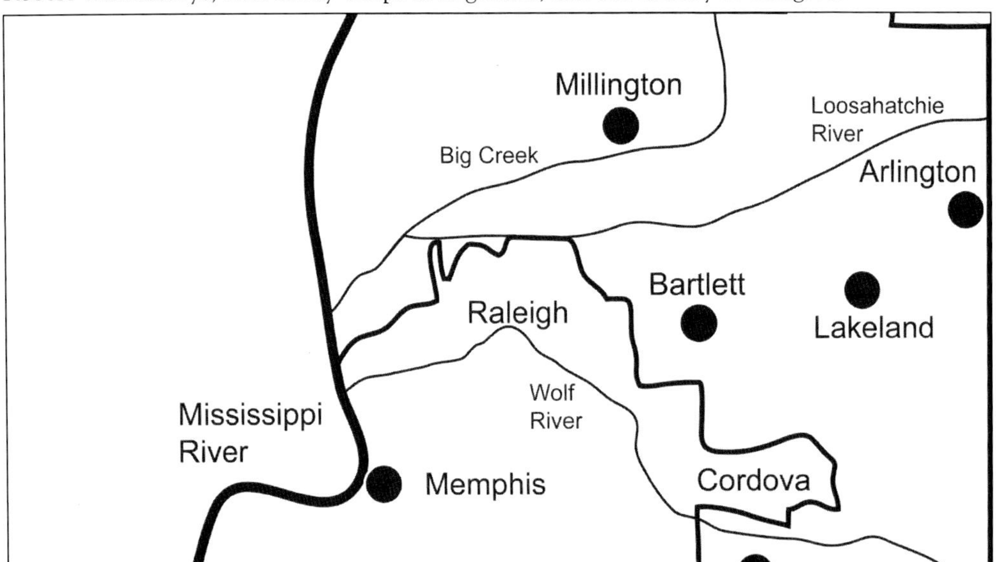

Shelby County is located in the southwest corner of Tennessee and occupies 755 square miles. Established in 1819, the county is the state's largest by size and population. Bordered on the west by the Mississippi River, Shelby County is the 44th largest in the nation with a population over 900,000.

INTRODUCTION

Shelby County was established in 1818 when Andrew Jackson and Isaac Shelby purchased what is today West Tennessee from the Chickasaw Indians for $300,000. Explorers had long known about the area. Marquette and Joliet had viewed the bluffs as they traveled down the Mississippi River in the mid-1600s. Foreign nations had set up forts on the bluff to extend their rights to new land. Settlers first reached the interior of Shelby County in the early 1800s, probably around Big Creek in northern Shelby County. A surveyor named John Ralston noted a family named McDaniel living near Big Creek in 1808. Clem McDaniel had settled there with his family a few years earlier. John Ralston eventually married McDaniel's daughter in 1822. The Big Creek Baptist Church was formed in 1812, and a post office was established in 1828. The population of Shelby County was under 500 in 1820 but grew to over 48,000 by 1860. The earliest communities grew up along rivers, which were major transportation routes before the advent of the railroads. Raleigh and Nashoba Plantation were developed along the Wolf River in the early 1800s. As railroads extended their lines out of Memphis, towns such as Bartlett, Germantown, and Collierville began to grow. Mind you, suburban growth in 1860 was going from 300 to over 600 citizens in a few years. Each community had its ups and downs. Raleigh's heyday was in the early to mid-1800s when it was the county seat. Bartlett saw tremendous growth when the circuit courts were placed there in 1875. When the courts moved back to Memphis in 1885, the city lost its charter and was not re-chartered until 1905. Millington saw tremendous growth in the 1940s with the addition of the Naval Air Station to the area. Today many Memphis residents are moving to Germantown, Collierville, and Bartlett because of the excellent school systems and the family-friendly neighborhoods. These suburban communities are beginning to deal with issues such as land use planning, environmental impact studies, historic preservation districts, and smart growth initiatives to help maintain the feel of a small town within a growing city. The photographs presented here show these cities before the Walmarts moved in, before a Walgreens was on every corner, and yes, even before Starbucks. If you needed the local news, you visited the post office or barber shop or attended a PTA meeting. There are many who remember the cotton gins, the day the first traffic light was installed, and walking to school. This book is dedicated to those who remember the days gone by and work to preserve and document for future generations the lives and lifestyles of the community they call home.

One

Memphis

The city of Memphis was officially chartered in 1819, but that is not to say there was not activity here before then. A series of Indian mounds lined the bluff south of present-day downtown Memphis. Created by the Mississippian Indians, the mounds were abandoned in the 16th century and are today known as Chucalissa and Desoto Park. Marquette and Joliet traveled down the Mississippi River in the 1660s and noted the Memphis bluffs in their journals. The Spanish built a fort in 1795 called Fort San Fernando de las Barrancas. This was situated north of downtown Memphis in what is now called the Pinch District. John Rice purchased a 5,000-acre land grant covering much of what is today downtown Memphis. Unfortunately, he never saw his new land as he was killed by Native Americans in 1791. His brother inherited the land and sold it to John Overton for $500 in 1794. Also investing with Overton were Andrew Jackson and James Winchester. The area was surveyed by William Lawrence, and a town was laid out in 1819, with Marcus Winchester, son of James Winchester, acting as sales agent. Benjamin Foy, a local trader who had been on the bluff for many years, was given the first deed.

The population of Memphis in 1820 was 354, and in 1826, the city of Memphis was incorporated with Marcus Winchester as first mayor. Thirty-six acres of land running parallel to the Mississippi River were set aside for a public promenade. This space was meant by the original proprietors to be a park for strolling and leisure. The courts decided in the mid-1800s that the land could be used for the betterment of Memphis. In 1877, the site for the Custom House was laid out, and in 1888, a site was dedicated for the Cossitt Library. Rail lines were allowed to pass through the space, adding train stations and switching yards. In time, Riverside Drive, a fire house, and several parking garages would be added, dramatically decreasing the size of the promenade. Today the public spaces include Confederate Park, Jefferson Davis Park, and the Cobblestone Landing.

Memphis was slow to grow, and by 1827, it was decided that Raleigh was a better location for the county courts. It was not until 1866 that the courts moved back to Memphis and not until 1910 that a permanent courthouse was built at Washington and Second Streets. Robertson Topp, who built the Gayoso Hotel in the 1840s, developed much of South Memphis. This area south of Union Avenue was eventually incorporated into Memphis in 1849. Topp was also instrumental in laying out the Memphis and Charleston Railroad into Memphis.

The Civil War had little impact on the city as the entire battle was seen by many citizens on their lunch hour from the bluffs. The city quickly fell into Union hands and was held throughout the war. Memphis continued to grow until the 1870s when the yellow fever epidemic reached its peak. In 1878, more than 5,100 lives were lost to yellow fever, with the city's population cut in half. Many who fled to St. Louis and Chicago never returned. Land speculators moved in, purchasing buildings and houses for next to nothing. The city slowly emerged from the disaster with the help of cotton and commerce. The Cotton Exchange grew in prominence, and Memphis became the largest inland cotton market in the world. Riverboats, sometimes as many as 50 a day, docked in Memphis, carrying cotton and other products around the world. Some 100 years later, another commercial carrier, FedEx, would gain fame for the same reason. The 1920s were a great boom for Memphis, with hotels, buildings, and theaters being constructed. Beale Street, once a residential area of the city's finest homes, became the great melting pot of the city. Italian saloon owners, Chinese restaurant owners, and African American businessmen all worked and lived in the Beale Street area. Clubs such as the Panama, King's Palace, and Pee Wee's Saloon became famous. Musicians played on the streets and in the clubs, cultivating a sound that would become known around the world as the blues. Years later, Memphis would be the center for a revolution in music. Elvis Presley would take his early influences in gospel, blues, and country music and create a new sound: rock-and-roll. Memphis was, for a number of years, the center of the music world with recording studios such as Sun, Stax, and American producing some of the country's best music. Memphis has seen many challenges through its almost 200-year existence. From the days of the earliest settlers through yellow fever and the Depression, Memphis has maintained its importance, not only as a river town but as a distribution center to the world.

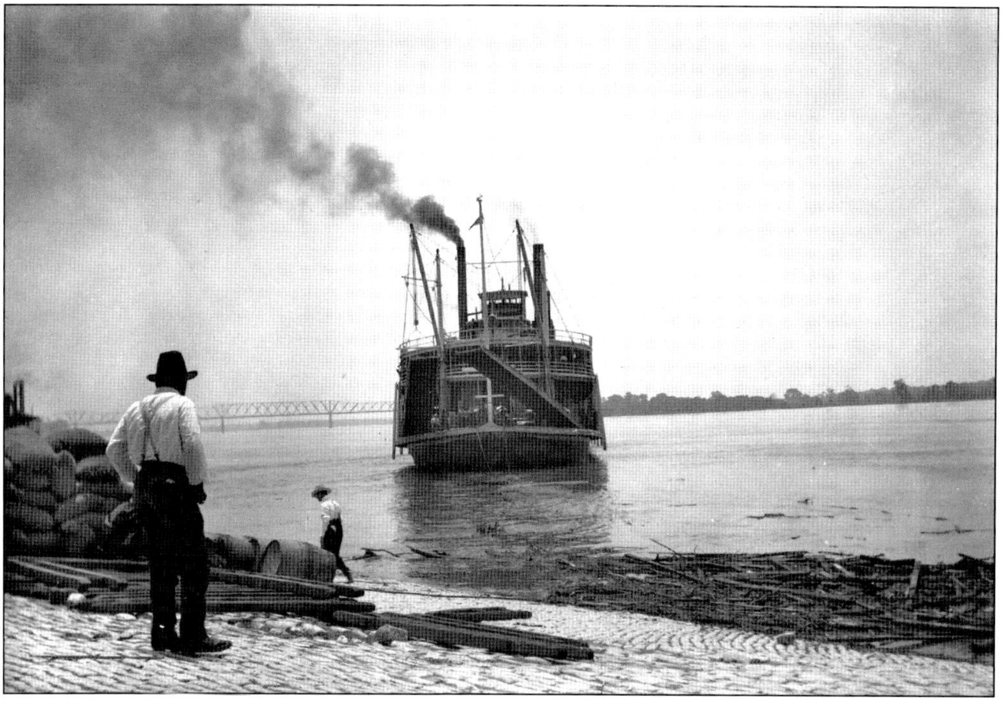

Before the railroads arrived in Memphis, the city was dependent on the Mississippi River for its commerce. If it was brought in or shipped out, it went through the Cobblestone Landing.

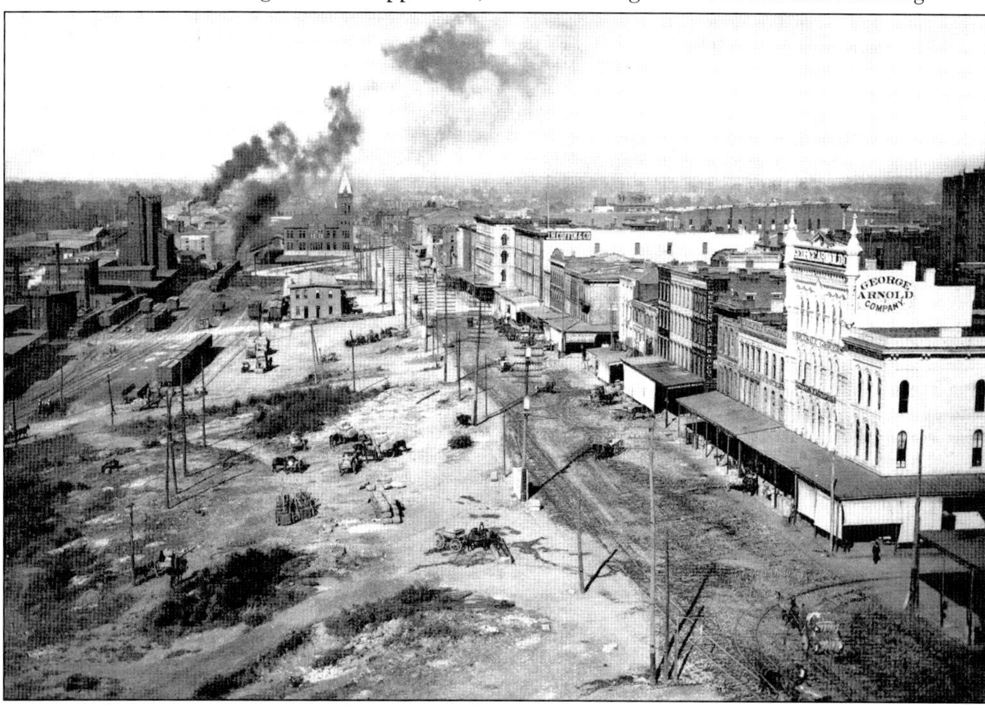

Front Street, shown here in 1888, was one of the busiest streets in Memphis. Hardware stores, cotton factories, hotels, and restaurants lined the first major street as visitors arrived from the riverfront. Poplar Street Train Station can be seen in the distance.

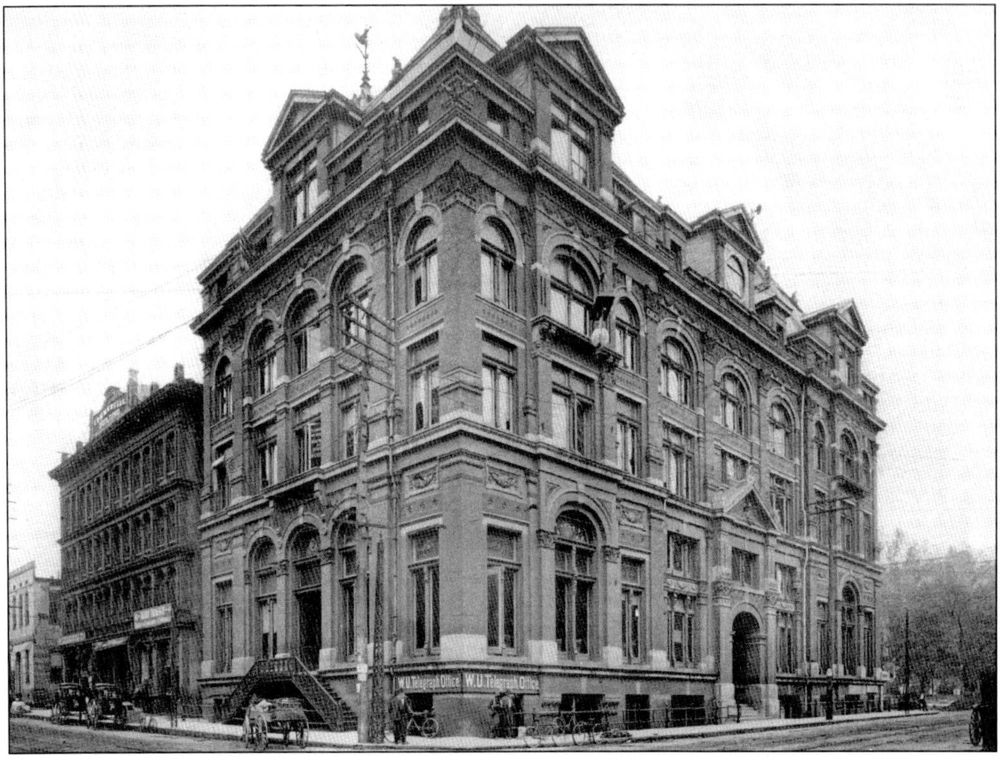

The Memphis Cotton Exchange, located at the corner of Second Street and Madison Avenue, was built in 1885 and stood until it was replaced in 1910 by the exchange building at the same location. In 1925, the exchange was moved to Front Street and Union Avenue.

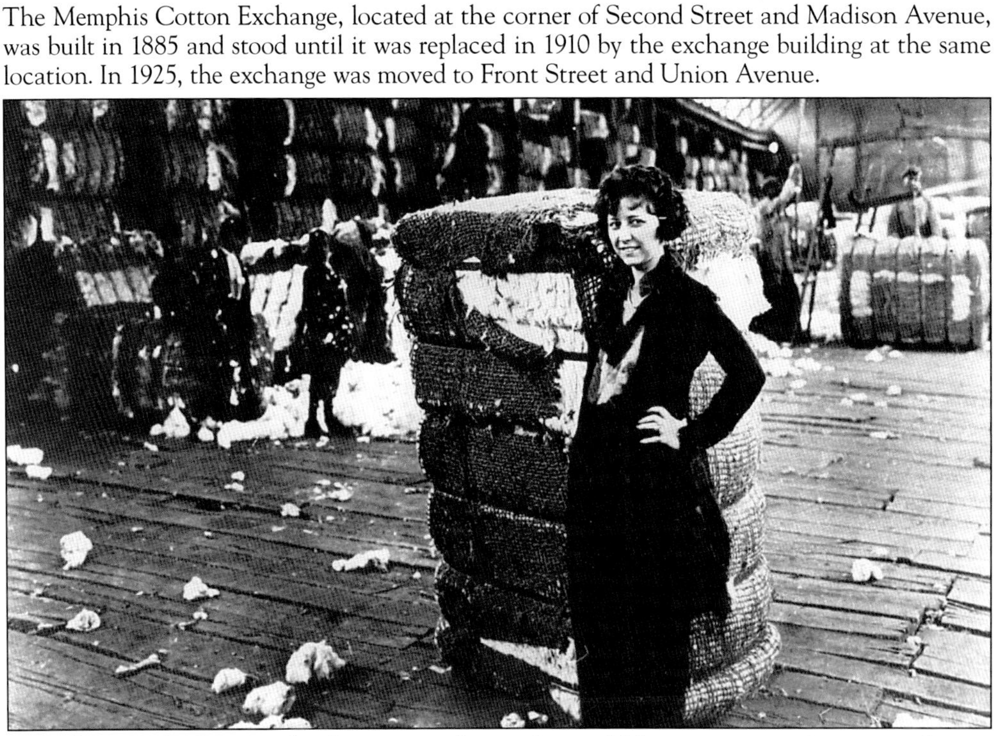
Memphis was the largest inland cotton market in the world for many years. A young girl poses in one of the many cotton warehouses in the South Main district of Memphis.

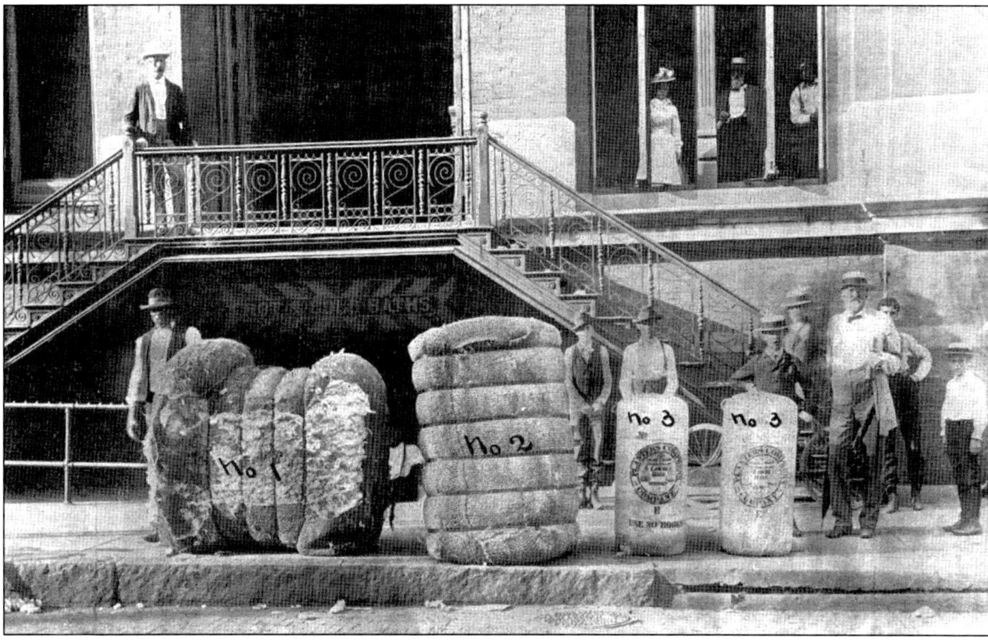

Growers stand in front of the original Cotton Exchange on Second Street, showing the different types of cotton bales being produced at the turn of the century. The exchange moved to its present location at Front and Union Avenue in 1925.

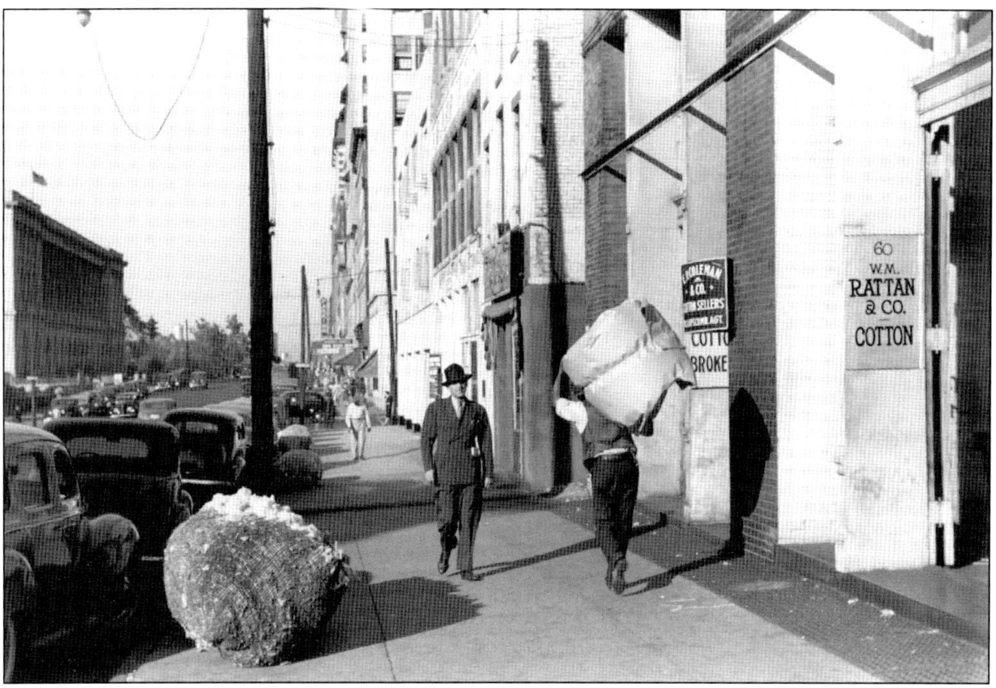

Front Street, seen here in 1937, was home to most cotton brokers and classing offices. Cotton was graded for quality and priced accordingly. It was not uncommon to see "cotton snakes," long strands of loose cotton, rolling down Front Street.

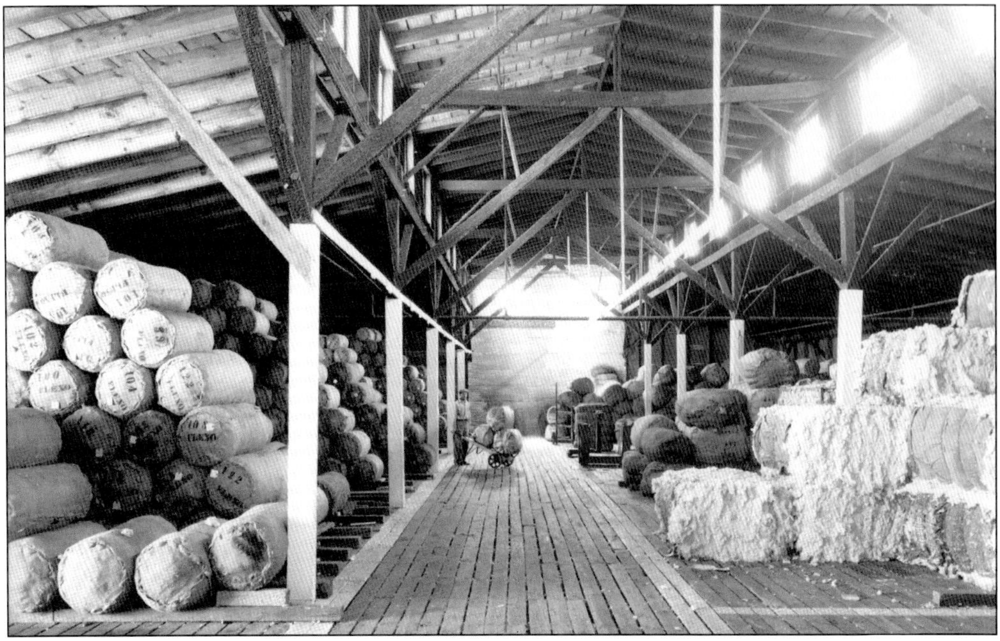

Large warehouses were built throughout Memphis to store cotton bales. Many such warehouses were built near the train stations on Calhoun Street, south of downtown.

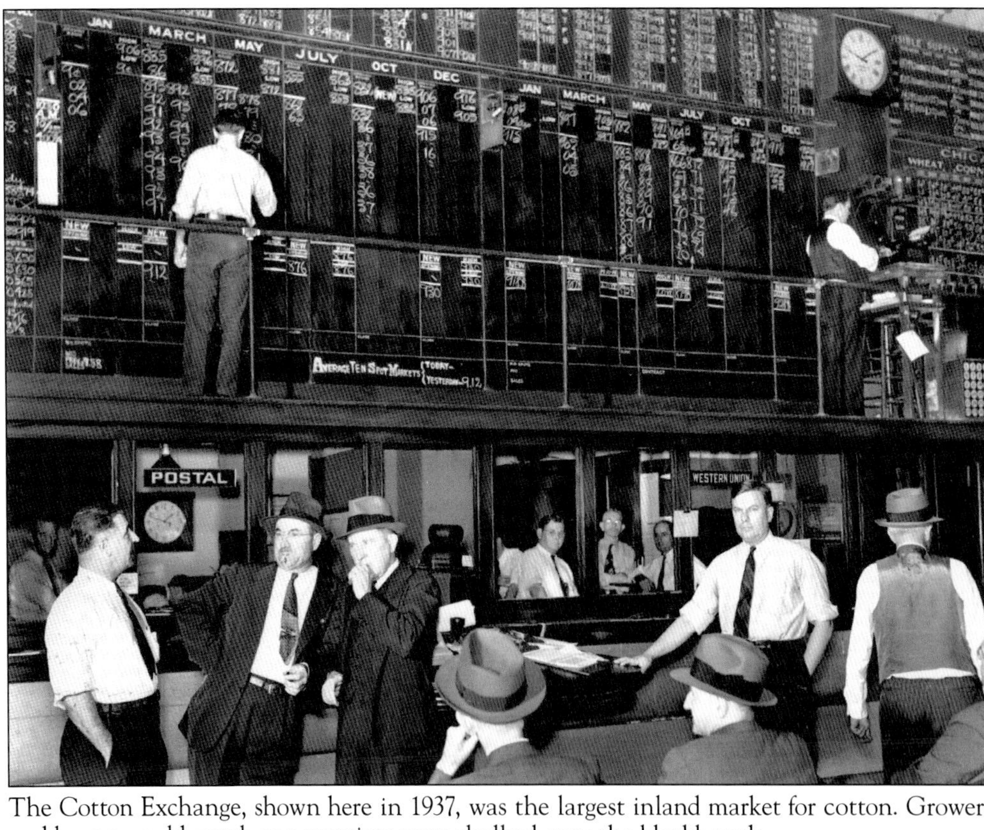

The Cotton Exchange, shown here in 1937, was the largest inland market for cotton. Growers and buyers would watch as new prices were chalked onto the blackboards.

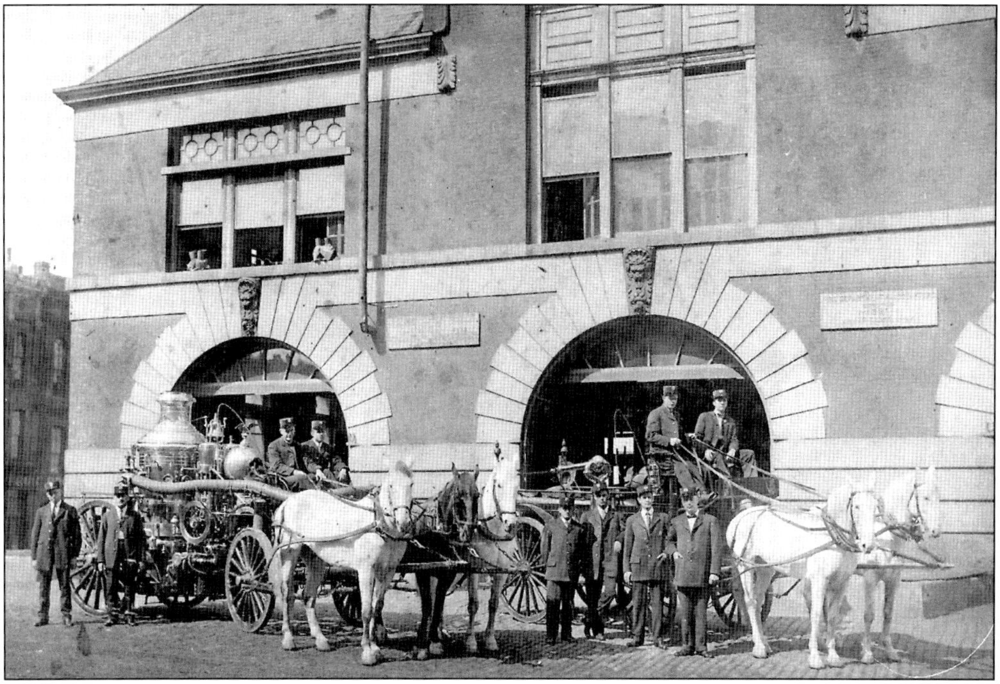

The Memphis Fire Department shows off new equipment at its headquarters located on Front Street in 1900.

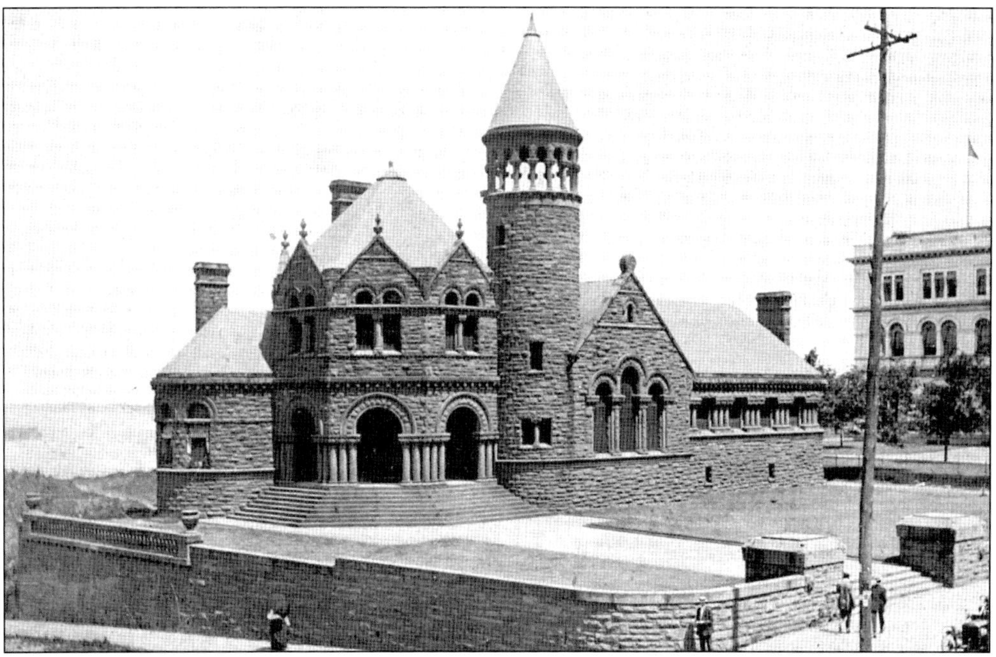

F. H. Cossitt arrived in Memphis in 1843 and began working as a wholesale dry goods merchant. He developed many of the properties on Main and Front Streets, and in 1861, he moved to New York and became a successful businessman. Upon his death, his daughters provided the money to set up the first public library in Memphis. The Cossitt Library, although much altered through the years, is situated on the corner of Front and Monroe Streets.

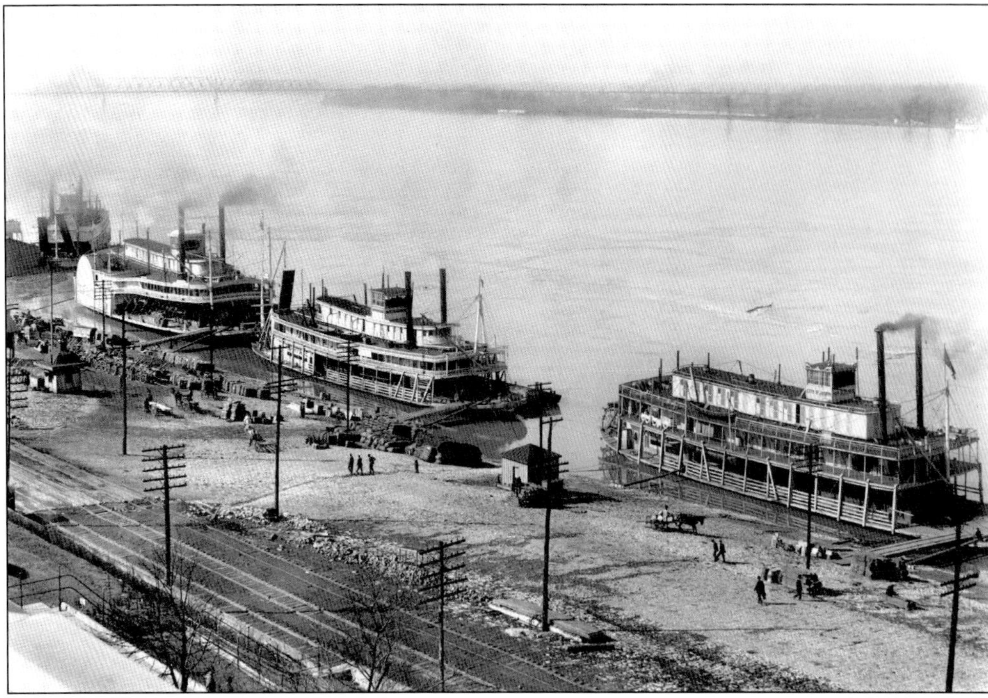

The laying of the Cobblestone Landing began in the 1850s and continued until the late 1880s. The landing was a hub of activity with cotton being loaded on riverboats on their way to the factories in England and the American Northeast.

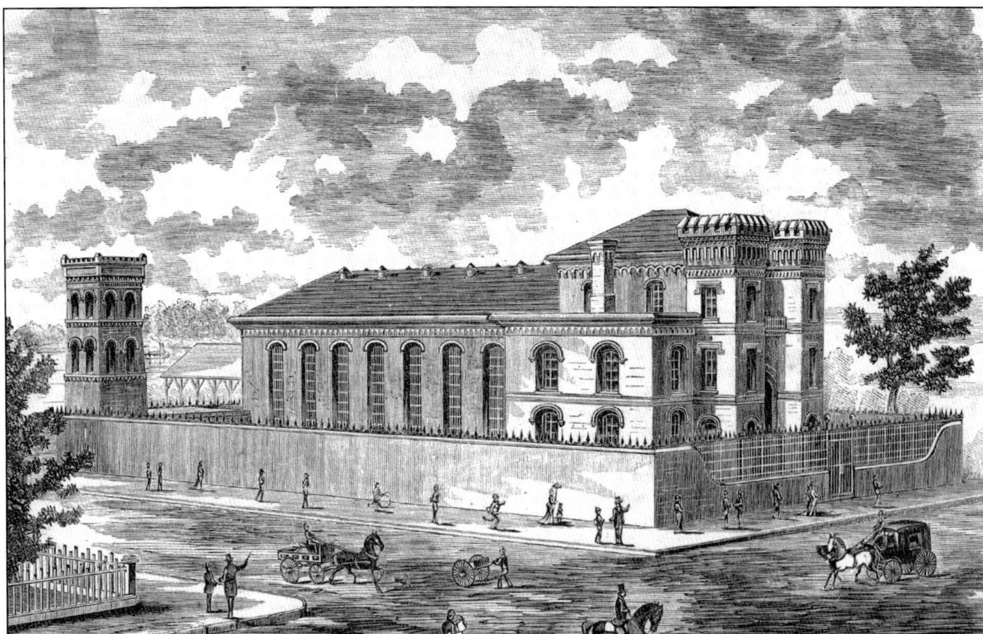

The Memphis Jail, designed by James B. Cook, was located at Front and Auction Streets. The walls were hollow and filled with sand to keep prisoners from digging out. Today the ornamental iron gates are all that is left of the building.

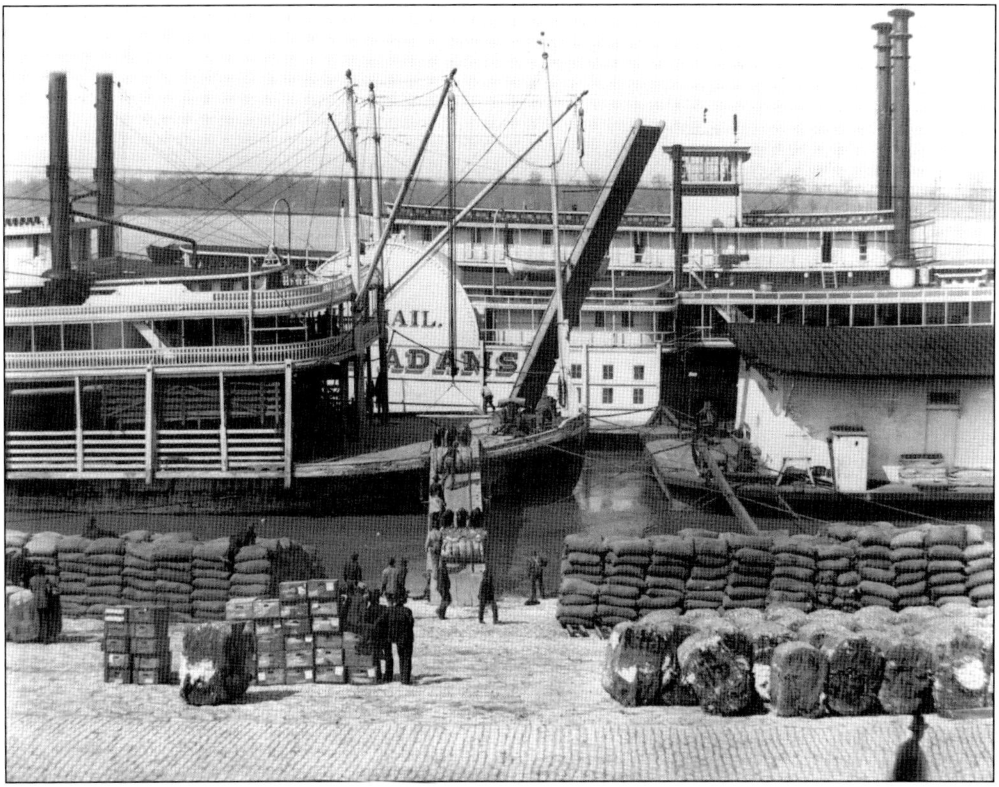

Before railroads, riverboats delivered everything from food and liquor to pianos and wagons. Shown here in 1906, the Memphis riverfront would see as many as 30 boats a day.

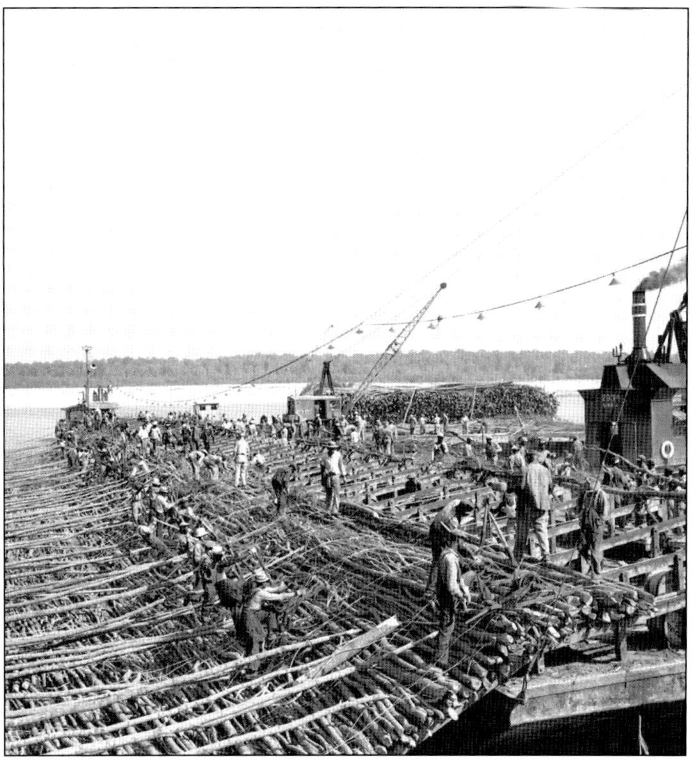

Ever since Shelby County was founded, there has been a constant struggle to control the Mississippi River. Sand bars blocked entry into the harbor, floods changed the course of the river, and erosion of the levee was always a problem. Willow mats were laid out in front of the Memphis Harbor by the corps of engineers to control erosion. These were replaced with concrete mats in the 1940s.

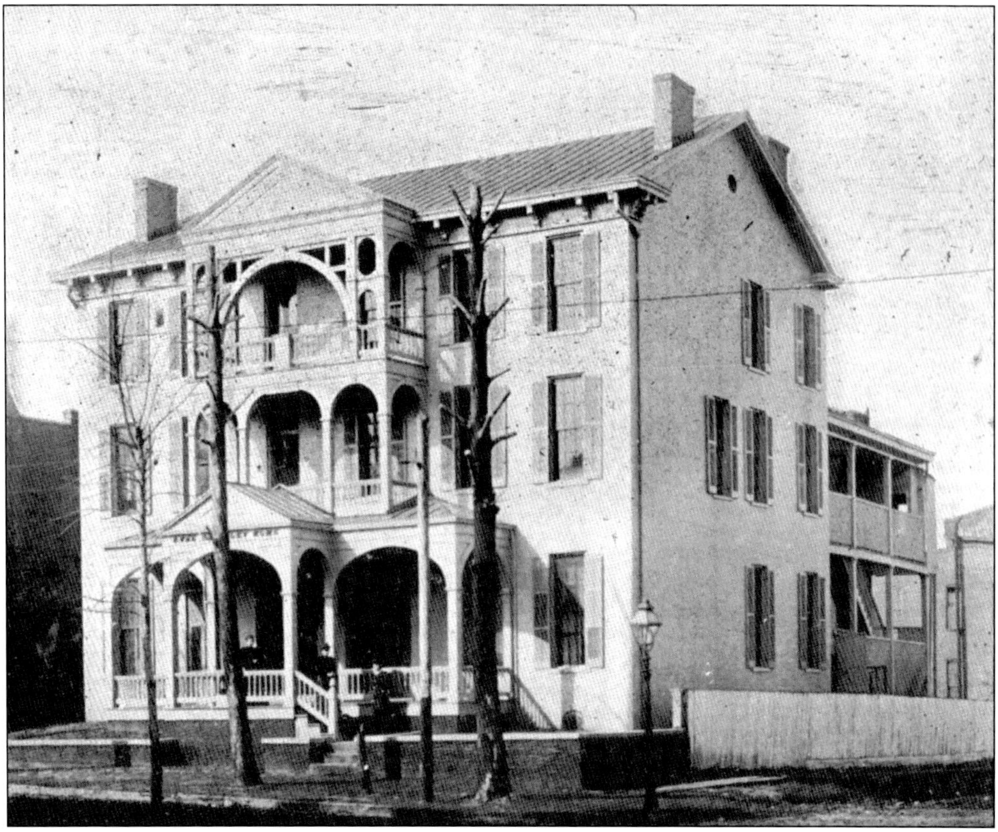

The Anne Brinkley home for young women, located at 291 South Second Street, was established by Hugh Brinkley and named for his mother. Anne Brinkley was the daughter of Judge John Overton, one of the original founders of Memphis. The seven-floor home was run by the Young Women's Christian Association.

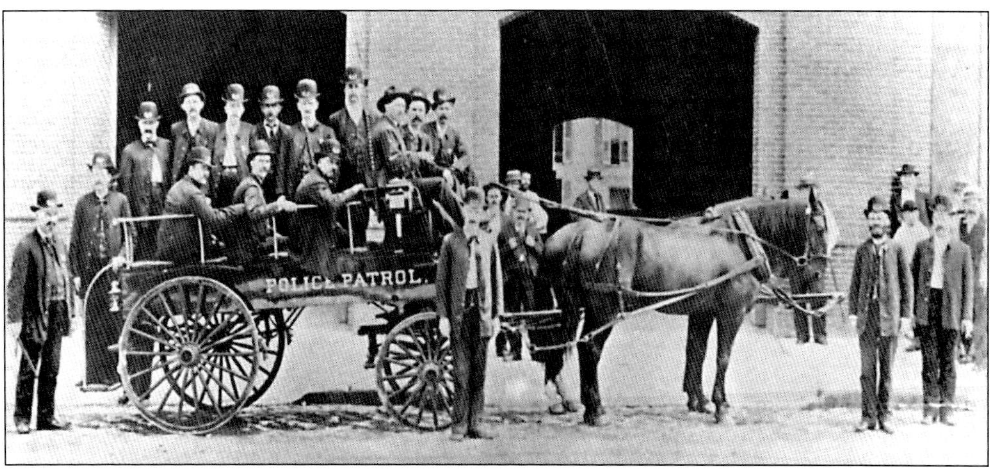

The police department shows off its new "Black Maria," used to transport criminals in 1905.

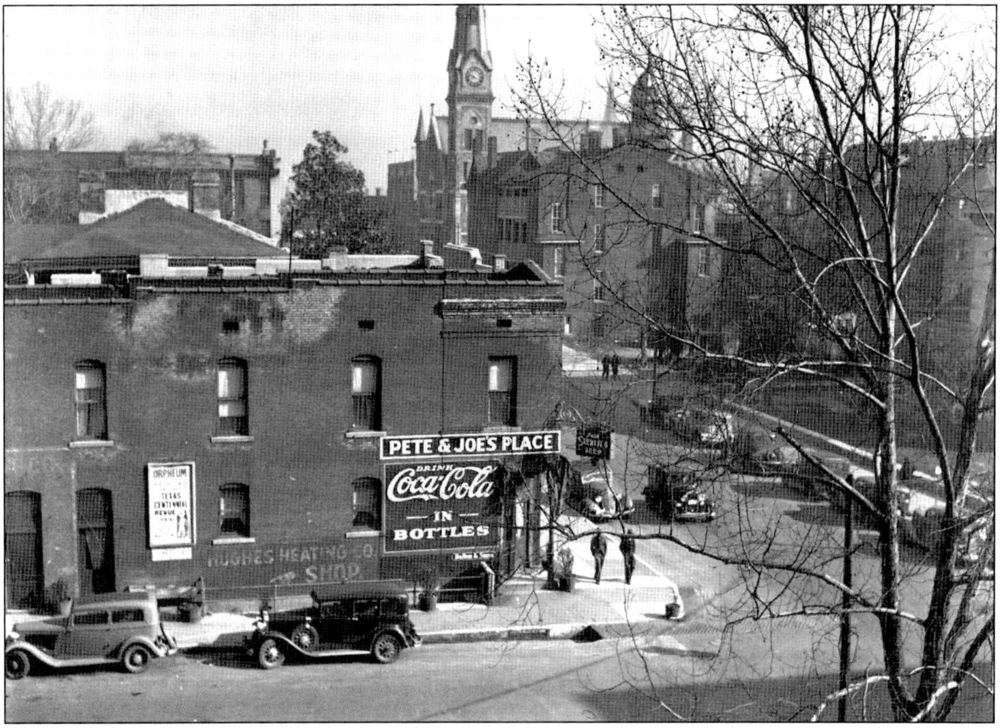

Situated next door to the Memphis Police Station on Second Street, Pete and Joe's Place was one of the most popular restaurants in Memphis during the 1920s and 1930s. One reason for its popularity was that frequent guests were served a small teacup filled with wine, an illegal beverage during Prohibition.

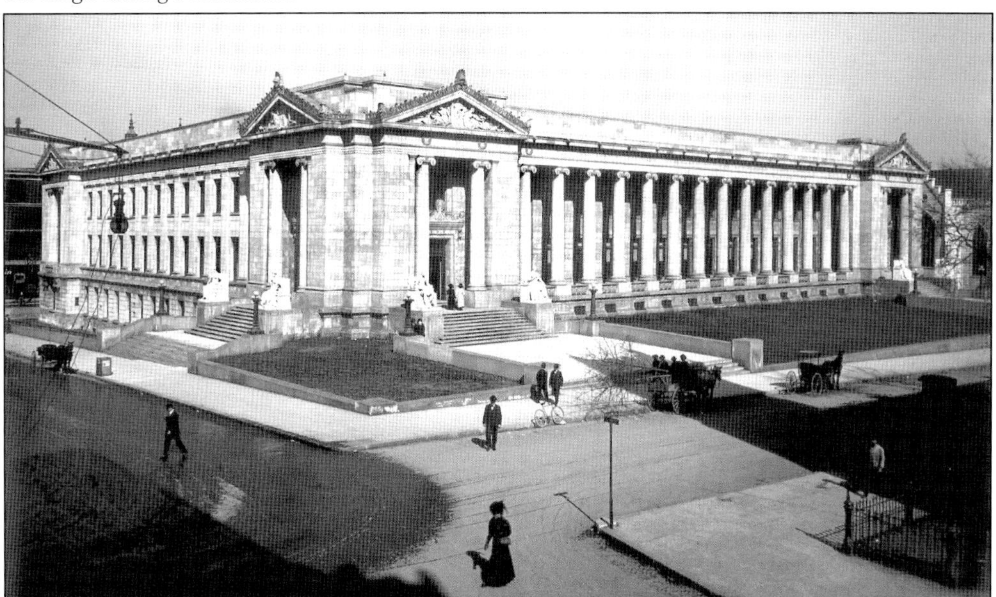

The Shelby County Courthouse was constructed in 1909 at the corner of Third Street and Adams Avenue. Made of blue Bedford limestone, this impressive building covers an entire city block. The first courthouse was a small log cabin located on Court Square.

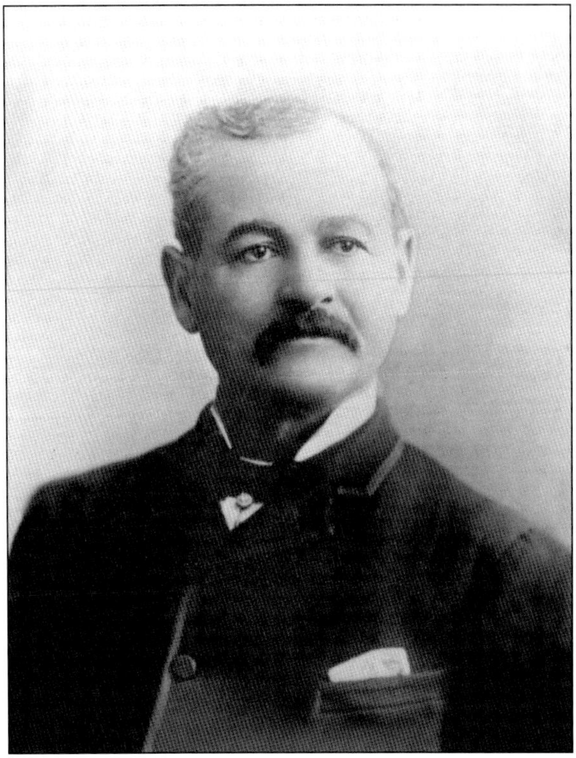

Robert Church was born in 1839 and came to Memphis in 1851 from Holly Springs, Mississippi. He owned several saloons, a 135-acre subdivision, a cab company, and more than 300 rental properties in Memphis. He built a 2,000-seat auditorium on Beale Street, which was visited by Theodore Roosevelt in 1902. He founded the Solvent Savings Bank in 1906 and bought the first bond to help Memphis recover after the yellow fever epidemic of 1878.

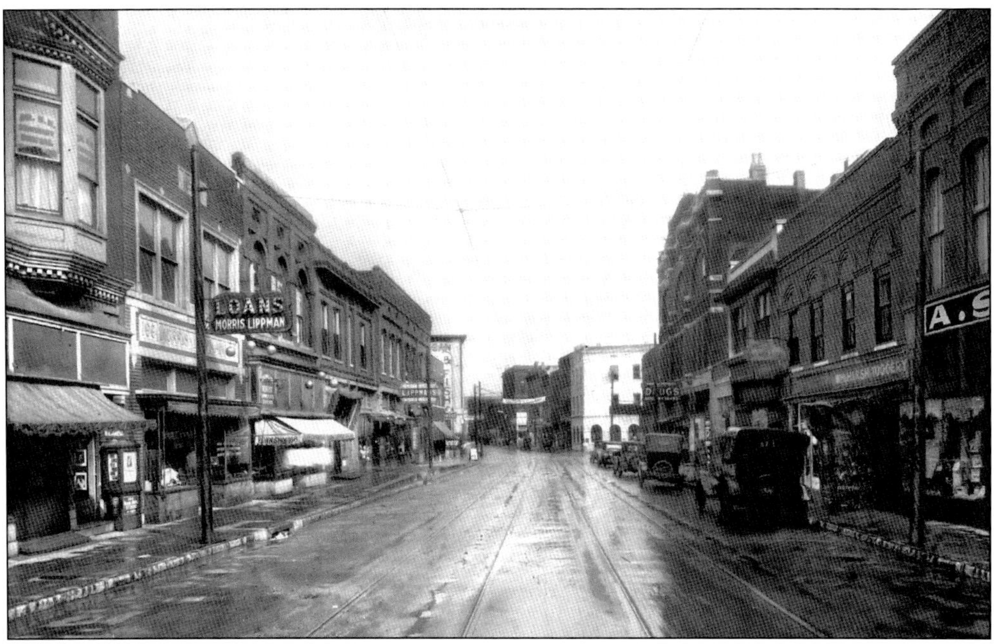

Known as the "Birthplace of the Blues," Beale Street has a long history, not only of music, but also of civil rights, entrepreneurship, and preservation. Martin Luther King marched down Beale during the sanitation workers' strike of 1967. Robert Church built the Beale Street Auditorium and helped Memphis financially after the yellow fever epidemic of the late 1800s. Preservationists stepped in to help save parts of Beale Street during the urban renewal of the 1970s.

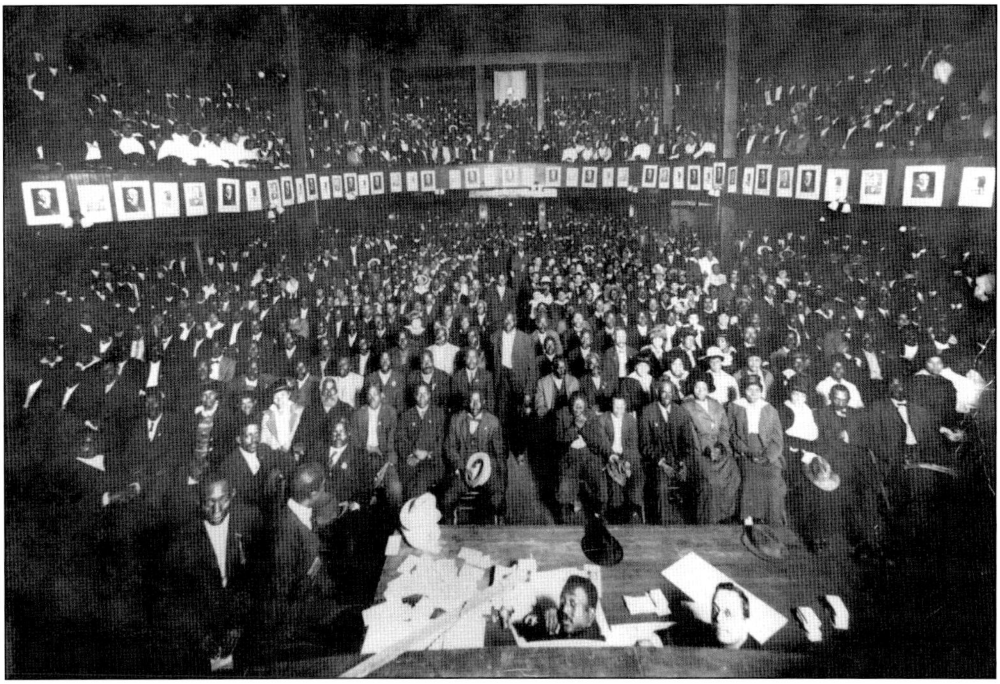

Built by Robert Church Sr. as an auditorium for the African American community, Church Park Auditorium was the site of various political and religious meetings. Located on Beale Street, it was replaced with a more modern building in the early 1900s.

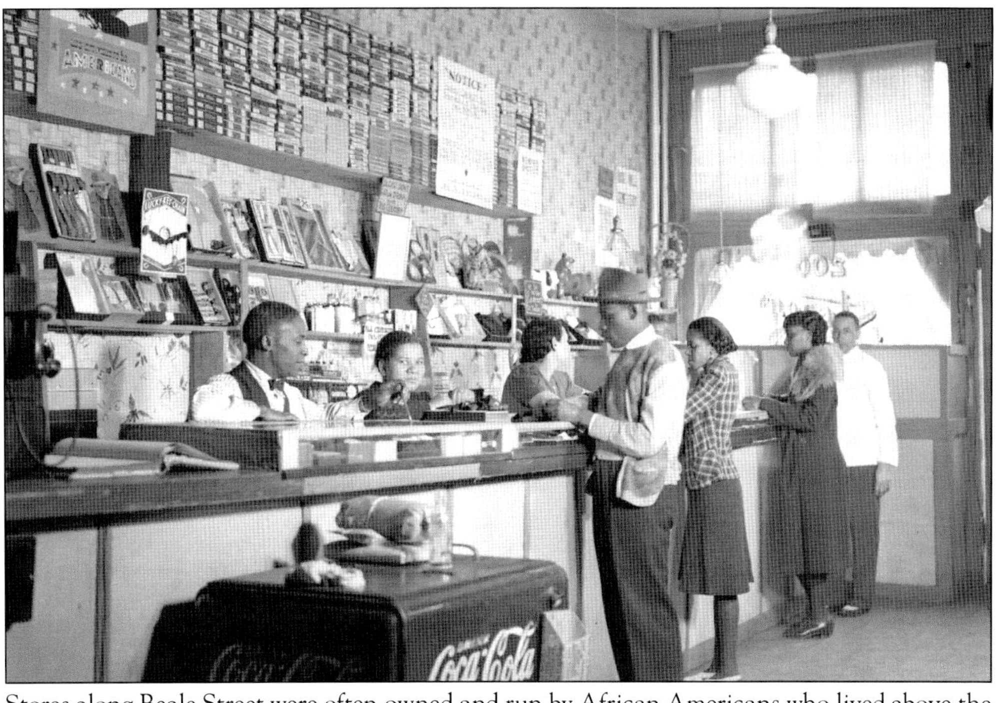

Stores along Beale Street were often owned and run by African Americans who lived above the business. The neighborhood around Beale was very diverse during the 1800s, with many Italian, Asian, and Jewish businessmen living and working there.

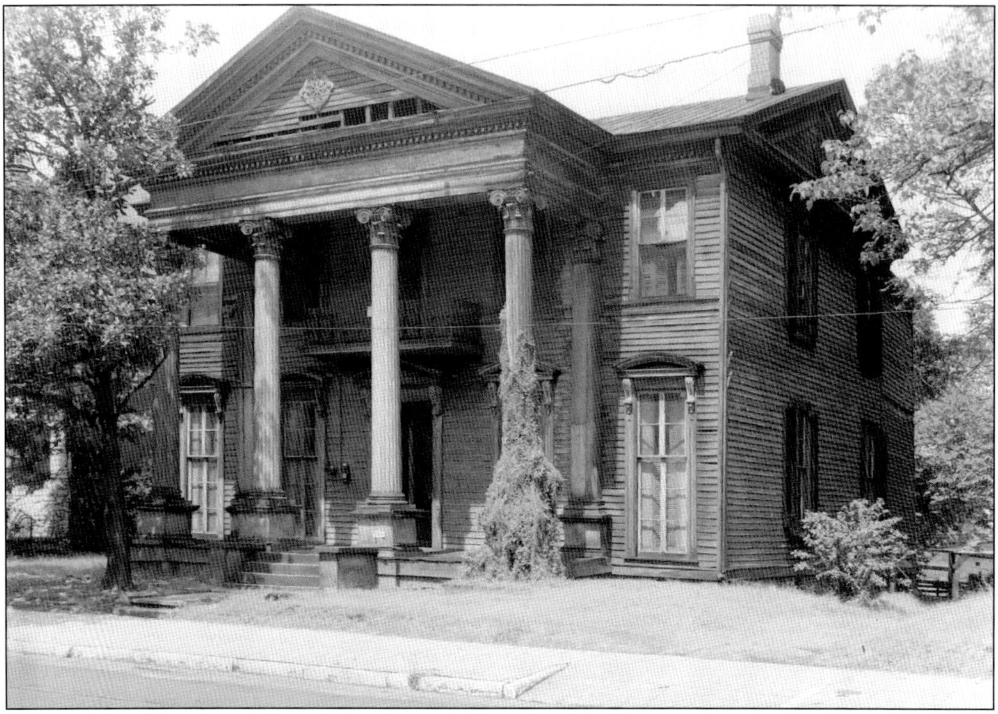

The home of James T. Pettit was located on Beale Street near Danny Thomas Boulevard. Mr. Pettit arrived in Memphis in 1847 and worked his way up to become one of the leading businessmen in the city. He was twice elected president of the chamber of commerce and the Cotton Exchange. The home was torn down in 1939.

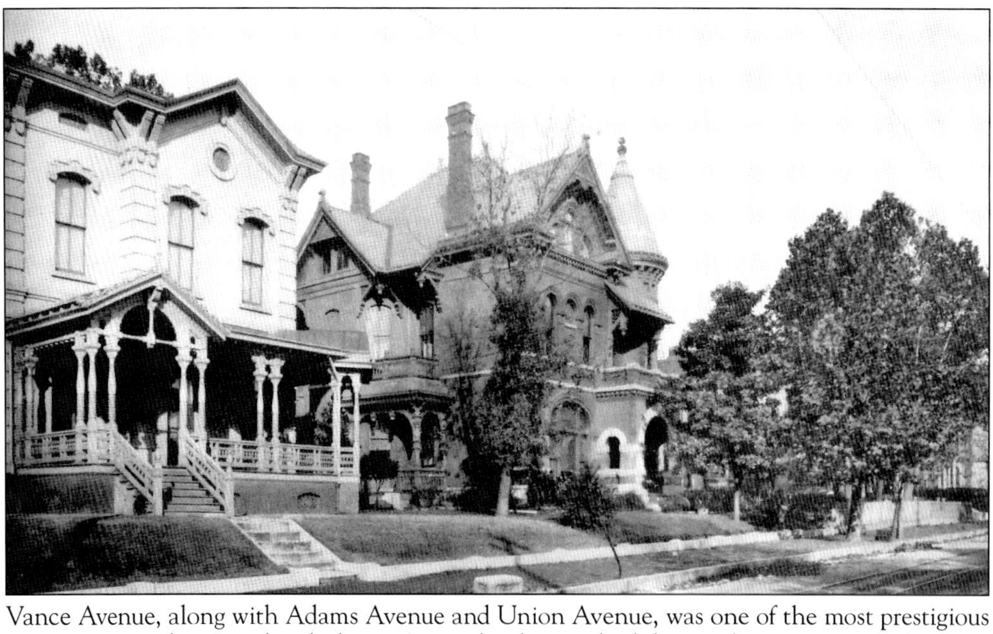

Vance Avenue, along with Adams Avenue and Union Avenue, was one of the most prestigious streets in Memphis. Lined with the city's grandest homes, built by riverboat owners and business tycoons, the street has but a single mansion left.

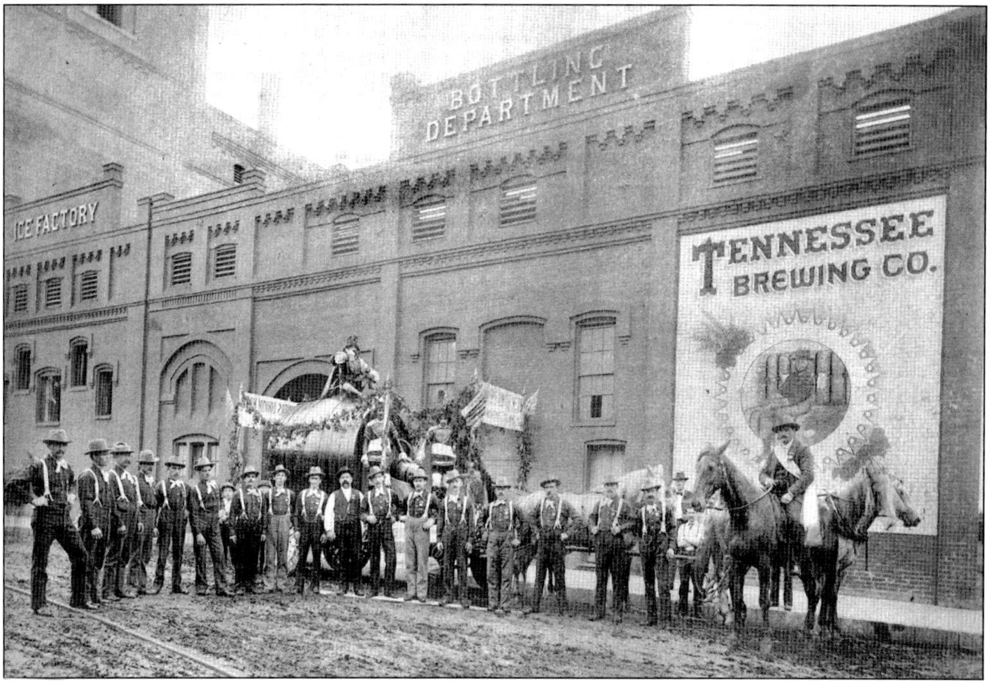

Built in 1890, the Tennessee Brewery, located on Tennessee Street, produced over 200,000 barrels of beer per year. Shown here in 1900, the brewery would continue to operate until the 1950s, producing Goldcrest Beer.

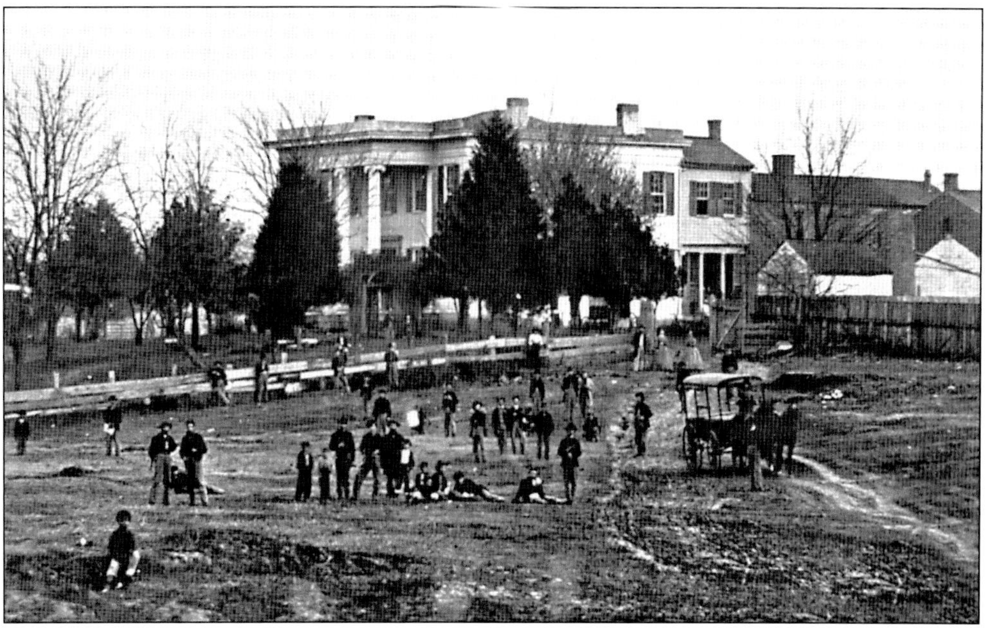

The Hunt Phelan home, located at Beale and Lauderdale, was built in the early 1840s and served as General Grant's headquarters briefly during the Civil War. The mansion was used as a soldiers' home after the war, lodging more than 19,000 persons in 1864 alone. The home today is still owned by the descendants of the original owners, although most of the furnishings and valuable archives were auctioned in 1999.

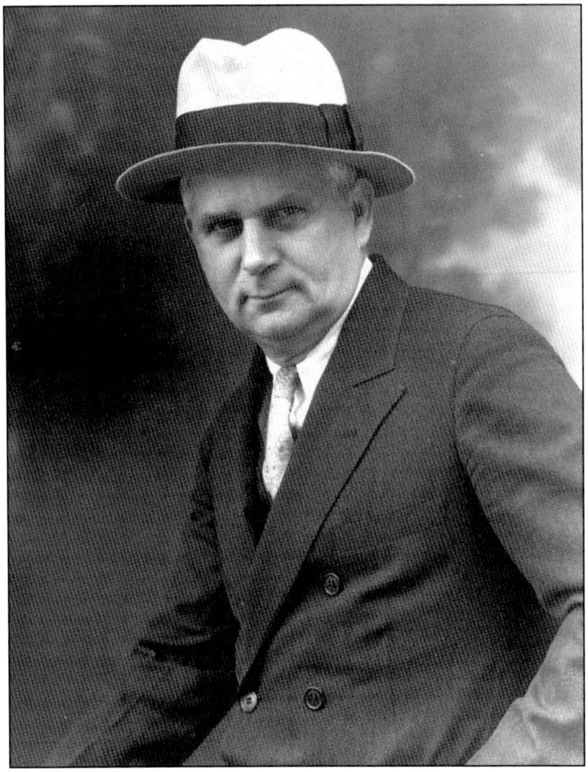

Clarence Saunders was one of Memphis's best-known entrepreneurs, having created the Piggly Wiggly grocery stores in 1916. After losing most of his money in a Wall Street battle in 1922, he created the "Sole Owner of My Name" stores and made a second fortune. He died at his home in Bartlett in 1953.

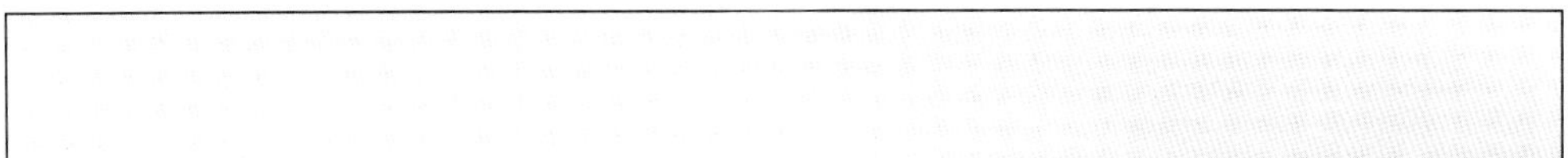

The grand pink marble building known today as the Pink Palace Museum was originally planned to be the residence of Clarence Saunders. The home contained a bowling alley, indoor swimming pool, and shooting gallery. Built in 1922, the home was never lived in by Saunders, who lost the residence to creditors just before completion. The mansion was donated to the city and has been used as a museum since 1930.

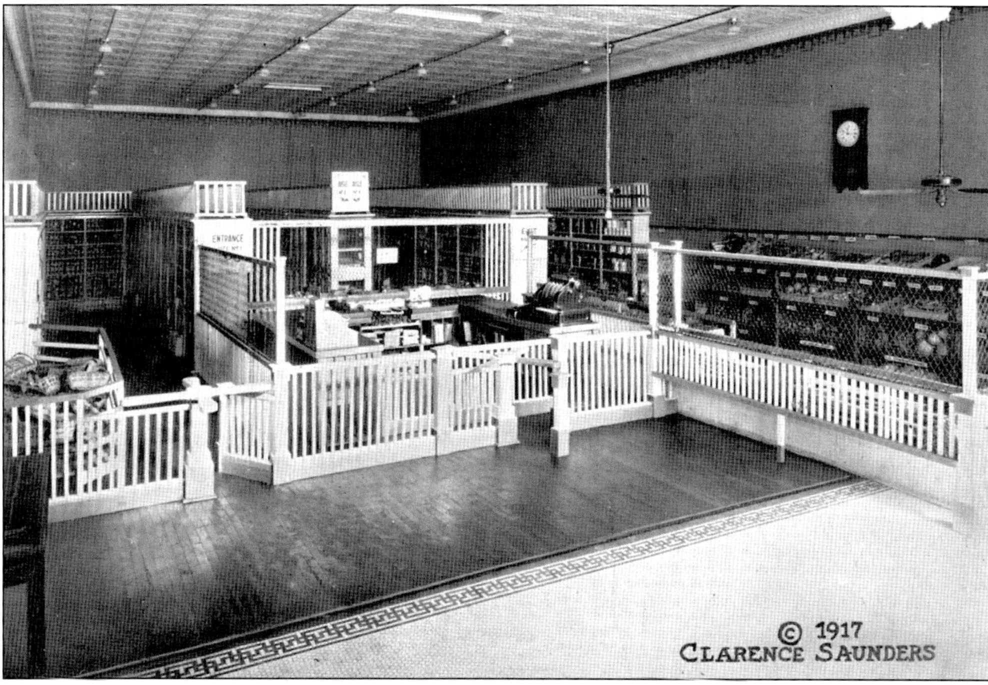

Clarence Saunders made history when he opened the first Piggly Wiggly in 1916. This photograph shows the interior of a Piggly Wiggly in 1917. The store was one of the first self-service grocery stores in the country. The stores grew from one in 1916 to 1,200 in 1922.

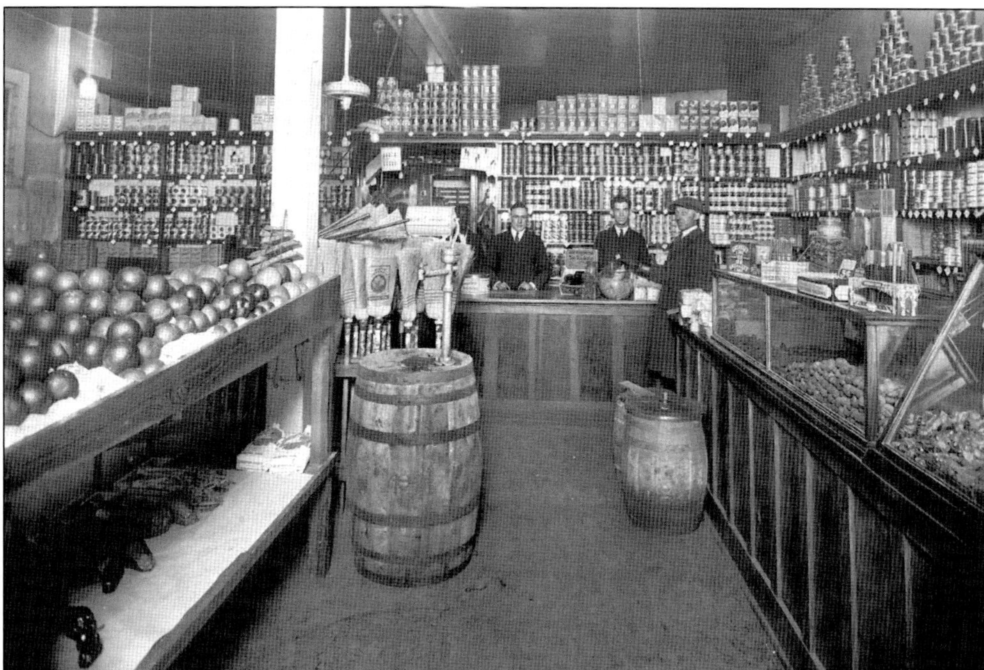

Mr. Bowers stores were located throughout Memphis. Seen here on Vance Street in 1921, Bowers was a self-service grocery store patterned after the Piggly Wiggly stores, which were developed in Memphis a few years earlier.

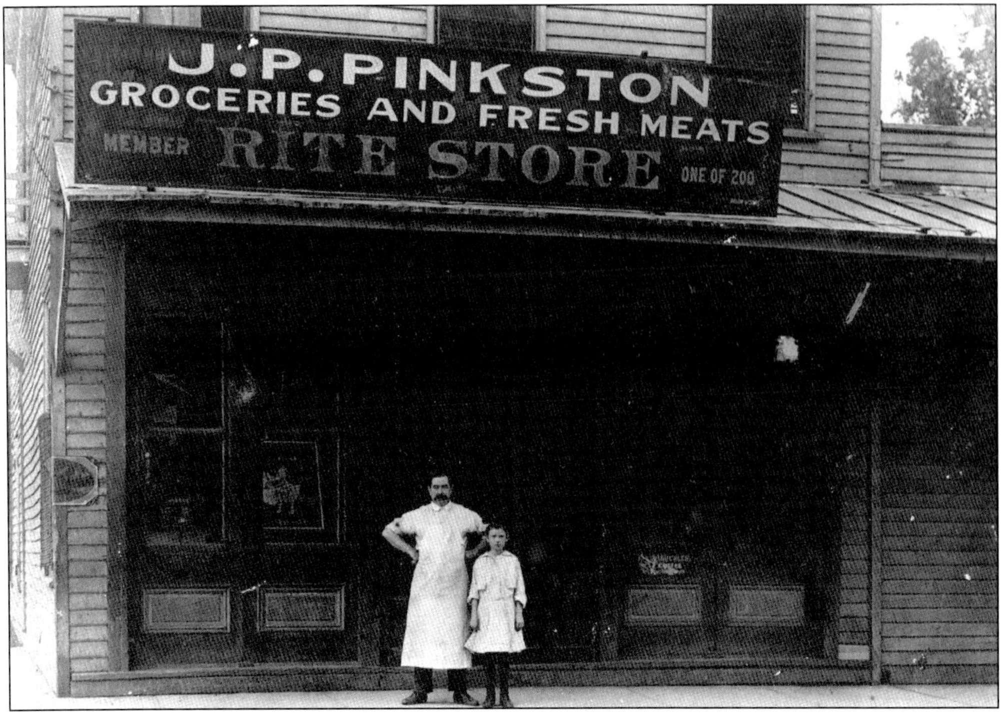

The Pinkston Meat Market was located at 169 Mill Street in the Pinch District and was in operation until the late 1920s. Operated by John P. Pinkston, shown here with his daughter Alma Daisy, the store was known for its meats and produce.

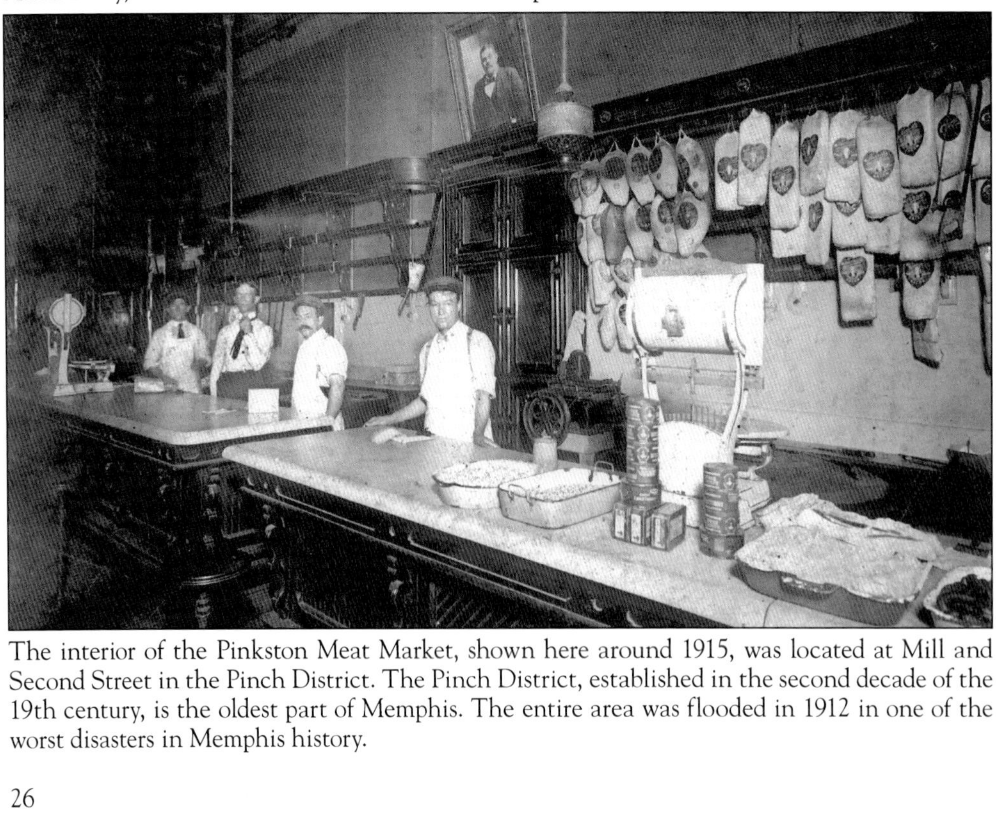

The interior of the Pinkston Meat Market, shown here around 1915, was located at Mill and Second Street in the Pinch District. The Pinch District, established in the second decade of the 19th century, is the oldest part of Memphis. The entire area was flooded in 1912 in one of the worst disasters in Memphis history.

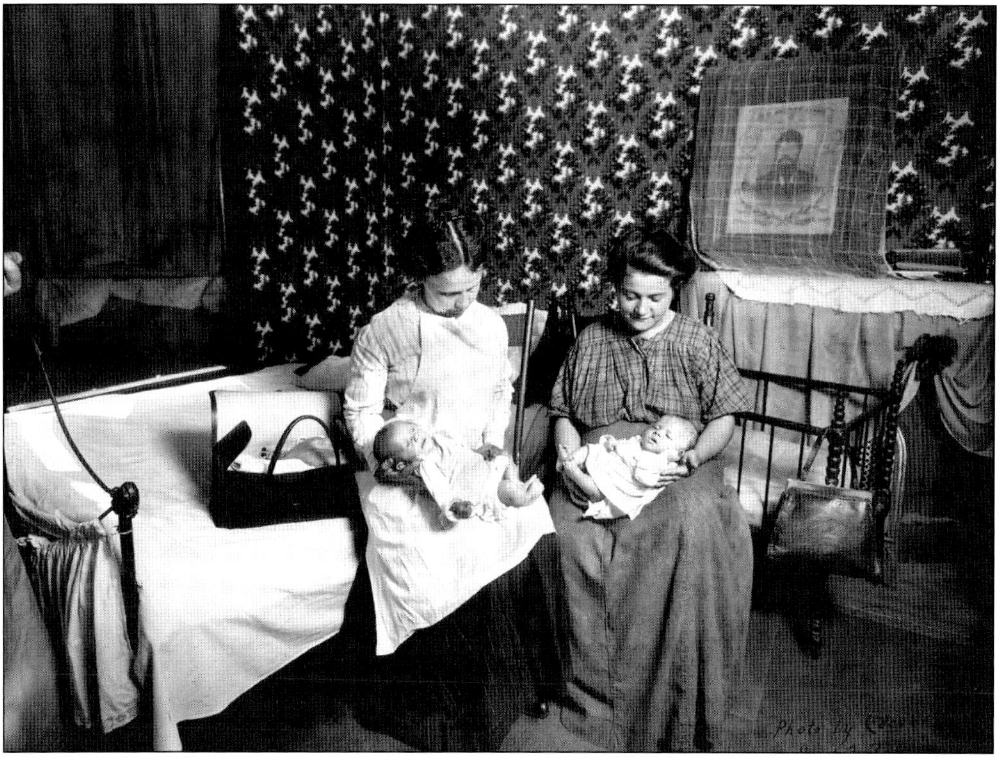

Following the yellow fever epidemic, Memphians saw a need for greater health control. The Memphis and Shelby County Health Department, shown here in 1915, worked hard to control tuberculosis, small pox, and polio.

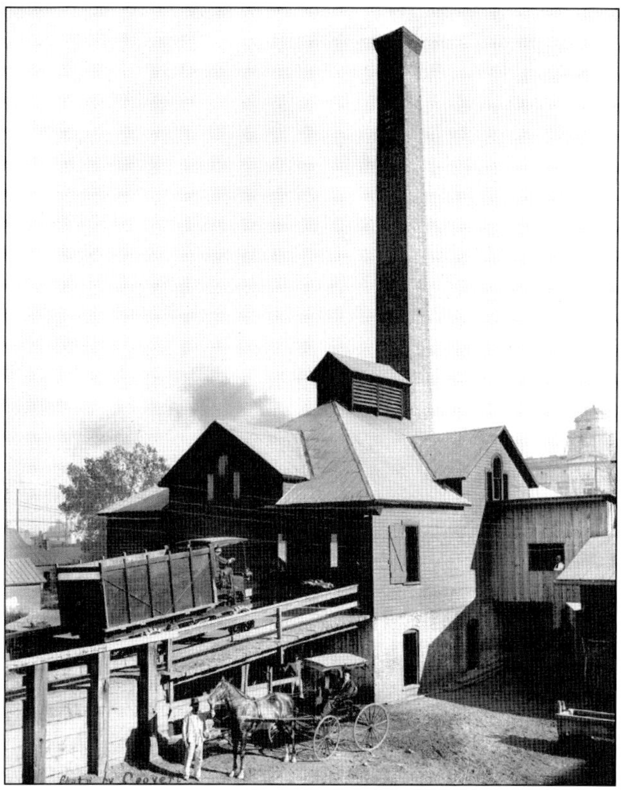

The health department facility, shown here in 1915, helped to destroy infectious items and keep the city clean.

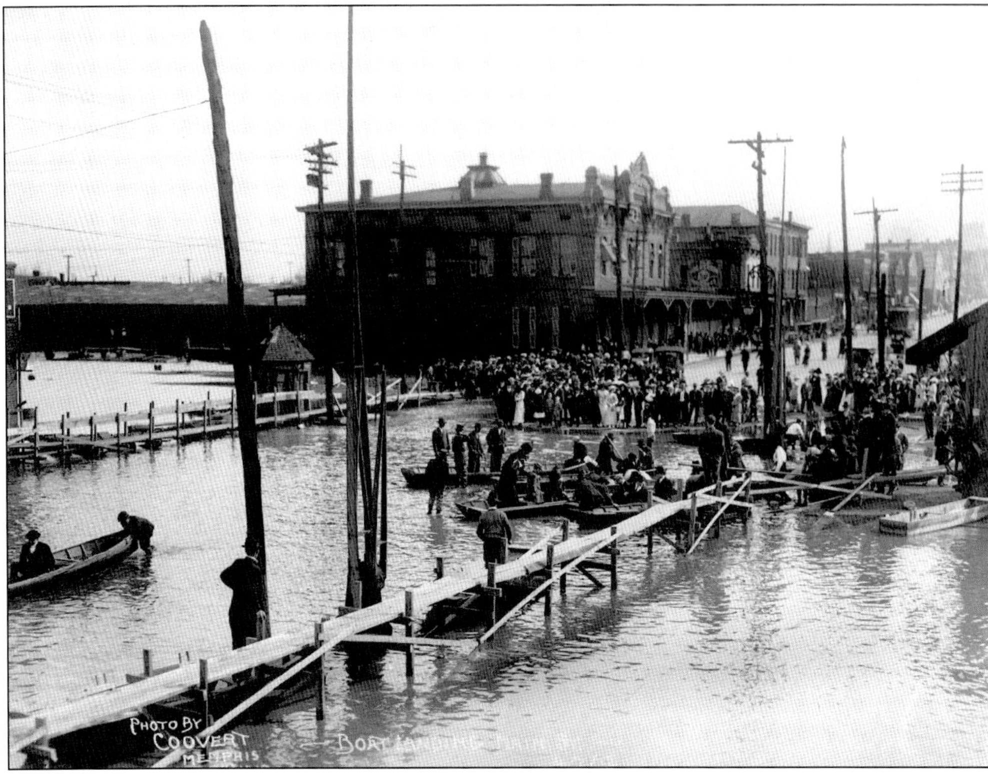

The great Mississippi River flood of 1912 was one of the worst on record and especially hard on Memphis. The Pinch District north of downtown was completely underwater. Many residents resorted to canoes to get around, as seen here near Main Street.

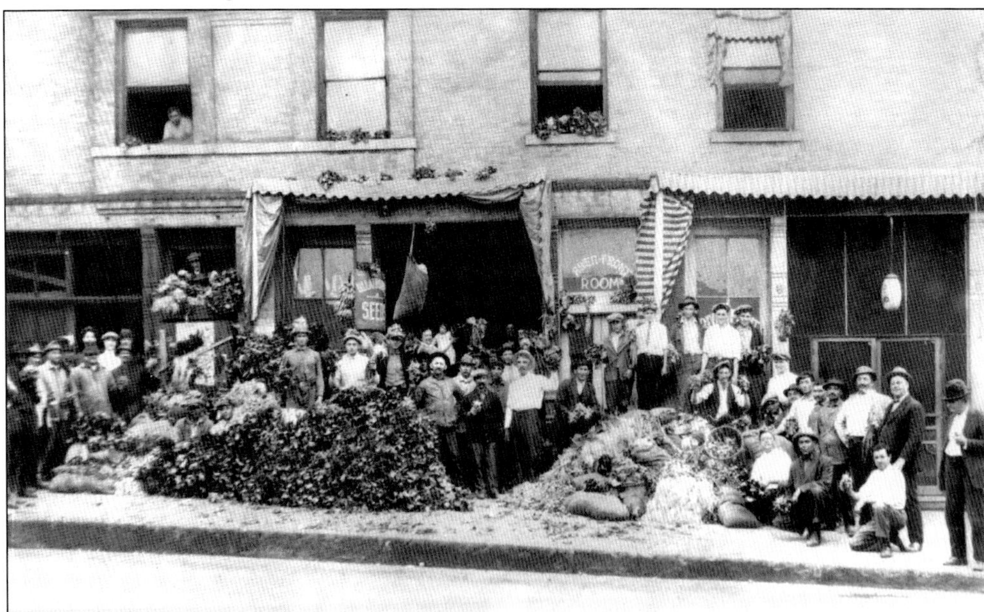

The Memphis curb market was a gathering place for local farmers to bring their fruits and vegetables for sale.

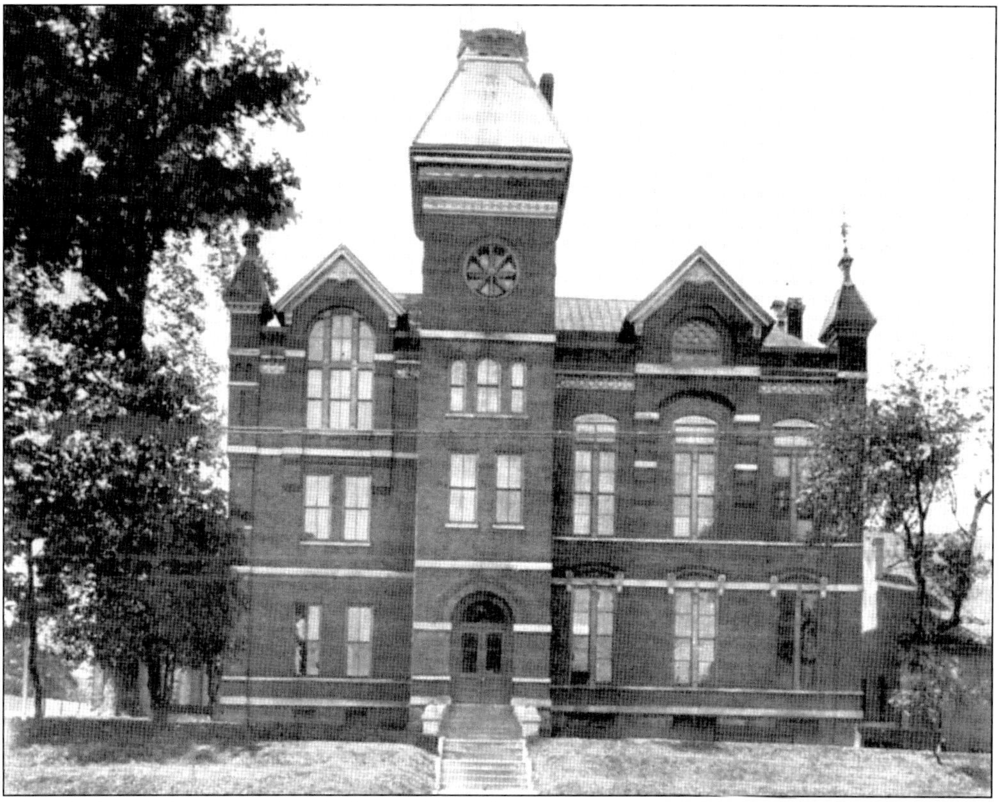

The Higbee School was founded in 1878 and was located at Beale and Lauderdale Streets. Miss Jenny Higbee arrived in Memphis just after the Civil War from New Jersey and taught for several years at the Memphis Female High School before buying the Robertson Topp estate and establishing her school there. The school closed in 1914.

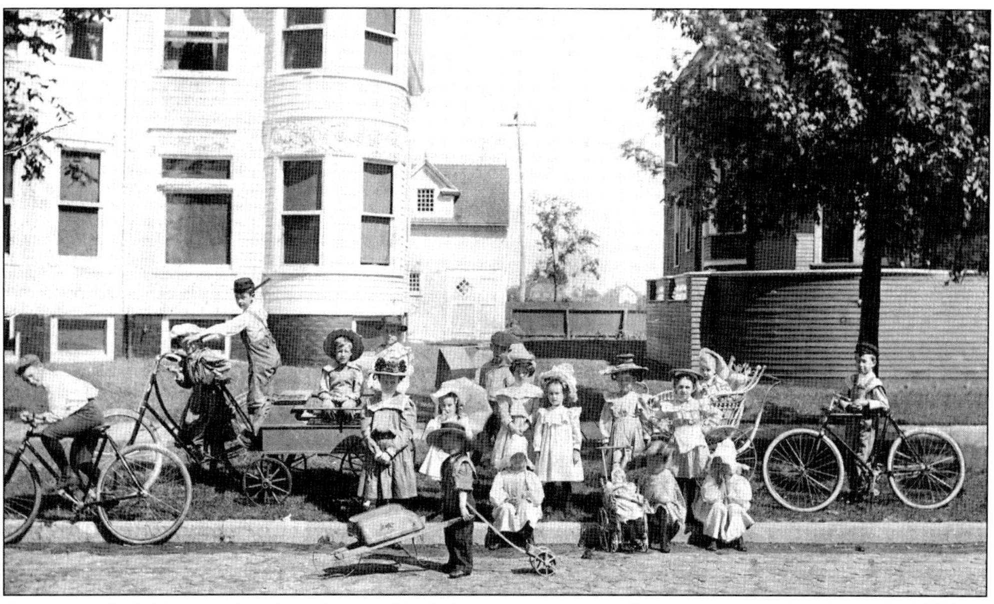

A group of children take time from a birthday party to pose for the camera in the early 1900s.

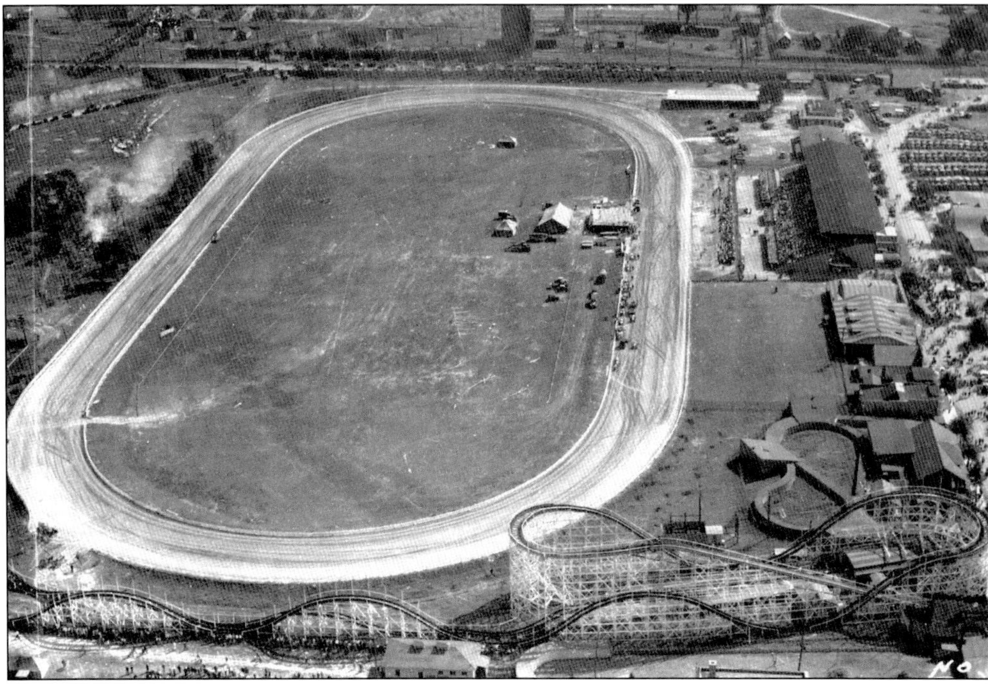

Montgomery Park was begun in the 1860s as a mile-long horse racing track. The track, shown here in 1920, was shortened and used for harness racing until the 1930s. The fairgrounds were to the right of the track and are today the site of Libertyland amusement park. The roller coaster shown at the bottom was brought to the fairgrounds from East End Park, located on Madison Avenue, and is one of the oldest in the country.

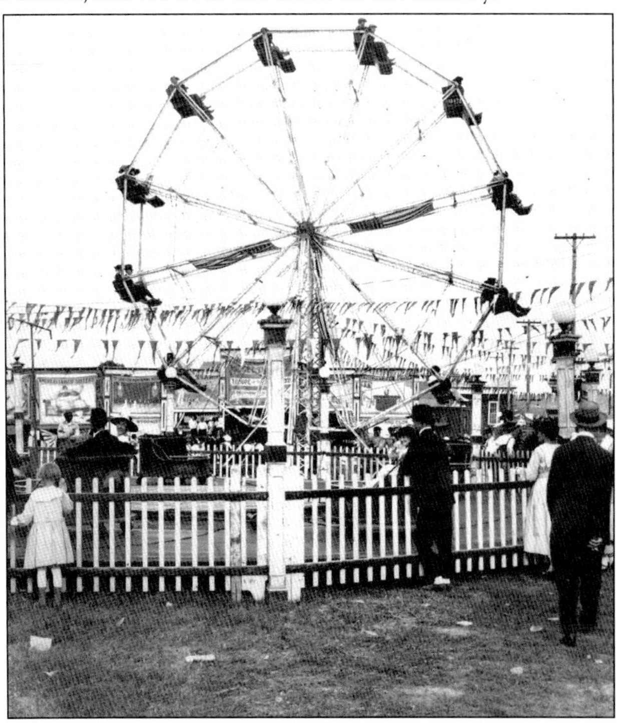

The Mid-South Fair began in 1856 as the Shelby County Agricultural Fair and was located at Poplar and Decatur Streets. In 1869, the fair moved to its present location on East Parkway. Shown here in 1912, the fair was the county's biggest day, bringing together small towns and rural farmers to compete or just to have fun.

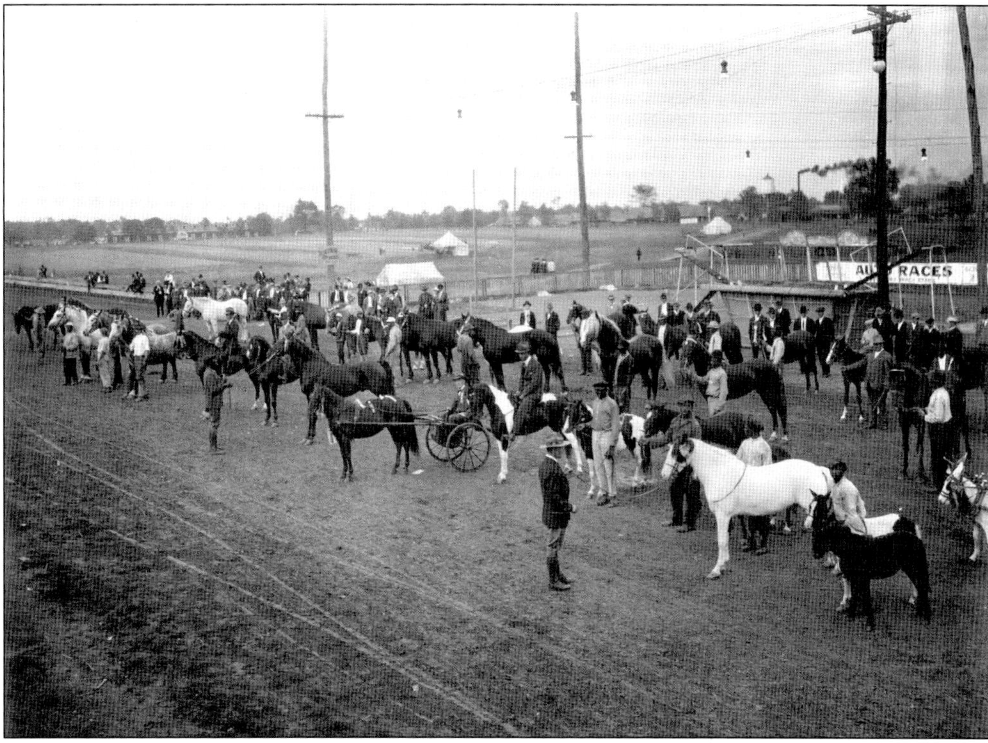

Horses and their owners line up at Montgomery Park during the early 1900s. The park was located just west of the present-day Mid-South Coliseum.

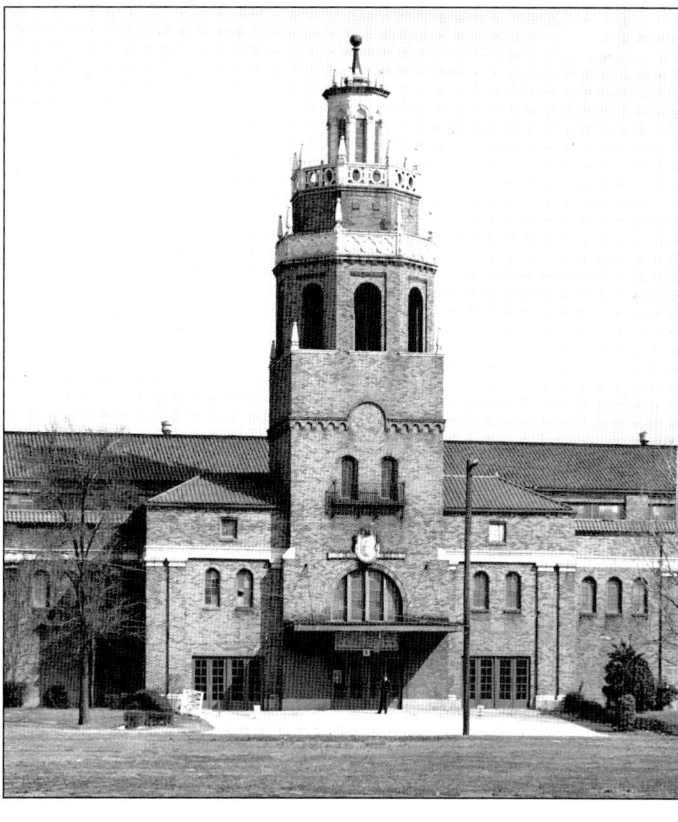

The Shelby County Building at the Mid-South Fair grounds was built in 1922 at a cost of $150,000. It was the largest open structure in the county until the building of the Auditorium North Hall downtown. The 37,000-square-foot building was one of the last remaining Spanish Renaissance public buildings in the city. The building tragically burned in 2003.

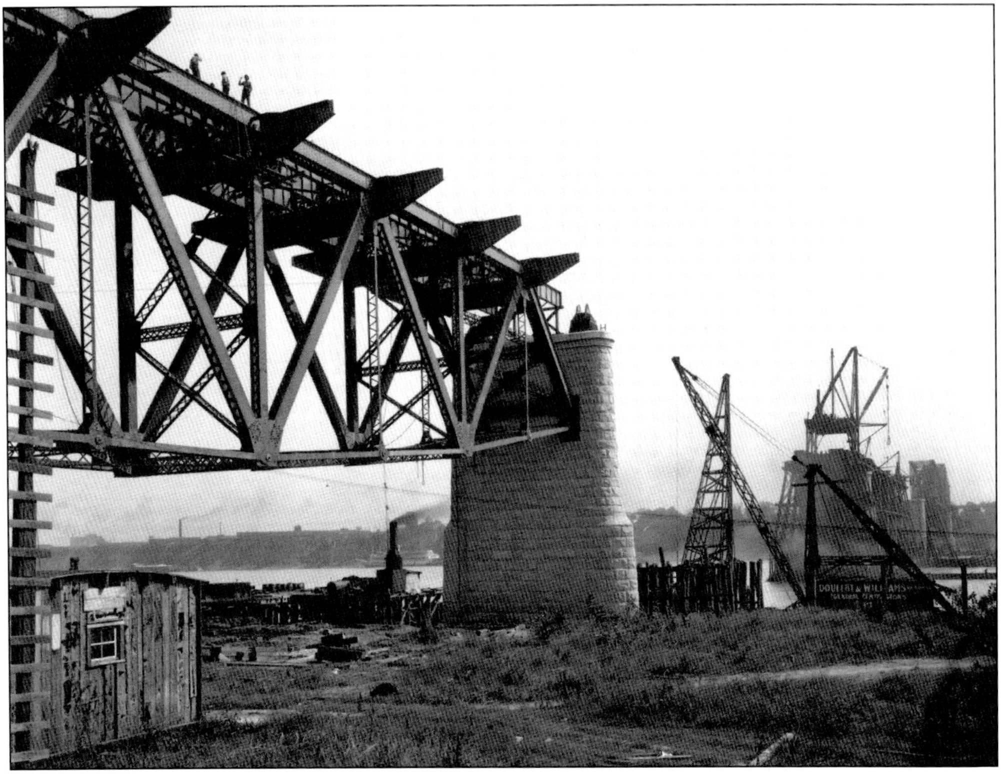

The Great River Bridge was opened in 1892, with 50,000 people turning out to see the first train cross.

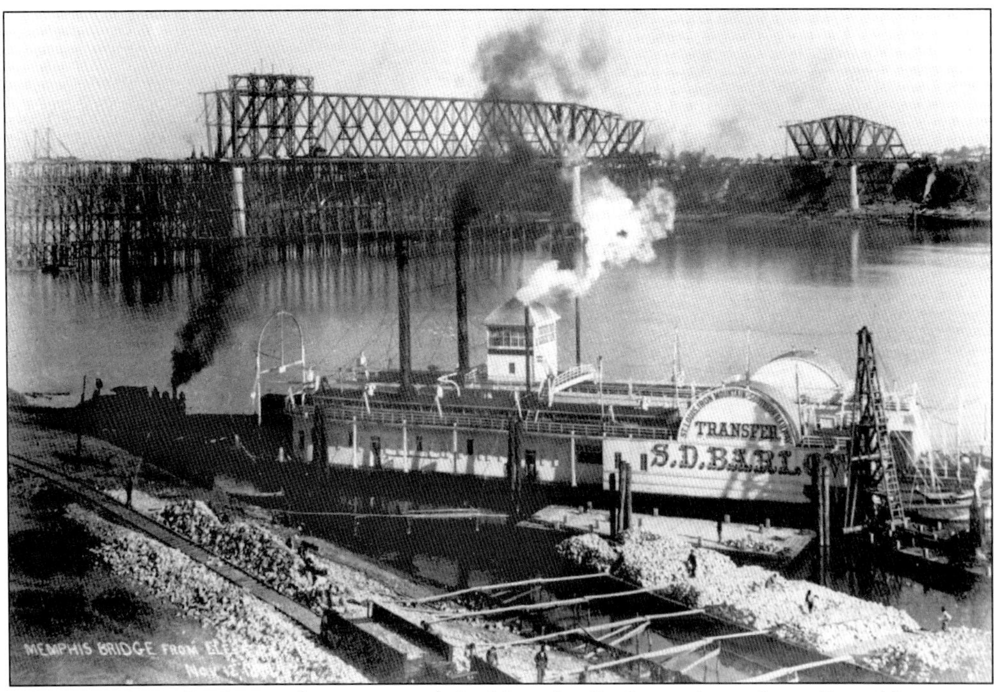

The Great River Bridge was later renamed the Memphis Bridge and is today still used by trains.

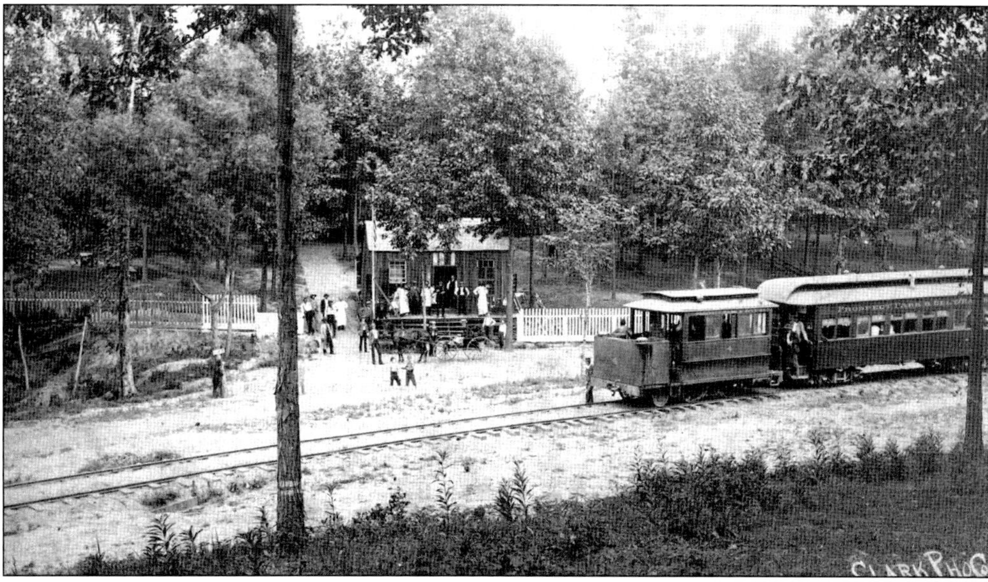

The Prospect Park rail line opened in 1887 to transport riders to a new subdivision located south of downtown Memphis. The area was once part of the Richard Person plantation and could be rented out for private parties and festivals. In 1895, the line merged and became the Memphis Street Railway Company.

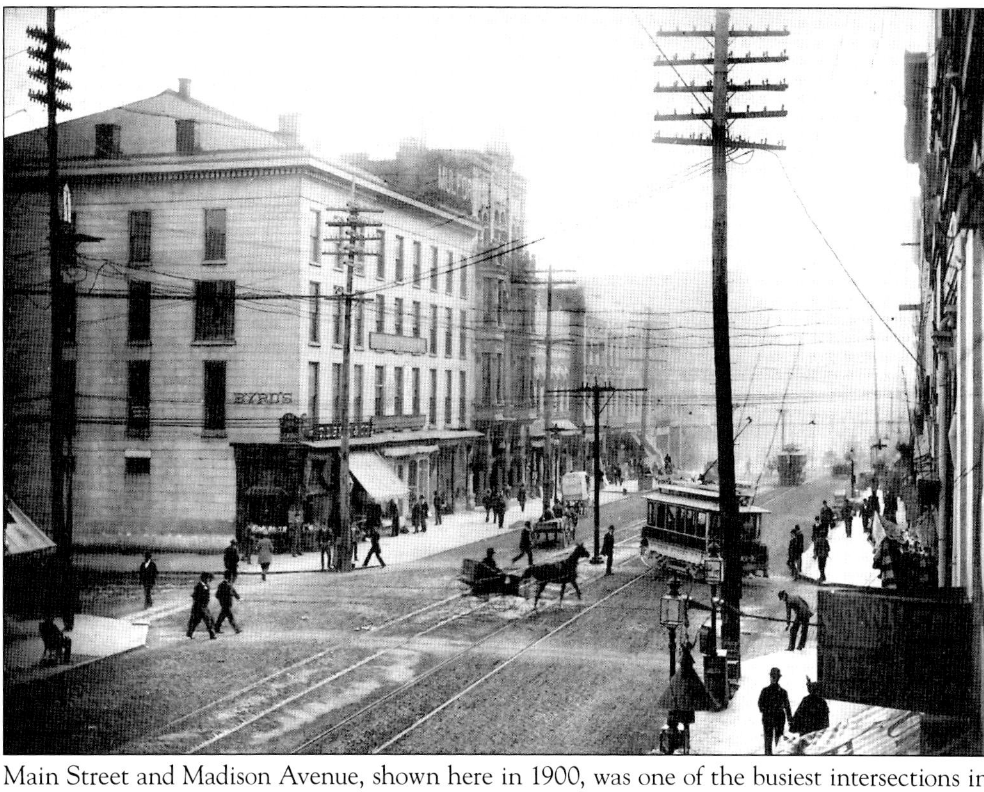

Main Street and Madison Avenue, shown here in 1900, was one of the busiest intersections in the early days of Memphis. On the left is the Byrd marble block building, which was built in 1885 and is still standing today.

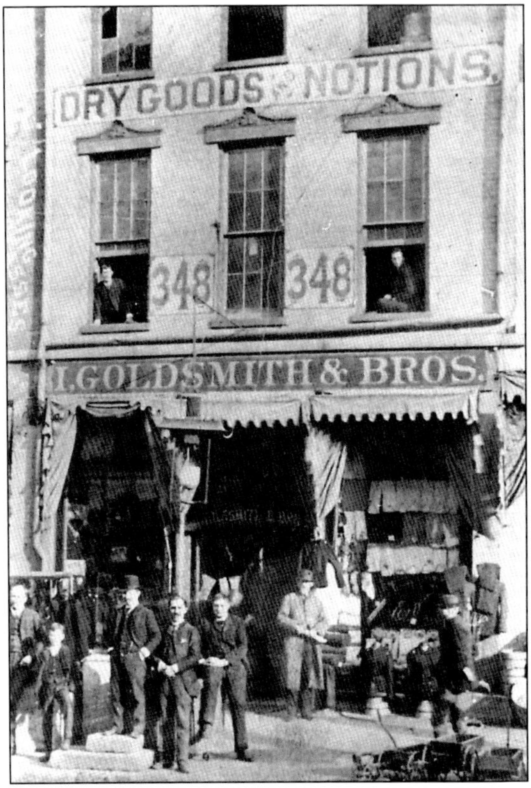

Originally located on Beale Street, Goldsmith's moved to Main Street in the 1890s. Shown here in 1895 at 385 Main Street, the store eventually moved across the street to Main and Gayoso, a move that was accomplished in just two days. Goldsmith's Department Store, in business since 1870, was sold to Federated Department Stores in 2003 and is now called Macy's.

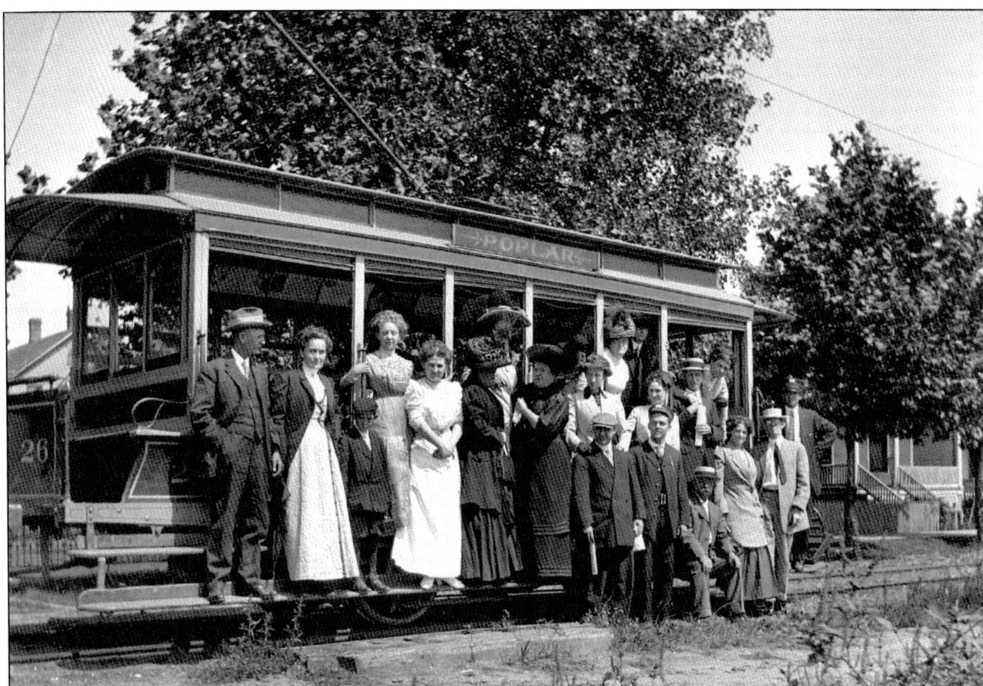

The first Memphis trolleys were mule-drawn and only in downtown. By the turn of the century, most of the young city was accessible by trolley, as seen here on Poplar Avenue in 1915.

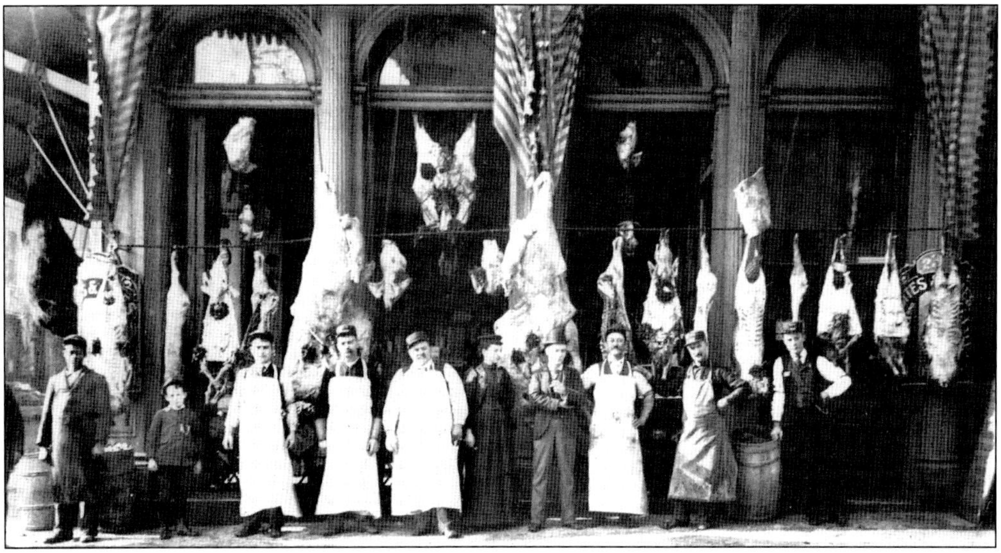

Located on Second Street, the Sites and Ames Fulton Meat Market showcased the latest in meats and fish. The store, shown here in 1893, serviced local restaurants such as the Peabody Hotel and Luehrman's on Main Street.

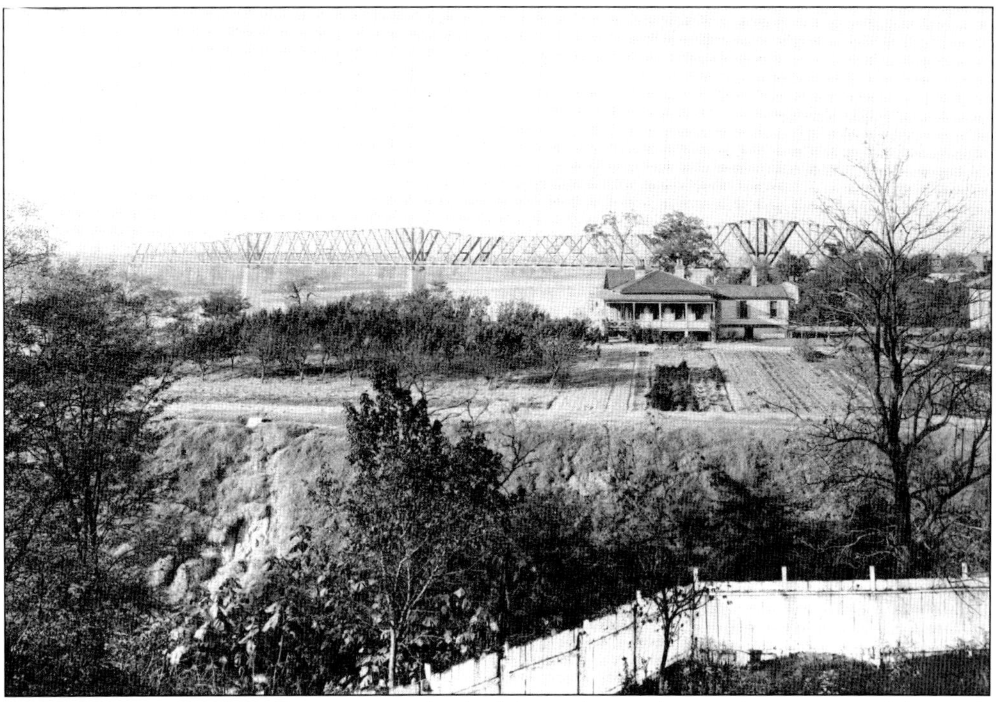

Located just north of the Desoto mounds, the Marine hospital grounds were part of the town of Fort Pickering. The hospital was built in 1884 and, for many years, was the only government hospital in Memphis. The grounds today are part of the Ornamental Metal Museum.

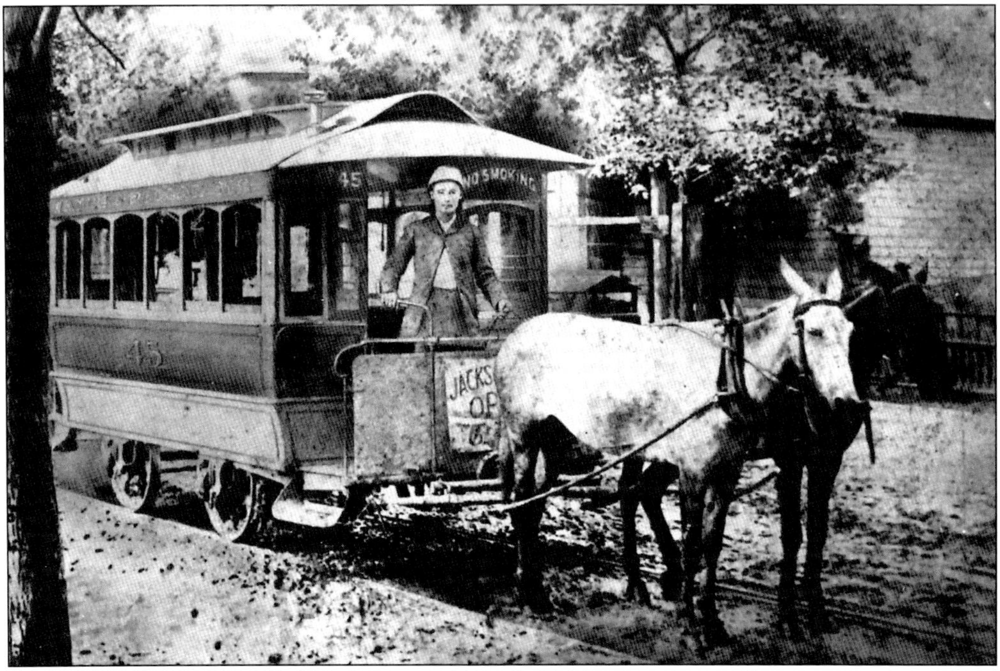

The first trolleys were pulled by mules; in the early 1900s, they ran on electricity.

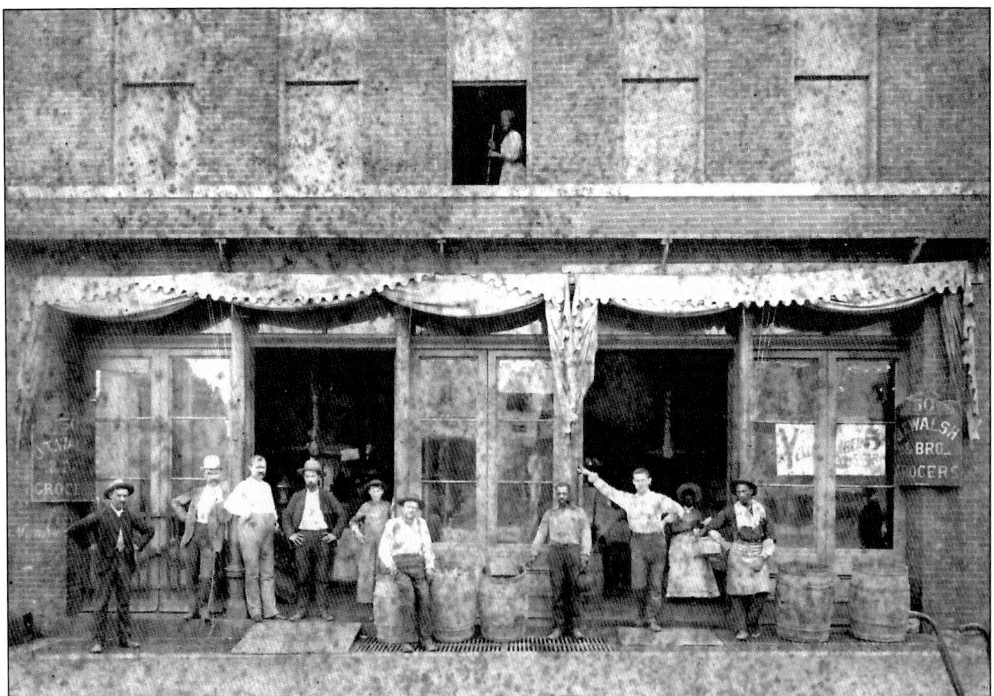

Many of the family grocery store owners were immigrants who had lived in Memphis for many years and often resided above the store, as seen here in 1900.

Elmwood Cemetery was founded in 1852, with the superintendent's cottage being built in 1866. Politicians, musicians, soldiers, and yellow fever victims lay side by side in one of the most beautiful cemeteries in the South. The cottage was added onto in 1903 and 1978. In 1978, it was placed on the National Register of Historic Places.

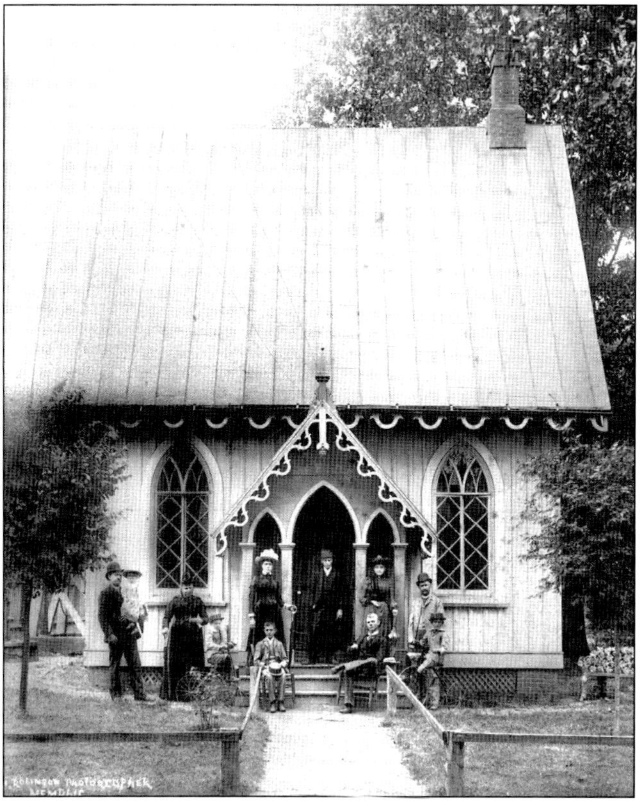

The Peabody Hotel, shown here in 1912, was originally located on Main Street at Monroe. The hotel burned in the early 1920s and was rebuilt in 1923 at the corner of Union and Second Streets.

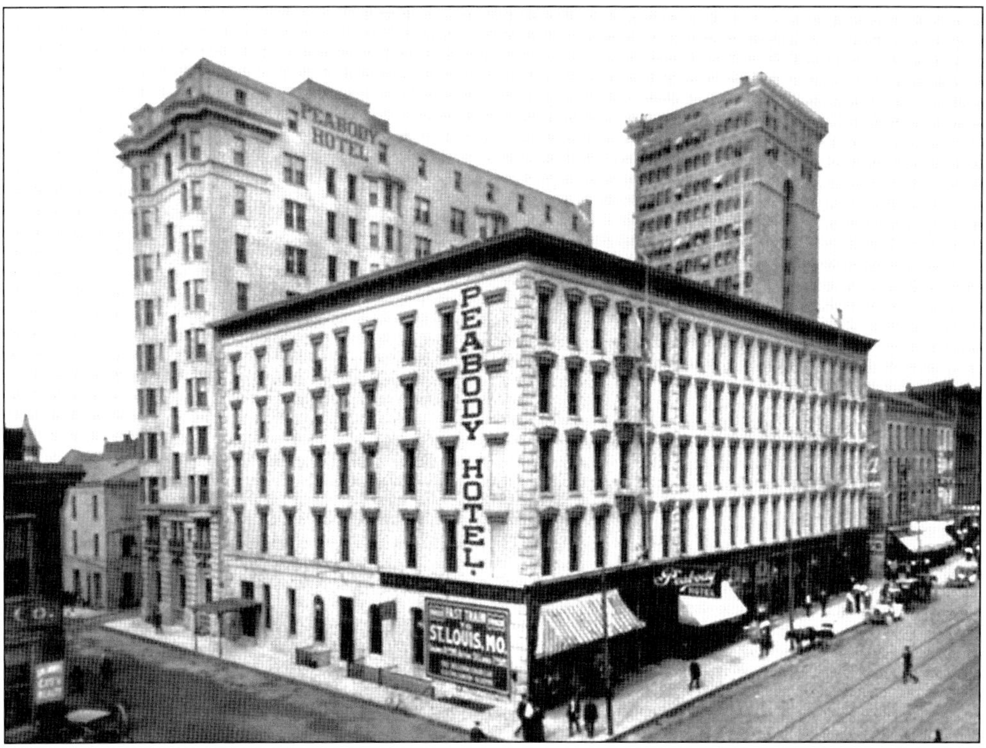

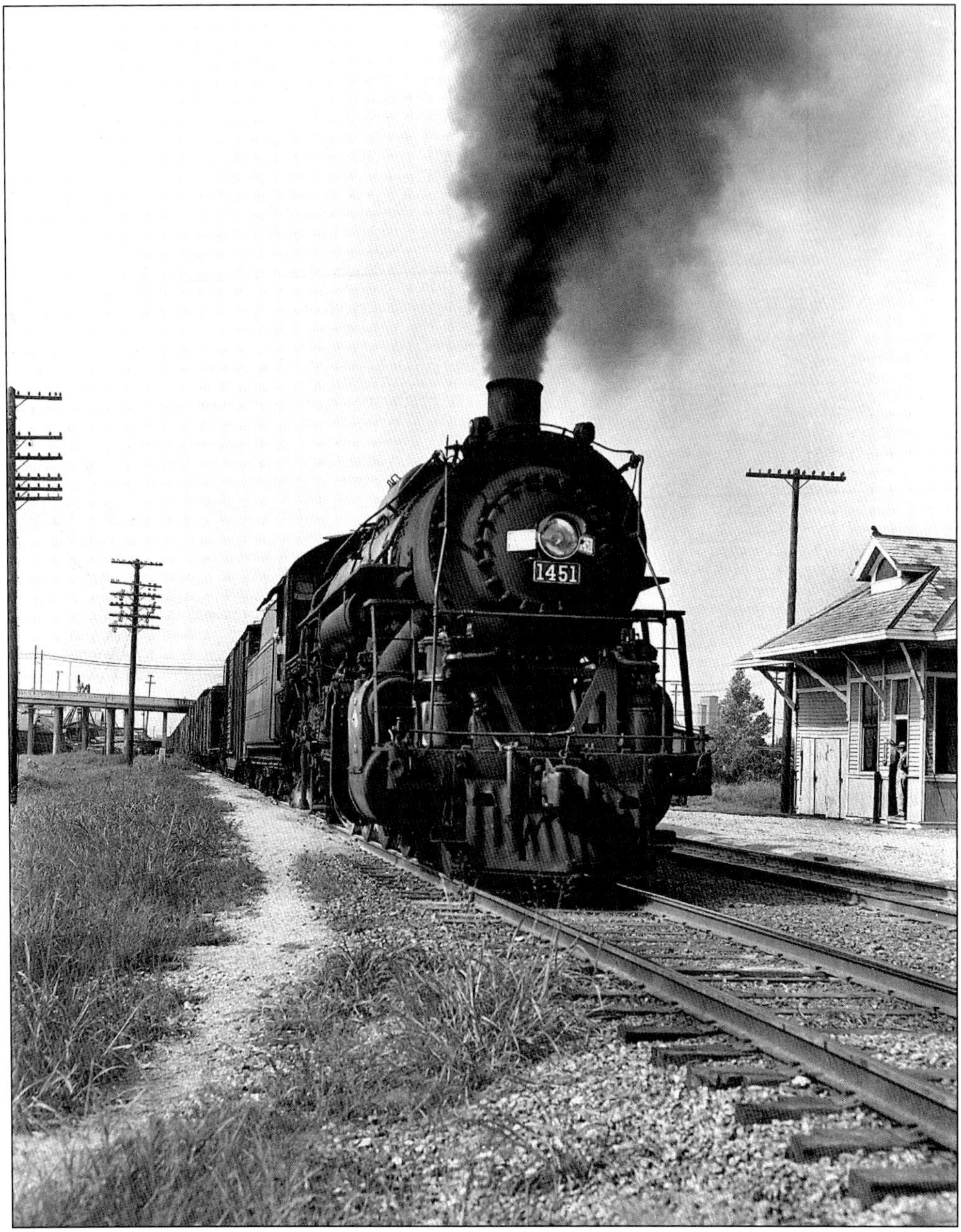

The first completed train line in Shelby County was the Memphis & Charleston line that ran out of downtown Memphis toward Germantown, Collierville, and Corinth in 1852. The railways in Shelby County played an important role in the growth of the county. By the end of the decade, Shelby County had more than six major rail lines coming into Memphis, including the Illinois Central, Louisville and Nashville, Memphis and Charleston, and the Southern Railway.

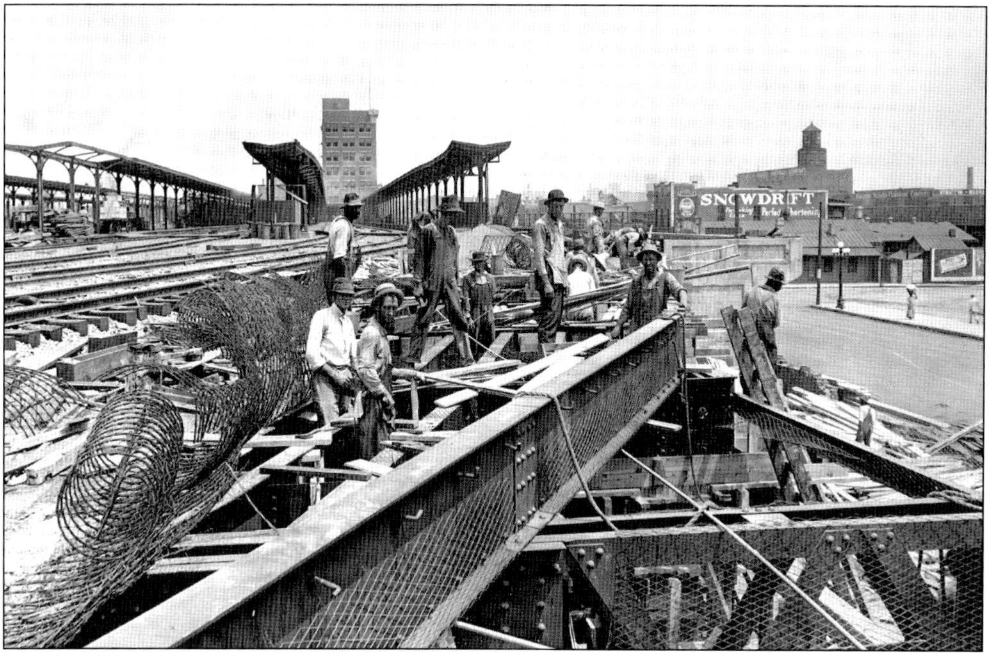

Seen here in 1914, workers complete track on Central Station, located at Calhoun and Main Street. The station, seen in the background, was the Memphis headquarters for the Louisville and Nashville train line. Union Station, a few blocks east on Calhoun, was the local headquarters for the Union Pacific.

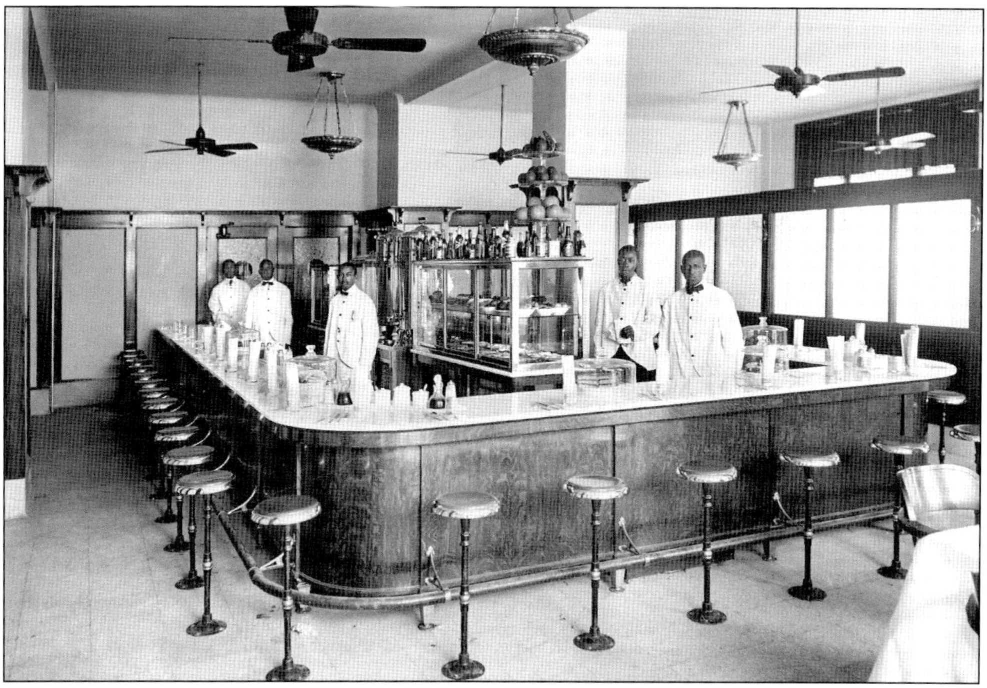

The Interstate Café in Central Station, shown here in 1914, was a popular spot to catch a quick snack before boarding the *City of New Orleans*, a popular passenger train that traveled between New Orleans and Chicago.

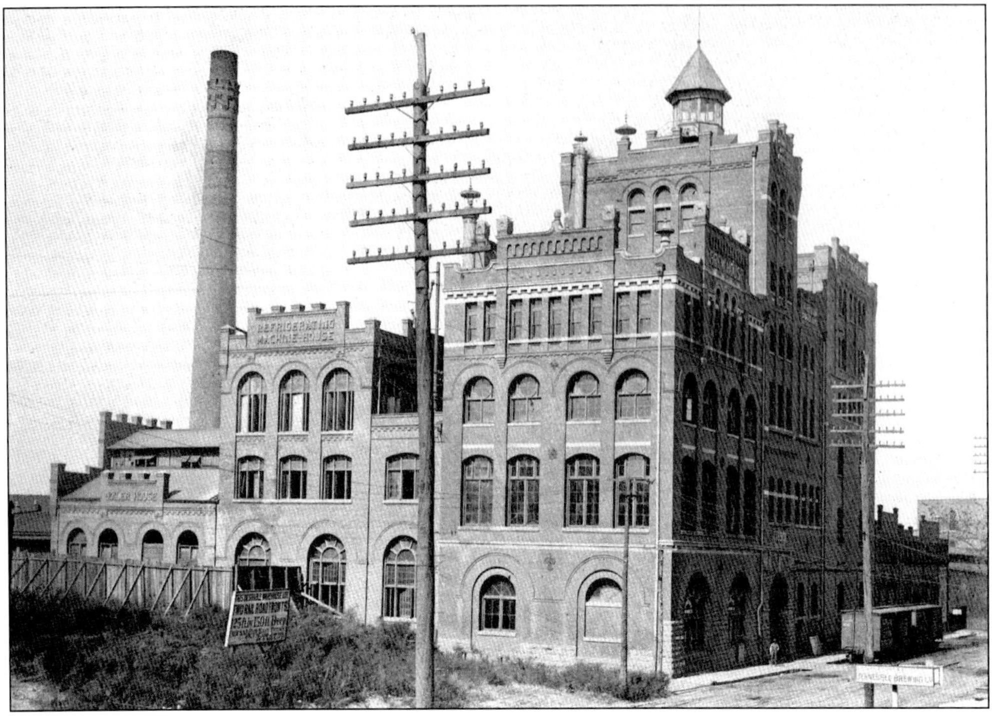

The Tennessee Brewery was built in 1890 and produced many fine beers, including Budweiser and Goldcrest. The building still stands today on Tennessee Street and is being renovated.

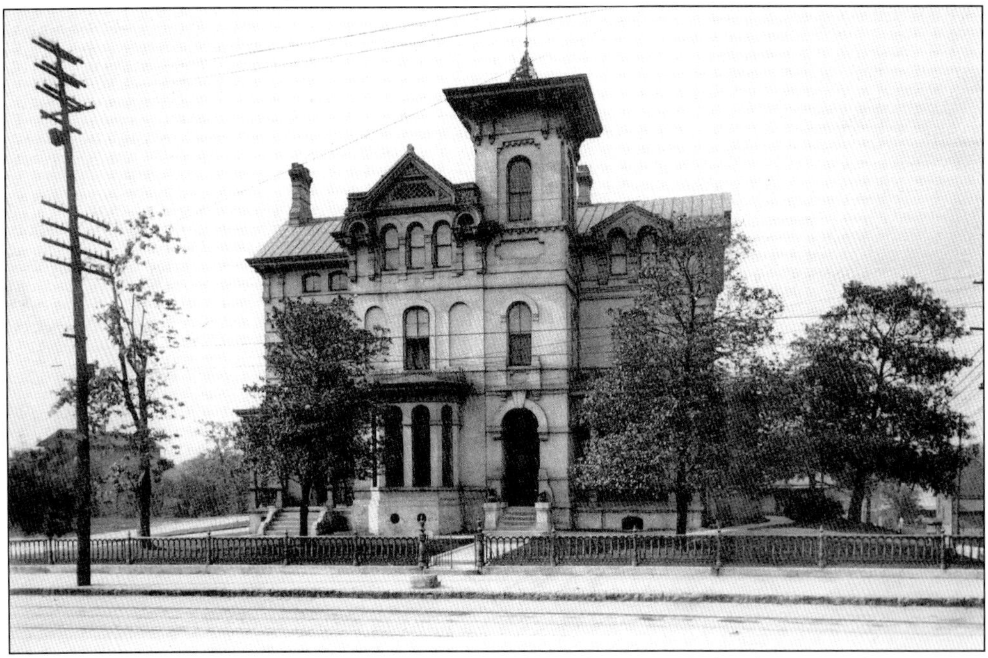

The Randolph house was located across the street from the Hunt-Phelan home, on the corner of Lauderdale and Beale Streets. The home was built in 1874 by William M. Randolph, a Memphis attorney and judge. He also built the Randolph Building on the corner of Main and Beale Streets in 1891. The Randolph mansion was demolished in 1976.

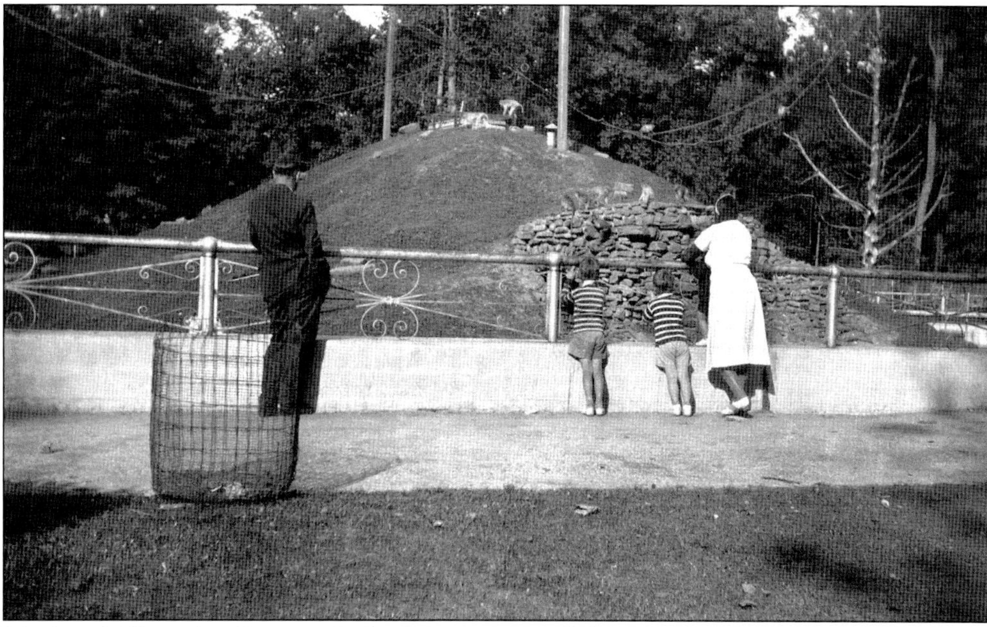

Monkey Hill at the Overton Park Zoo was one of the zoo's best remembered enclosures. Surrounded by water, the island was home to various monkeys who would often escape and have to be recaptured from the roofs of startled neighbors' homes.

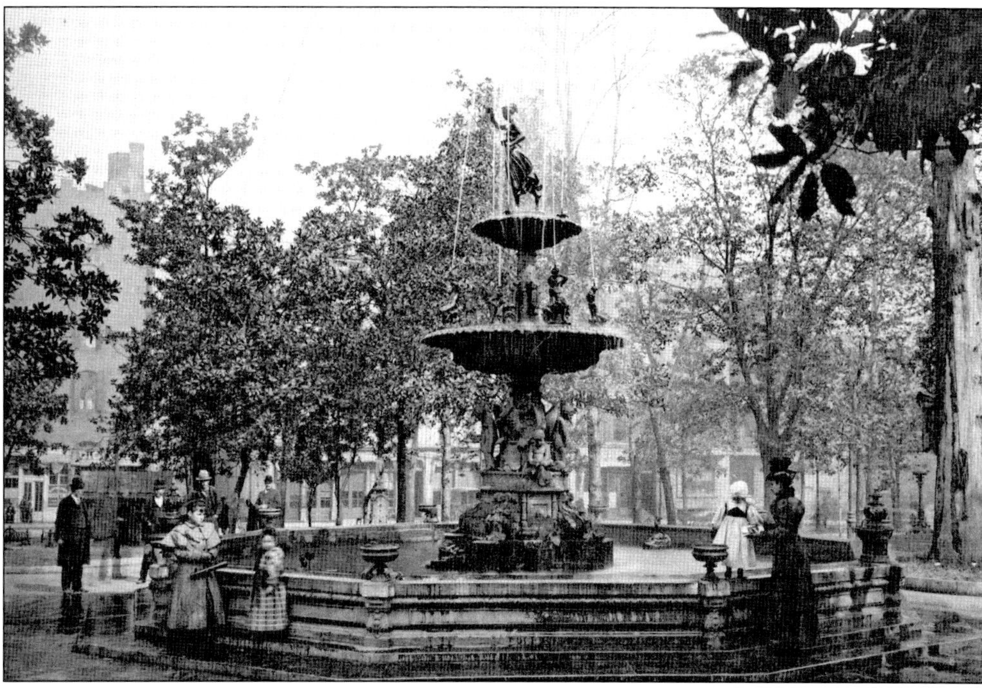

Court Square was one of four original squares laid out in 1819. The other squares are Auction, Market, and Exchange. The fountain was donated by local citizens in 1876 to mark the centennial of the United States. The Hebe Fountain in Court Square contains at its top a reproduction of Antonio Canova's statue of Hebe, cupbearer to the Greek gods. The statue was badly damaged during a storm in 1942.

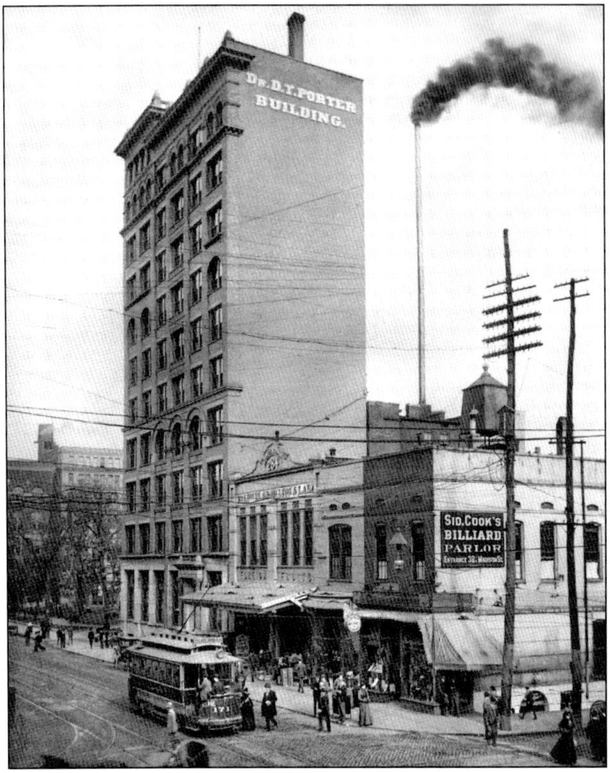

Built in 1895 by Jones, Hall and Kirby architects, the 11-story D. T. Porter Building was the first steel-frame skyscraper in Memphis. At the time of its construction, it was the tallest building in the world to have a circulating hot water heating system. The building was purchased in 1898 by the family of D. T. Porter and renamed in his honor. Dr. Porter helped Memphis recover financially from the yellow fever epidemics of the late 1870s.

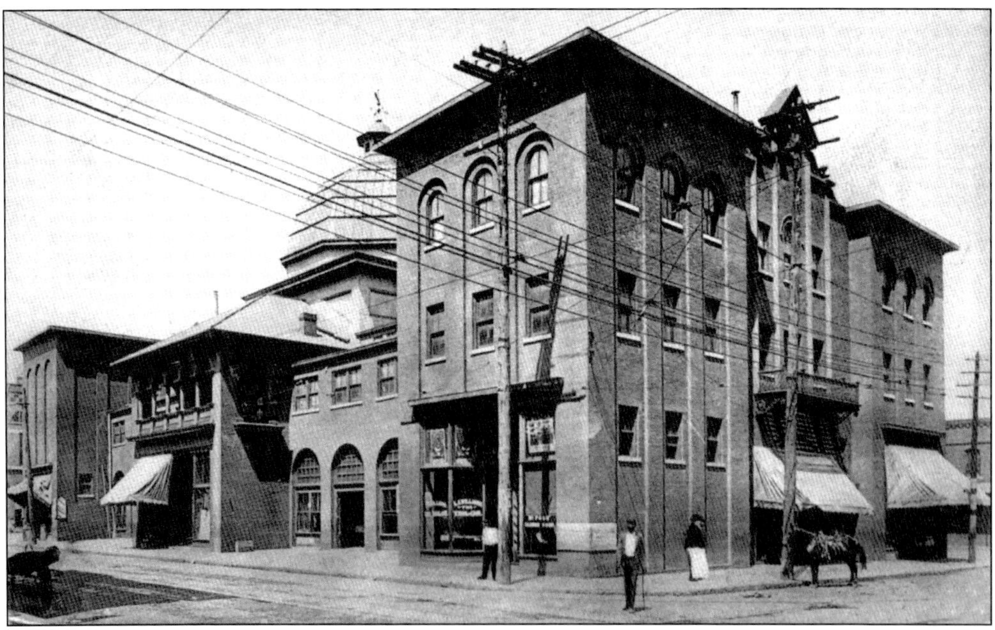

Built in 1899 as a market for a variety of businesses including groceries, dentists, barbers, and shoemakers, the Beale Street Market was one-stop shopping for residents of the famous neighborhood. The Market House was razed in 1930 to make way for a public park in honor of W. C. Handy. A statue of Handy was added in 1960, and for many years, the park was host to local musicians and jug bands.

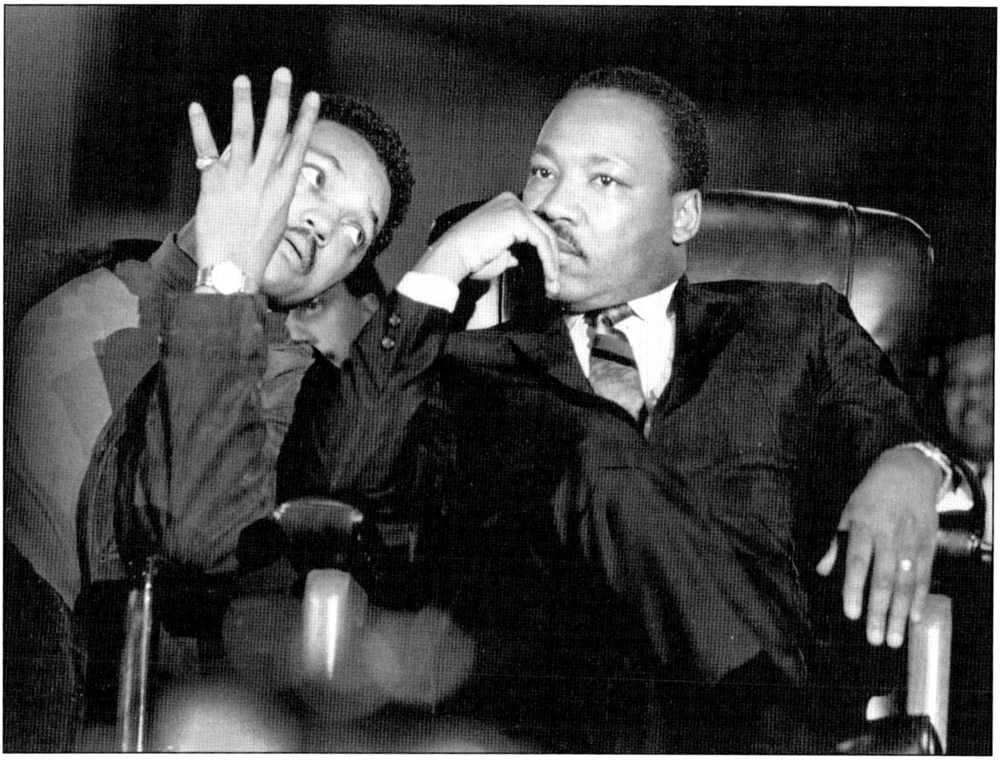

Rev. Martin Luther King speaks with Jesse Jackson while in Memphis to help the sanitation workers who were on strike. A protest march down Beale Street ended abruptly when crowds became out of control and started looting stores.

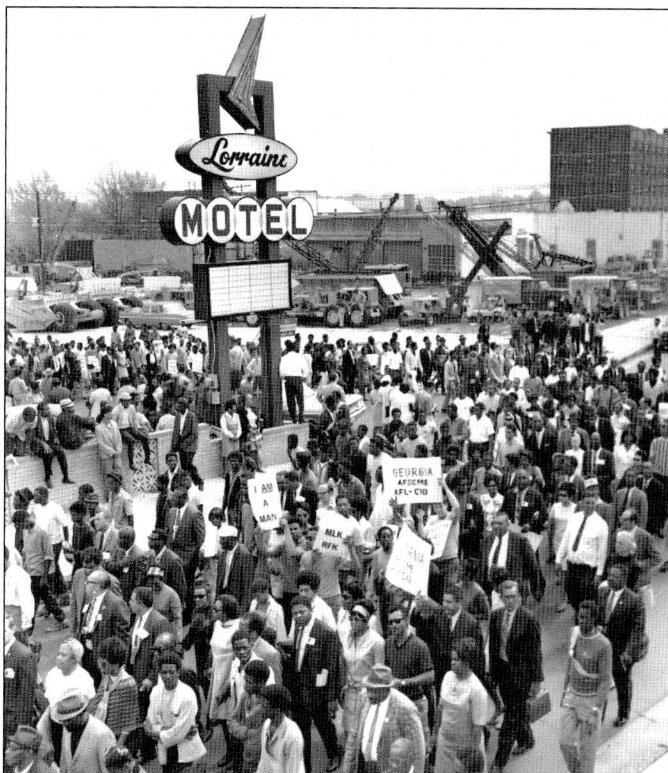

After the assassination of Rev. Martin Luther King, a memorial march was held, which passed by the Lorraine Motel where he was killed a few days earlier.

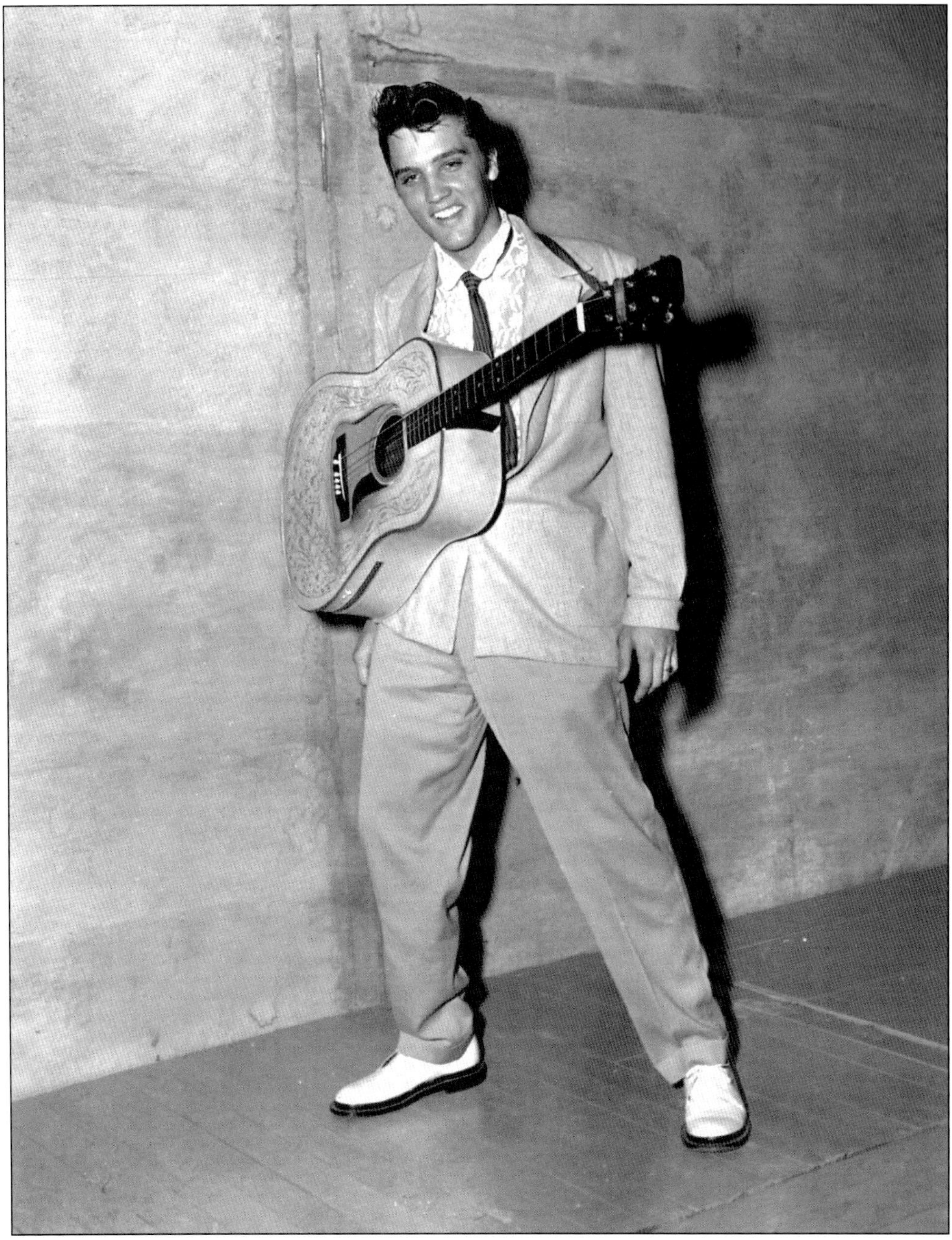

Elvis Presley arrived in Memphis from his boyhood home of Tupelo, Mississippi, in 1948. It was here that he was influenced by gospel, blues, and country music. Shown here on August 5, 1955, at the Overton Park Shell, Elvis was on the verge of stardom.

Riley "B. B." King was born in Indianola, Mississippi, and moved to Memphis as a young man. He often competed in the Beale Street amateur contests, emceed by Rufus Thomas in the 1940s. He received the "B. B." in his name when locals started calling him the Beale Street Blues Boy.

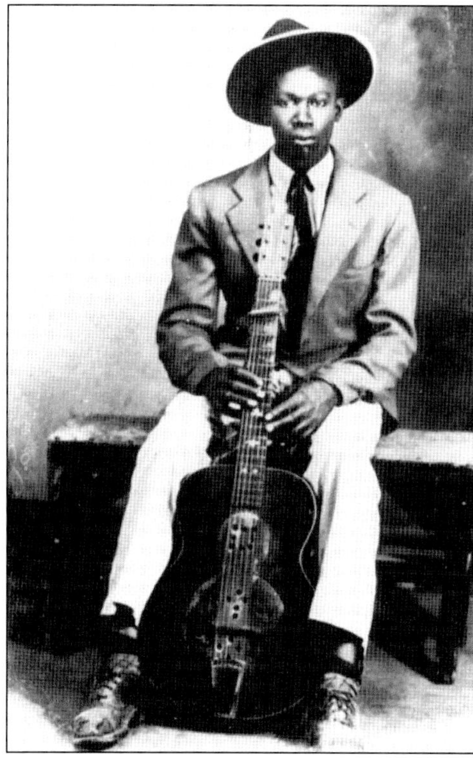

W. C. Handy, second from the right, came to Memphis from Florence, Alabama, in the early 1900s. In 1909, he composed a song entitled "Mr. Crump Blues, but soon changed it to the "Memphis Blues." He went on to write the "Beale Street Blues" and the "St. Louis Blues." Upon his death in 1958, a park on Beale Street was named in his honor.

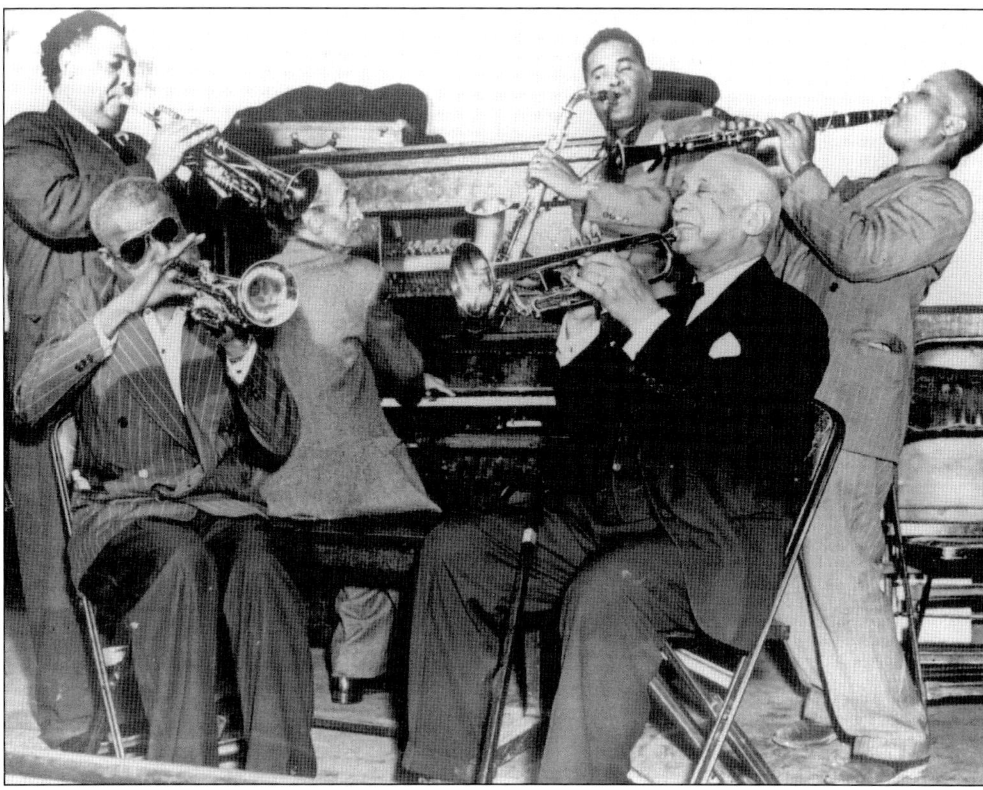

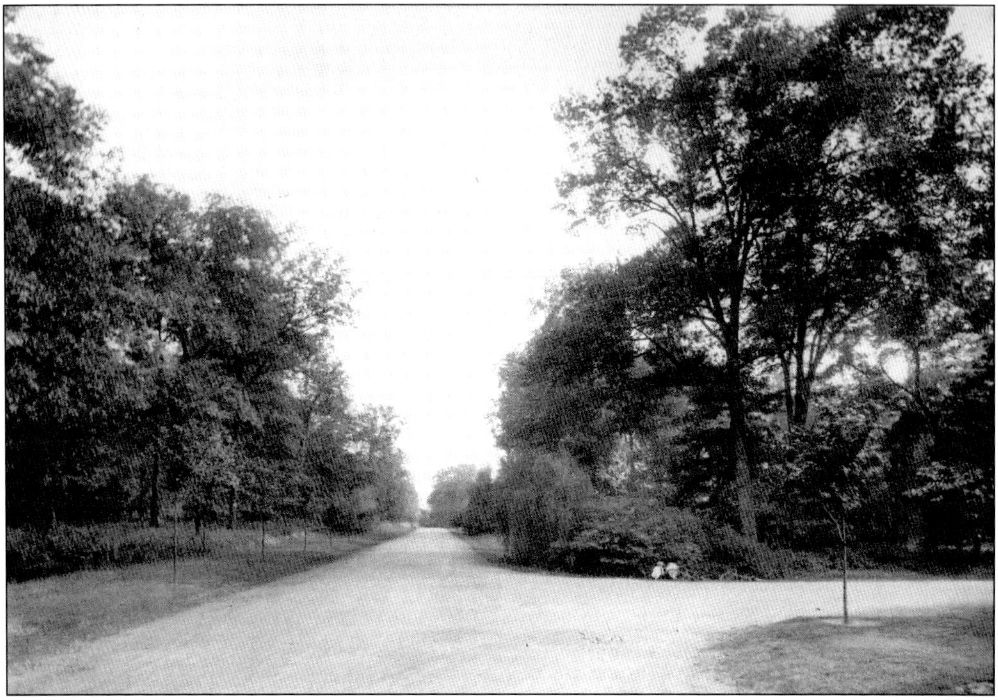

The Memphis parkway system, which includes North, East, and South Parkway, was designed by George Kessler and completed in 1910. Horse-riding trails were added to the median during the 1940s on East Parkway near Overton Park.

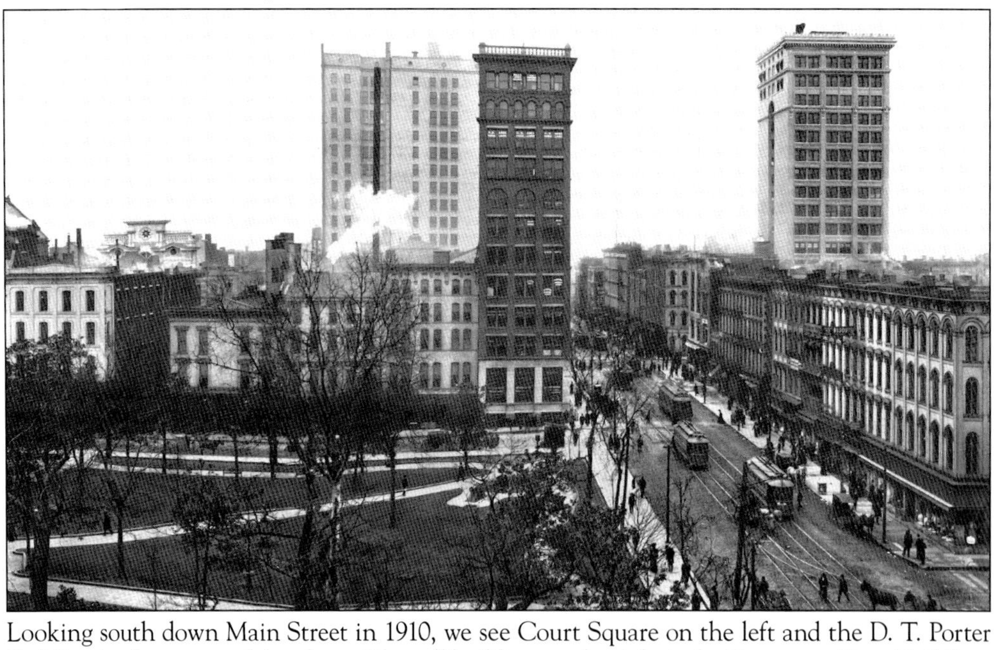

Looking south down Main Street in 1910, we see Court Square on the left and the D. T. Porter Building in the center of the photo. The tall building on the right is the Tennessee Trust Building, built in 1907, which is today the Madison, an upscale hotel. To the left of the D. T. Porter Building is Gaston's hotel and restaurant. John Gaston, a restaurateur and civic leader, donated land for a public park known as Gaston Park and helped to establish John Gaston Hospital.

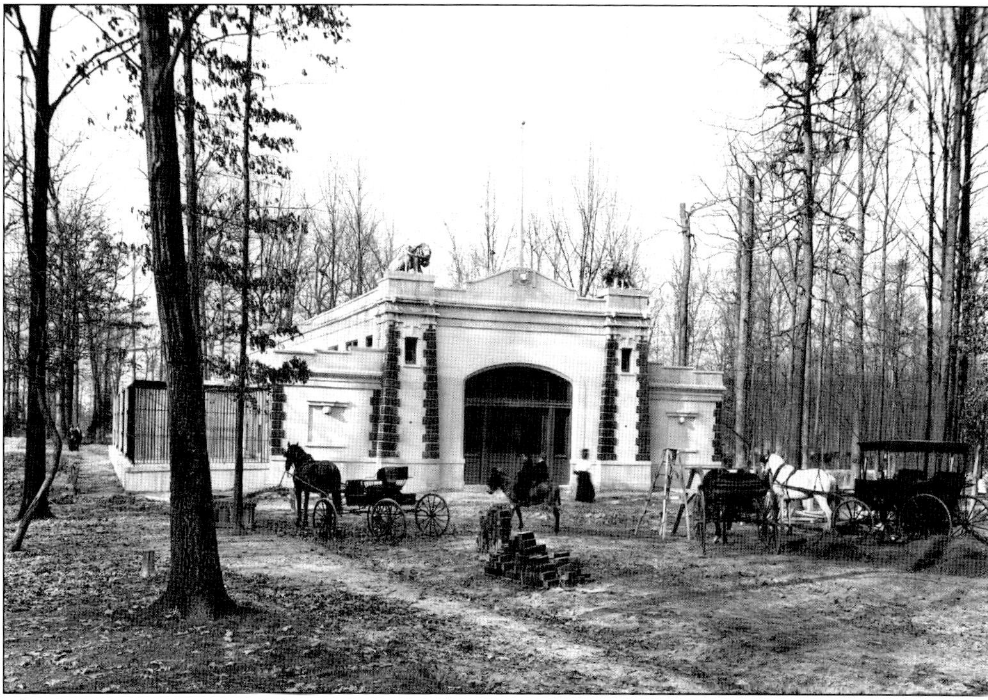

The Carnivora House of the Overton Park Zoo was designed by L. M. Weathers in 1909. For many years, it was the lion house, which included Leo, the famous MGM lion seen roaring at the beginning of movies. The building was converted into a restaurant in the 1990s.

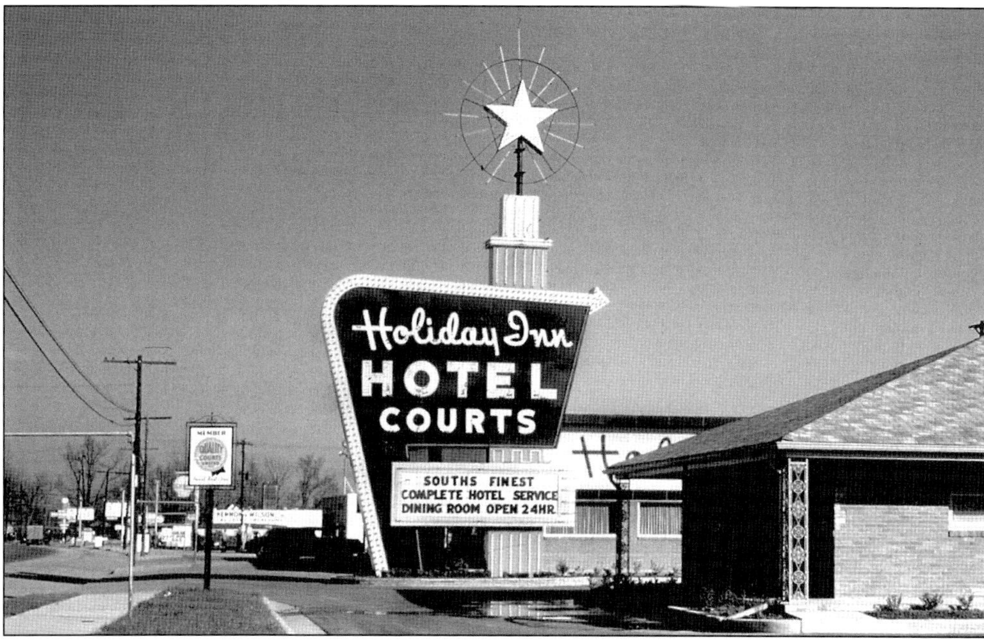

The very first Holiday Inn was located on Summer Avenue in east Memphis. Built by Kemmons Wilson in 1952, the new concept in overnight accommodations appealed to the traveler on a budget. Usually located outside of busy downtown, guests could pull their car right up to the door of their room. Today there are more than 1,500 Holiday Inns worldwide.

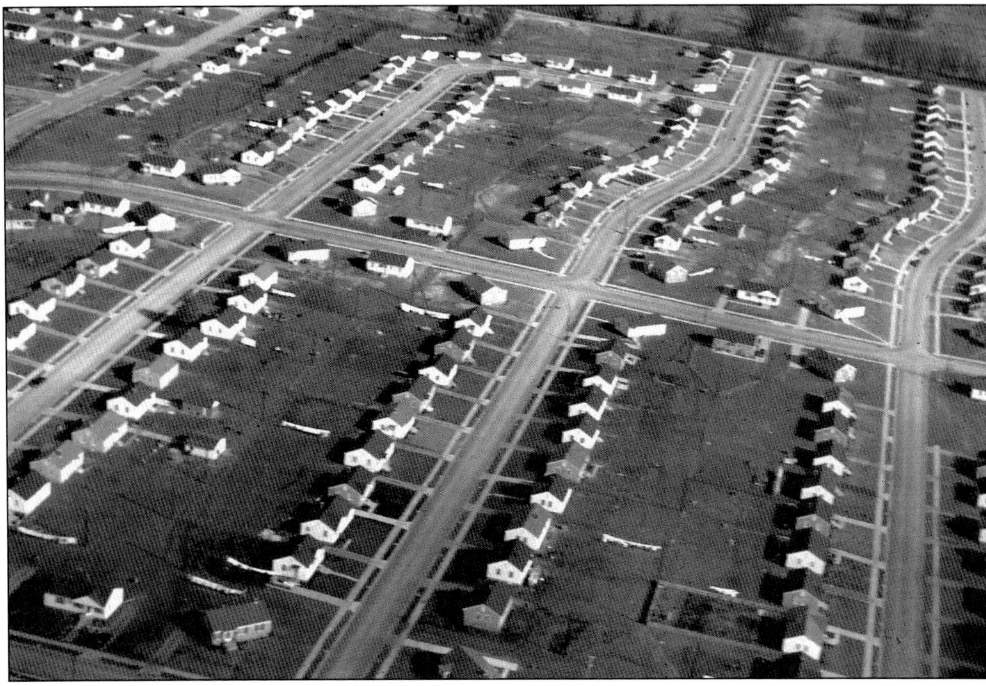

After World War II, Memphis saw a great housing boom. Subdivisions such as High Point Terrace, Sherwood Forest, and Berclair, shown above in 1947, enticed people to live in the suburbs. For many soldiers returning from the war, it was the first house they had ever owned.

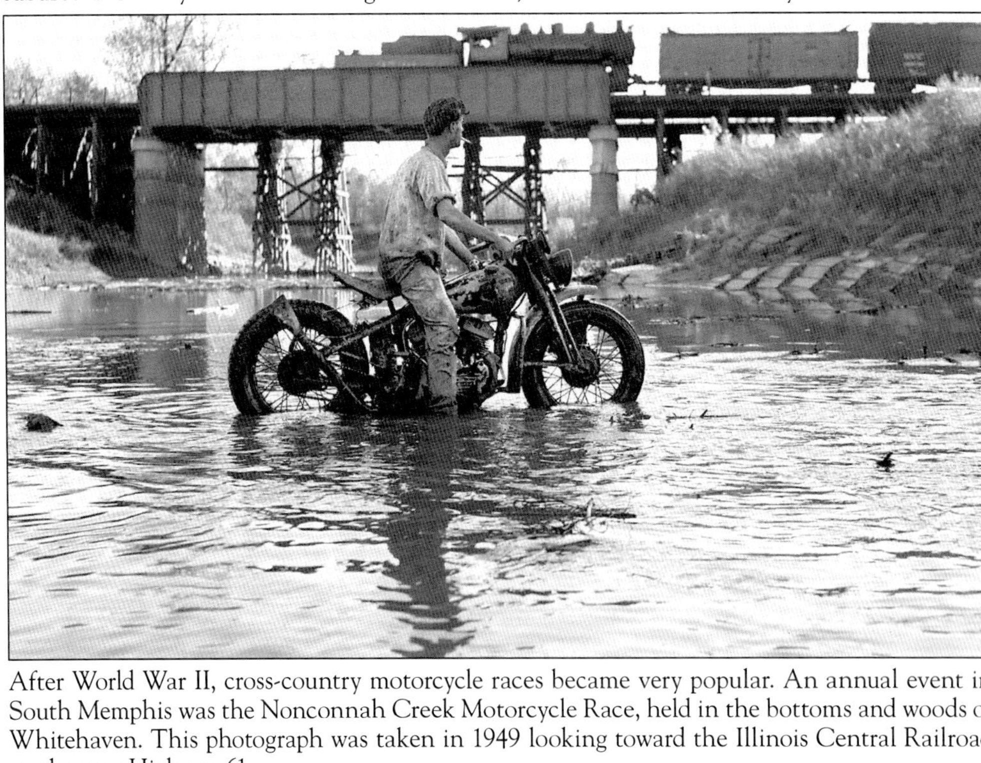

After World War II, cross-country motorcycle races became very popular. An annual event in South Memphis was the Nonconnah Creek Motorcycle Race, held in the bottoms and woods of Whitehaven. This photograph was taken in 1949 looking toward the Illinois Central Railroad tracks near Highway 61.

Two

SUBURBAN MEMPHIS

Over the years, Memphis has grown to incorporate many smaller communities and towns. Areas such as Binghampton, White Station, Buntyn, Frayser, and Berclair all were considered outside the city of Memphis. Raleigh, Cordova, and Whitehaven were all located within the city limits of Memphis. Raleigh was first settled by a trapper named Tapp, who hunted and trapped in the area around 1816. A few years later, Wilson Sanderlin and James Freeman purchased the land from the State of Tennessee and named the area Sanderlin's Bluff. In 1824, the State chose the area for the county seat despite opposition from John Overton, who wanted the courts located in Memphis. Land was purchased from Sanderlin and Freeman, and a new courthouse was built for $555. The new town was named Raleigh by Joseph Graham, in honor of his North Carolina home. The town quickly grew and, by 1837, had more than 1,500 residents. In 1866, the courts moved back to Memphis, and the once thriving town was now a sleepy community with just 300 inhabitants. Raleigh saw a revival in the late 1800s with the popularity of the mineral springs in the area. The first spa was advertised in 1842. For many years, the springs at Raleigh were noted for their purity and medicinal properties. Trains would bring out visitors for dances and fairs held on the grounds of the Raleigh Inn and other hotels. The Raleigh Inn burned in the early 1900s, and the springs eventually dried up as the local water table was lowered.

The first settlement in Cordova dates to 1835 when Robert and Joshua Ecklin arrived from North Carolina. A few years later, several other families arrived and began to farm the land. These included the Rogers, Cullen, Cole, Galloway, and Green families. They mainly raised cotton, which they would transport to Memphis in the fall. This took several days and often caused great hardships as the roads were dirt and there were few bridges. Thomas Crenshaw built his two-story home east of Cordova in the 1830s. Known as Mount Airy, the home still stands today and is listed on the National Register of Historic Places. Robert Ecklin built a large brick home on Hall Road near Macon in the early 1840s. Located where Woodland Hills is located today, it was the first home in the county to be built by an architect.

The community of Cordova was originally known as Marysville after Miss Mary Williams. It was later changed to Allentown around 1875 in honor of Jim Allen. Mr. Allen had donated land for a school, church, cemetery, and lots for both the Baptist and Presbyterian preachers. His store was located on Macon Road and became the center of the town. This was a common practice in several Shelby County towns including Millington, Bartlett, and Collierville. A large landowner would donate property in the center of his land for churches, schools, and courthouses, thus making his surrounding property more valuable. The city was renamed Dexter in 1888, when the Tennessee Midland Railroad was cut through. The only problem was there was another stop on the Midland line called Dexter, so the name was changed in 1903 to Cordova. The Cordova School was built in 1913 and is today a community center. In 1986, eight citizens purchased the old school for $150,000. Over the next four years, donation drives, bake sales, and arts and crafts festivals were held to help pay on the note. Proudly, in 1990, the final payment was made, and the community had their own civic center. Everything from karate classes to weddings are held in the historic building. During World War II, the National Fireworks Company built a factory in Cordova that produced an anti-aircraft gun called the Oclikeron, which fired a 20-mm shell.

Whitehaven was first settled by a pair of brothers, Benjamin and Daniel Hilderbrand. The brothers lived in Vicksburg, Mississippi, and often traveled to the Memphis Bluffs in the early 1800s to trade with the Native Americans. In 1818, when West Tennessee was opened for settlement, they purchased large tracts of land in the Whitehaven area. They were offered land near Court Square for a much lower price but decided on land near a large spring where they had traded and farmed for several years. In 1838, Benjamin Hilderbrand built a two-story home just west of the Memphis Airport on Airways Boulevard. This house stood until the late 1990s when it was torn down by the Memphis Airport Authority. Another large landowner was William Person, who owned 5,000 acres near Nonconnah Creek. He is said to have transported cotton seed from North Carolina in a Roman-style cart more than 65 times throughout his life. Some of the early settlers in the area included the Elam, Canada, Neely, Brooks, McCorkle, Weaver, and Raines families.

The area grew strong in the years preceding the Civil War. Nathan Bedford Forrest controlled most of northern Mississippi, and most farmers in the Whitehaven area were sympathetic to the cause and helped him when they could. As news of their sympathetic help for Forrest reached the Union army station in Memphis, the Union made raids into the southern part of Shelby County, burning farms and even killing civilians in front of family members. Belle Edmondson was a spy for the Confederate army. As the 18-year-old daughter of Capt. Andrew Edmondson, she would routinely carry medicine and documents concealed in her dresses to Memphis, flirting with Union guards until they would let her pass. Whitehaven recovered from the effects of the war and continued to grow. In 1929, land was purchased from the Elam family for the Memphis Airport. Few of the original inhabitants would recognize Whitehaven today, a community of large subdivisions and warehouses.

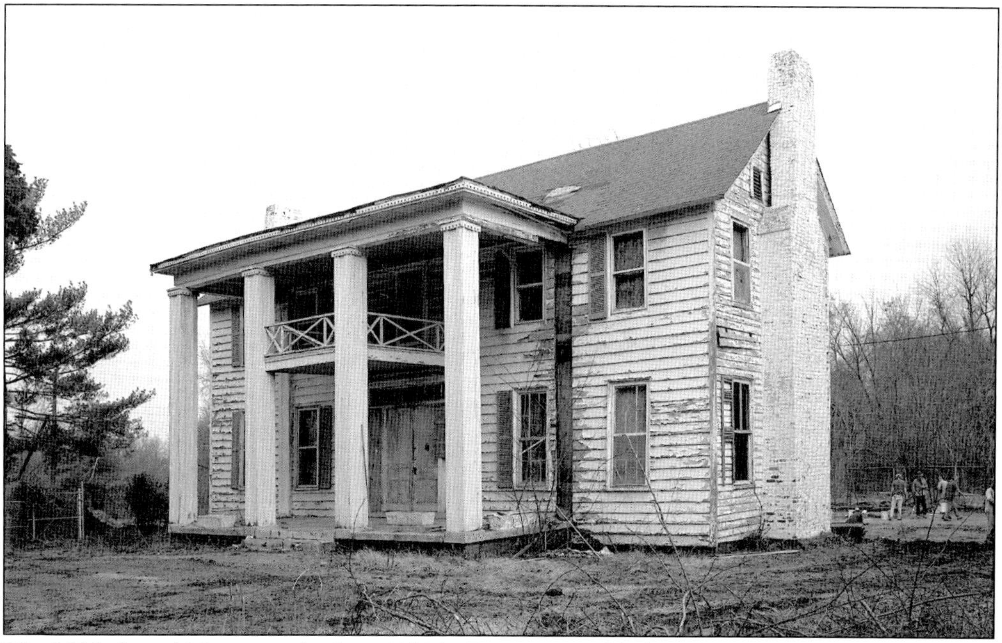

The Hilderbrand House was built in 1838 by Benjamin Hilderbrand, whose father had settled in the Whitehaven community around 1818. Benjamin's father and uncle had applied for a 7,000-acre land grant in 1818 near Whitehaven, where they had operated a trading post for several years. The house was torn down by the airport authority in 1998.

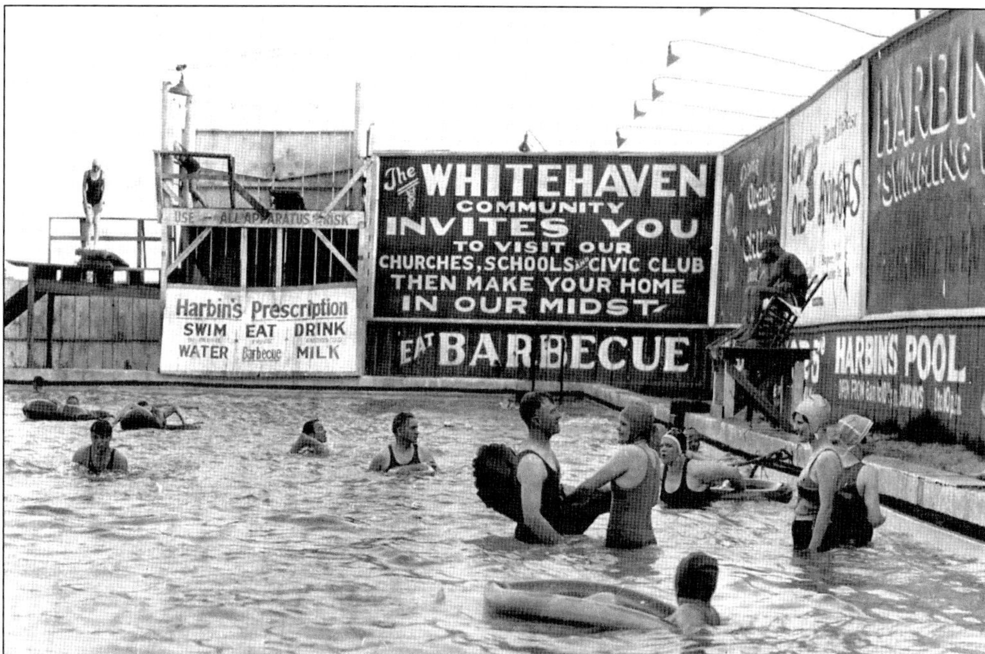

J. C. Harbin was an entrepreneur in the Whitehaven community from the 1920s until the 1980s. His Harbin Cabins were advertised along Highway 51, and his public swimming pool even promoted living in Whitehaven. He also owned a race track, an ice cream company, and a barbecue restaurant.

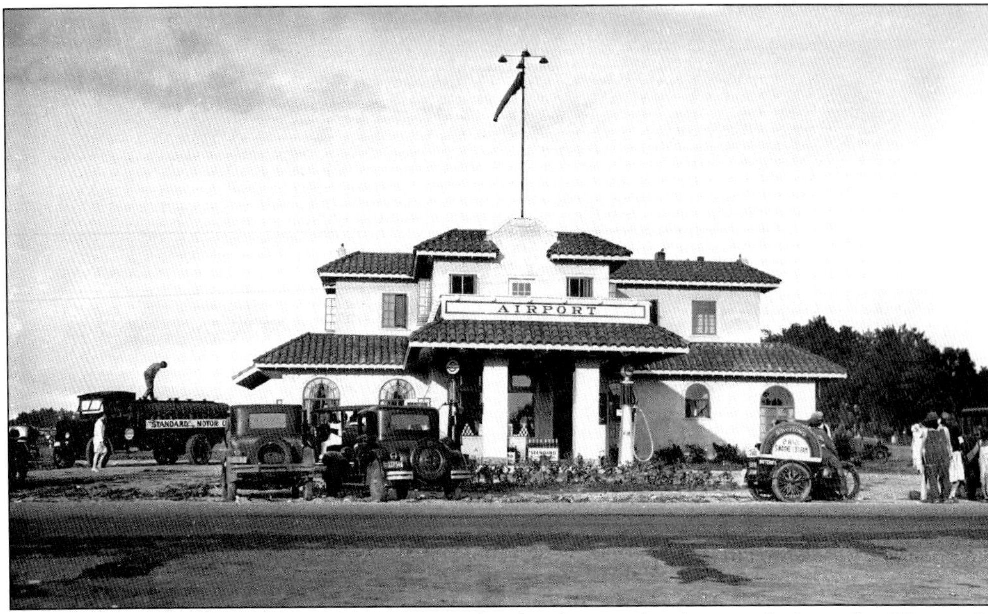

The City purchased 200 acres from several Whitehaven families, including the Elams, for $250,000. Over the next 70 years, the City added onto this, and today the airport covers more than 3,330 acres. The original airport handled four flights a day in 1929. A new terminal building was constructed by the Works Progress Administration in 1939. By this time, the airport was seeing 30 flights a day with such airlines as American, Eastern, and Southern (now Delta).

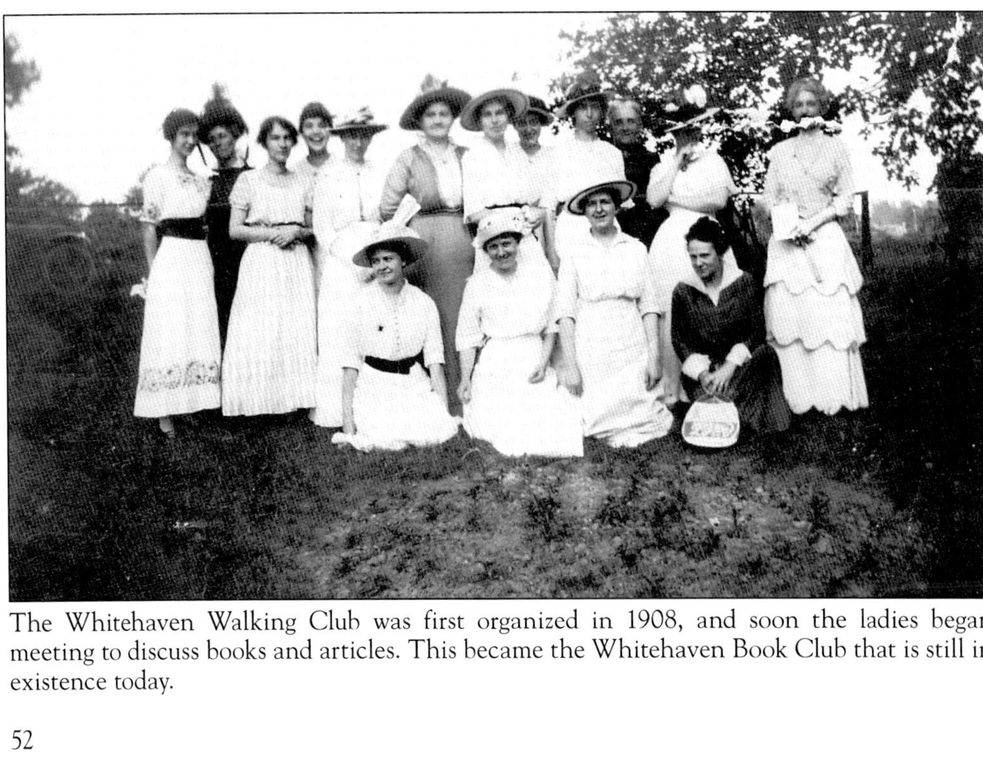

The Whitehaven Walking Club was first organized in 1908, and soon the ladies began meeting to discuss books and articles. This became the Whitehaven Book Club that is still in existence today.

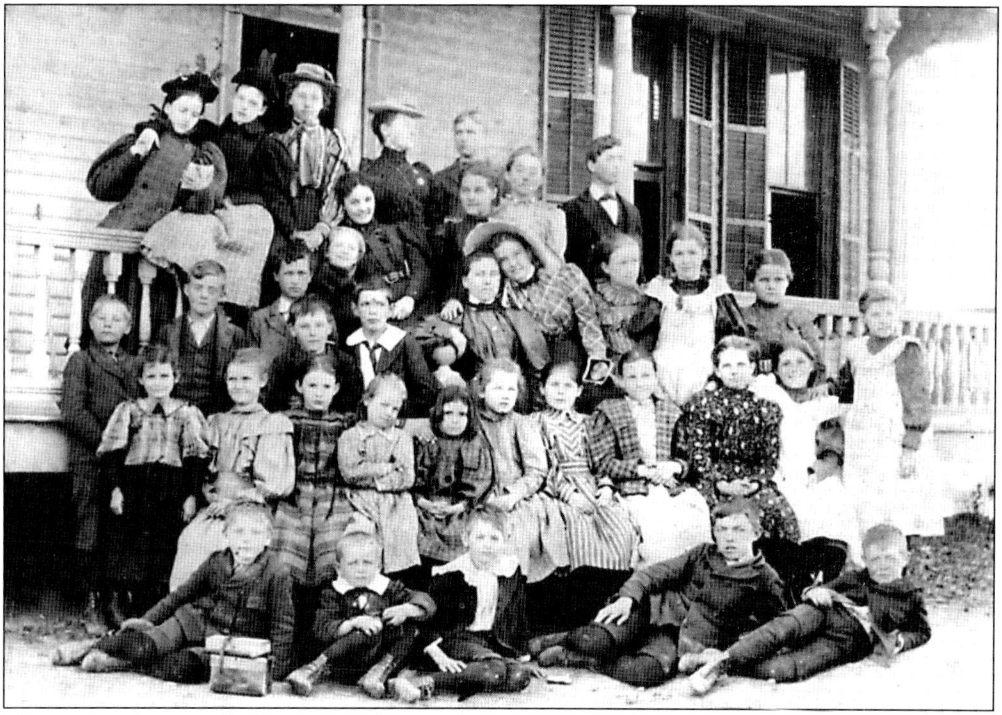

This early photograph from around 1900 shows the Whitehaven School. The school quickly outgrew the tight quarters of the converted house shown above, and a new, more modern school was built in 1908.

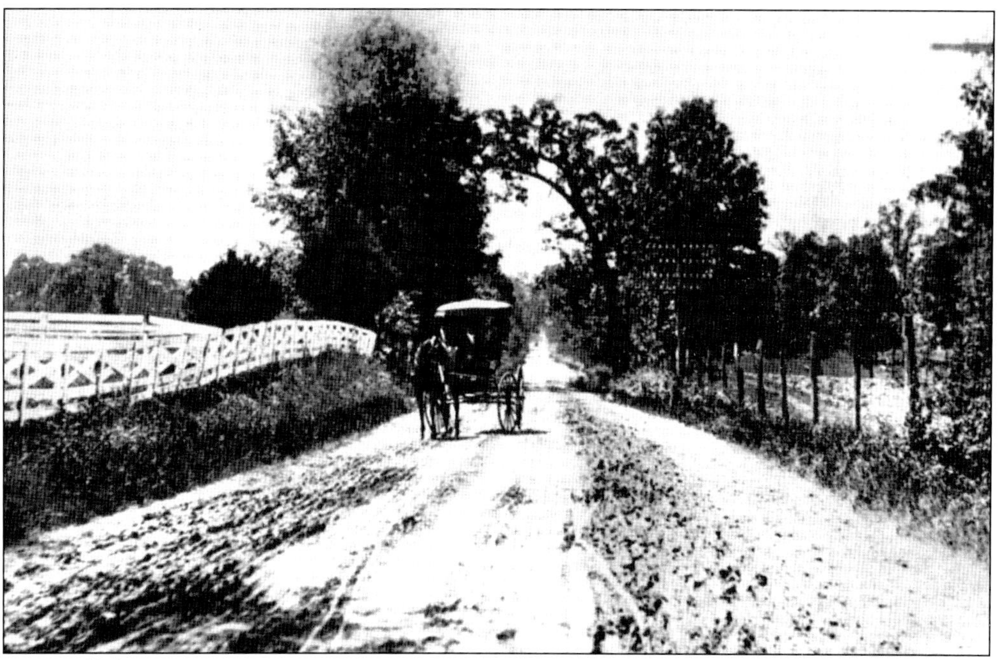

Originally known as Hernando Road, the street was officially changed to Elvis Presley Boulevard in the late 1970s to pay tribute to its most famous resident, Elvis Presley, who had purchased Graceland in 1957 for $150,000.

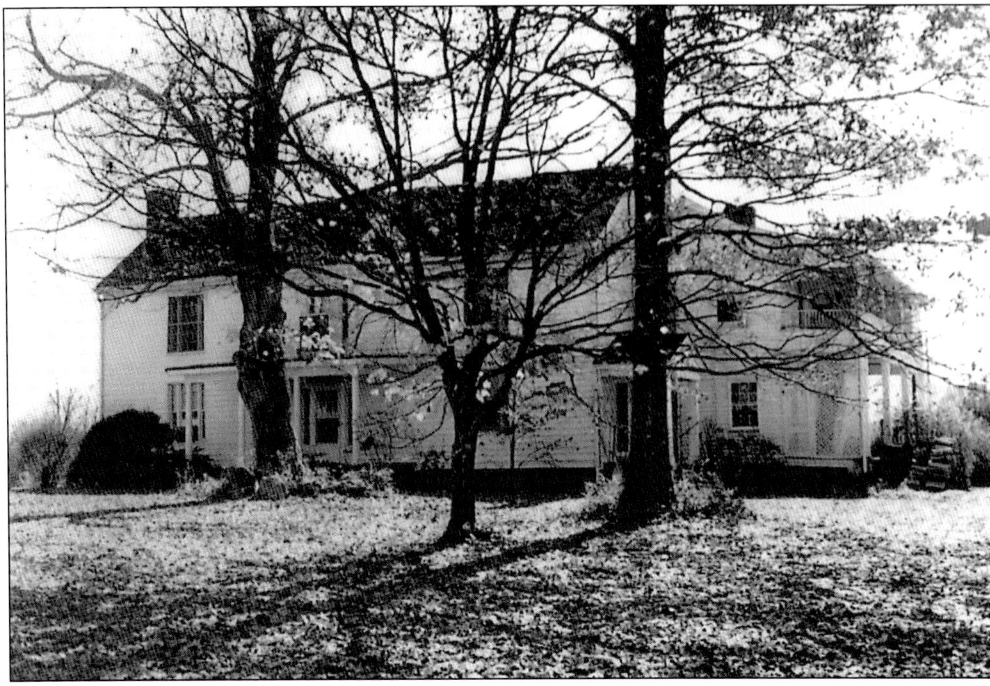

Mount Airy was built by Thomas C. Crenshaw in 1835 near Morning Sun. Mount Airy, with more than 2,000 acres, was a working plantation with its own gin, sawmill, barns, blacksmith shop, and smokehouse.

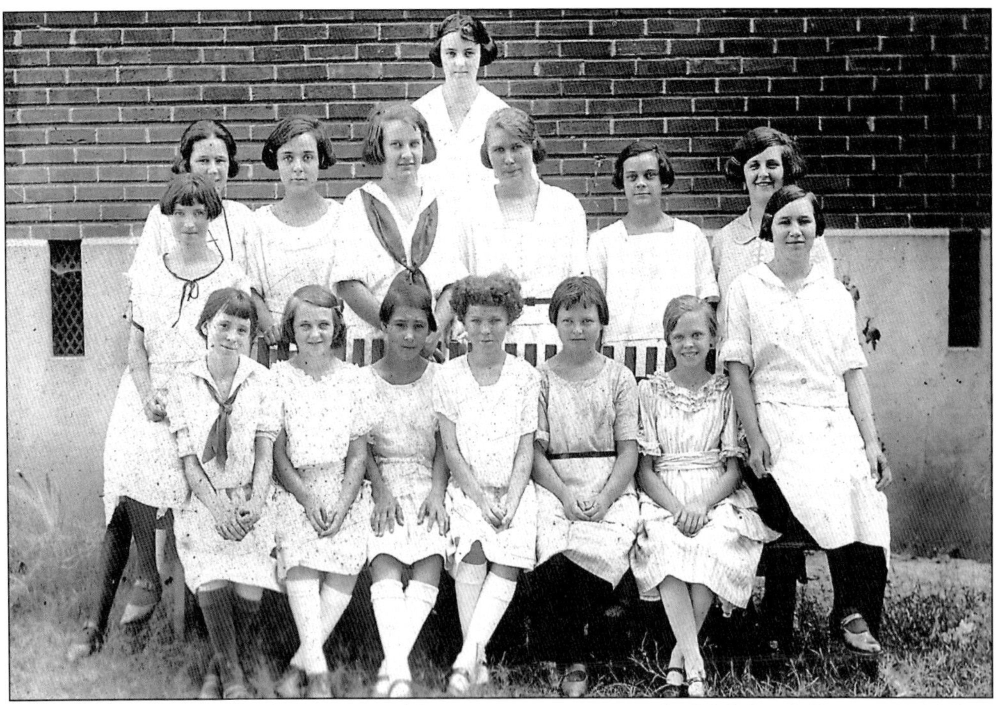

The girls shown above had just returned from winning a prize at the Mid-South Fair in 1923. They attended the Cordova School, which was built in 1913 and is today used as a community center.

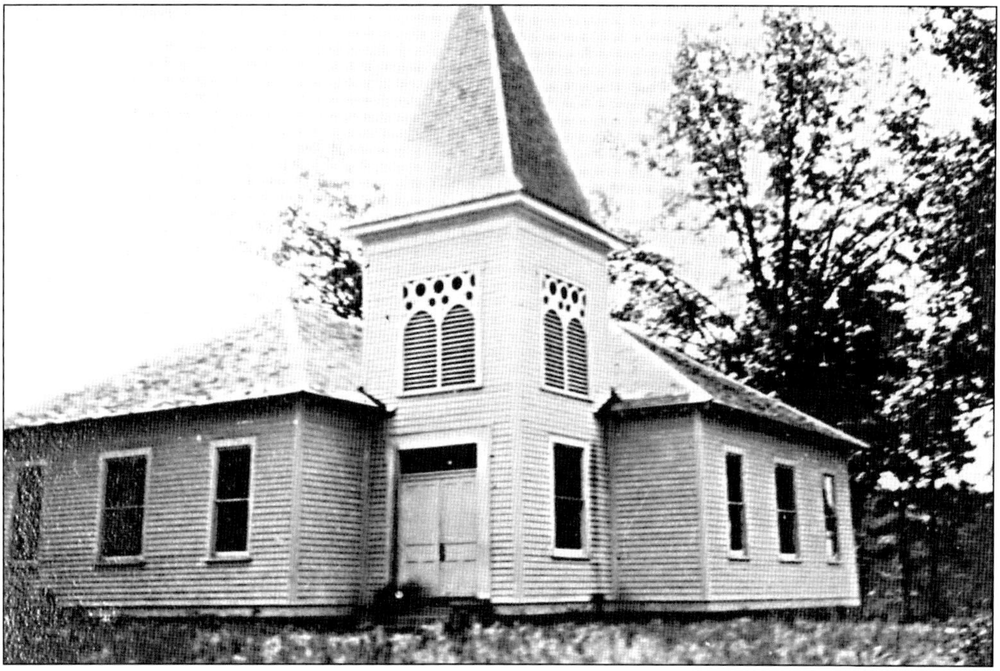

The Cordova Presbyterian Church was organized in the mid-1800s. There were 11 charter members of the church, all named either Allen or Rogers.

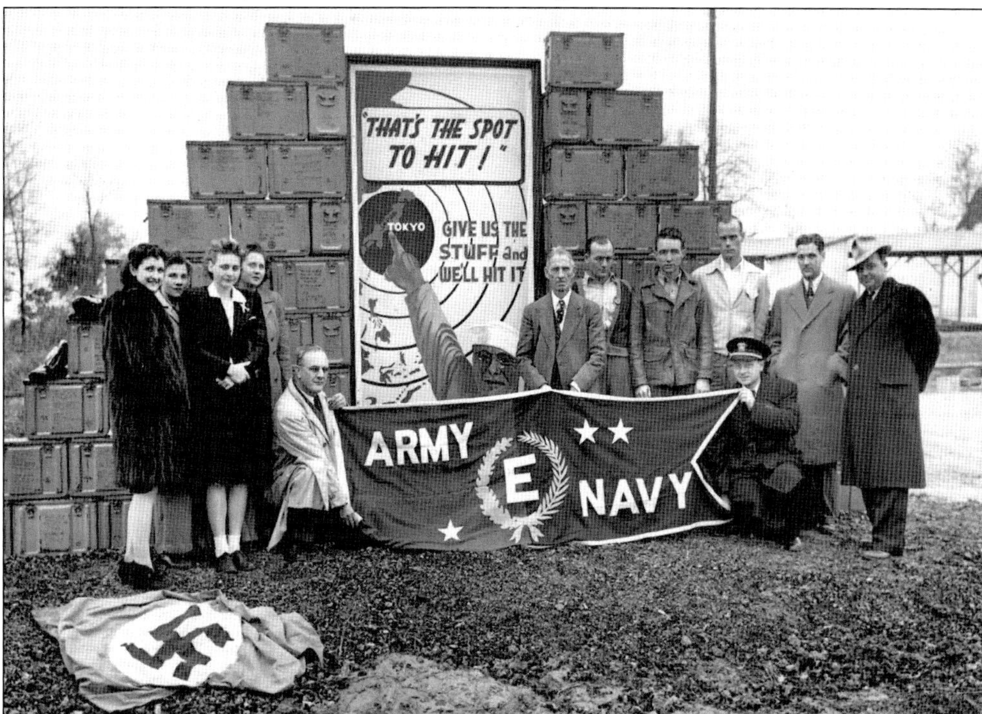

Shown here is the original crew who started with the National Firework Company in 1942. Third from the left is lifelong Cordova resident and historian Margaret Schwam. This photograph was taken in 1944. The plant produced a tank shell during World War II.

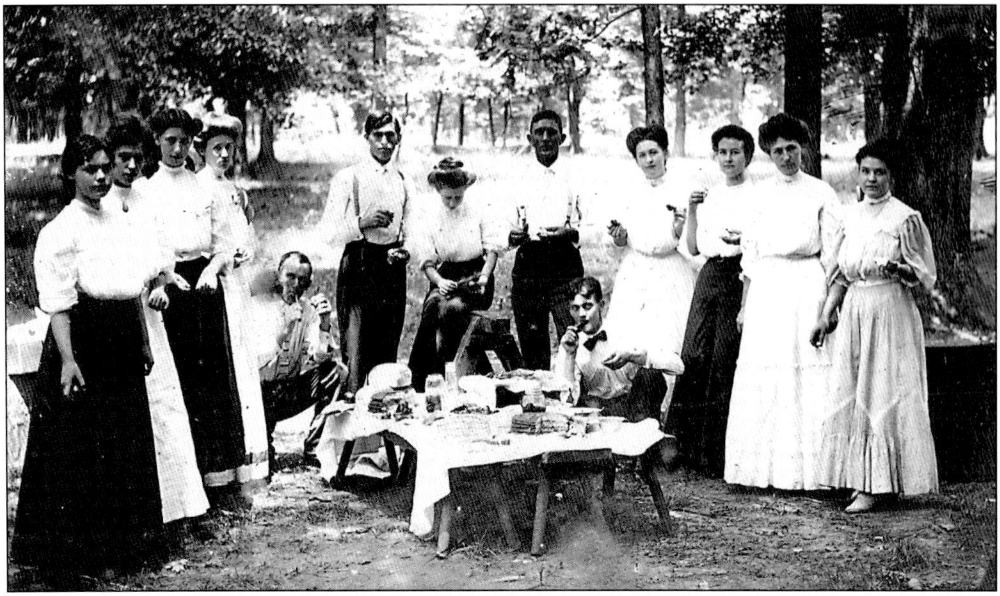

This early photograph shows a picnic near Cordova in 1908. From left to right are Lattie Kirk, Gertrude Strong, Irene Moore, Callie Woods, Clyde Yates, Joe Strong, Maude Moore, John Schwam, Joe Arrington, Annie Yates, Chloe Ruthledge, Glenda Strong, and Effie Mullins. The photograph was mailed for 5¢ with the simple address "J. H. Schwam, Cordova" written on the back.

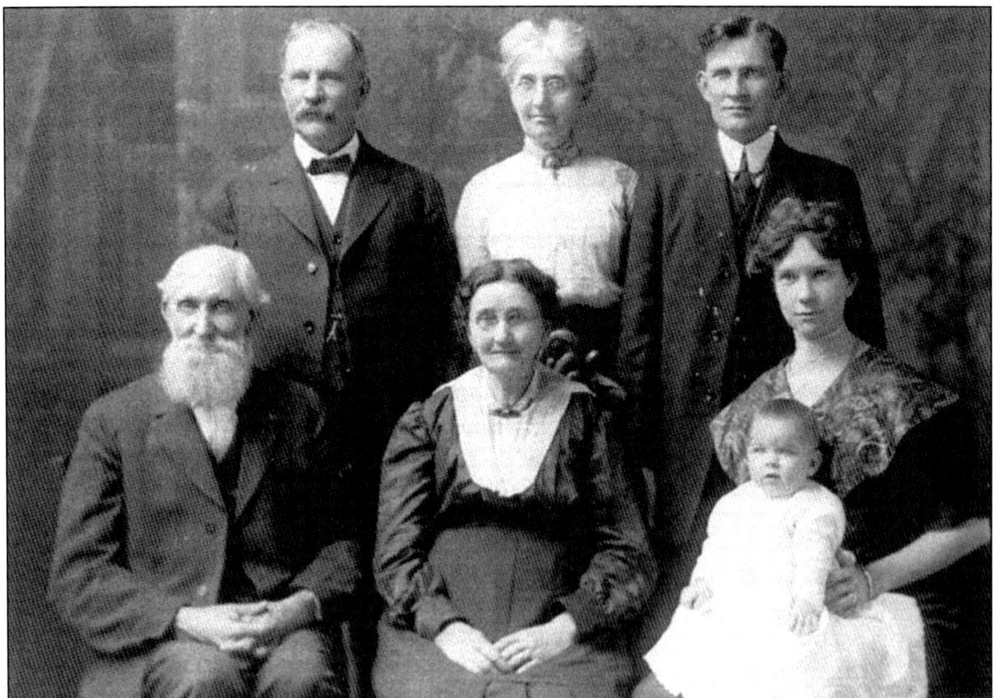

From left to right are (standing) Walter Granville Allen, Alice Agusta Allen, and Dr. Elroy Levert Hooper; (seated) Thomas Allen Jr., Roxanna Allen, and Marie Allen Hooper holding Agusta Sue Hooper. The first Allens arrived in Cordova around 1835.

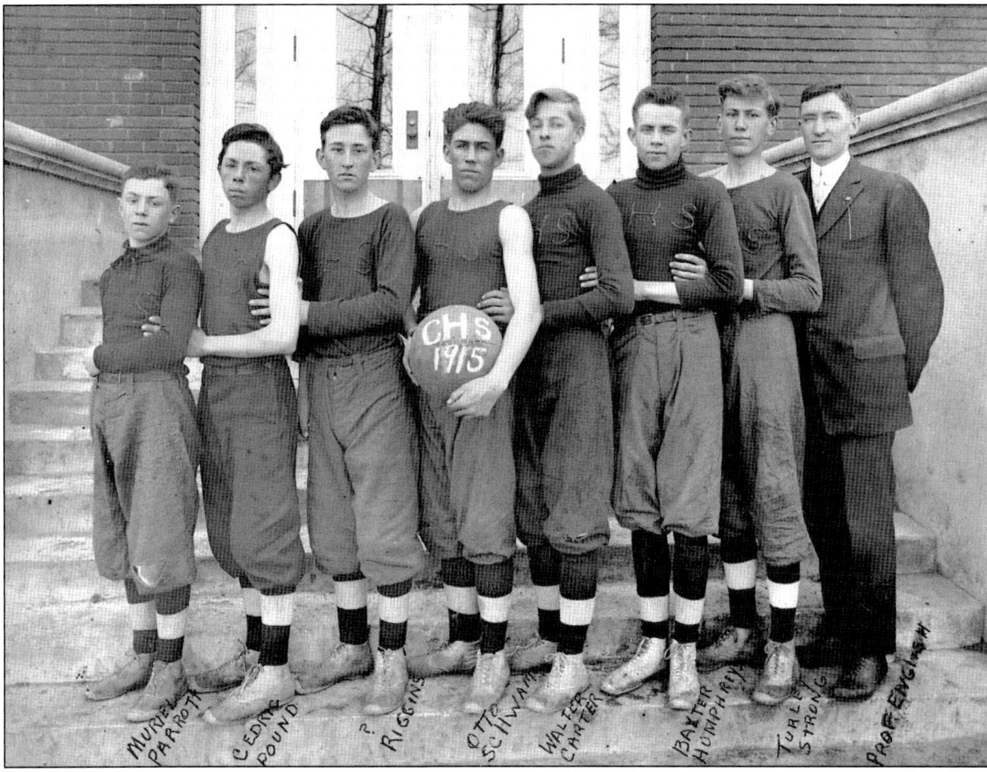

Pictured here are members of the Cordova boys' basketball team from 1915. From left to right are Muriel Parrott, Cedric Pound, John Riggins, Otto Schwam, Walter Carter, Baxter Humphrey, Turley Strong, and Professor English.

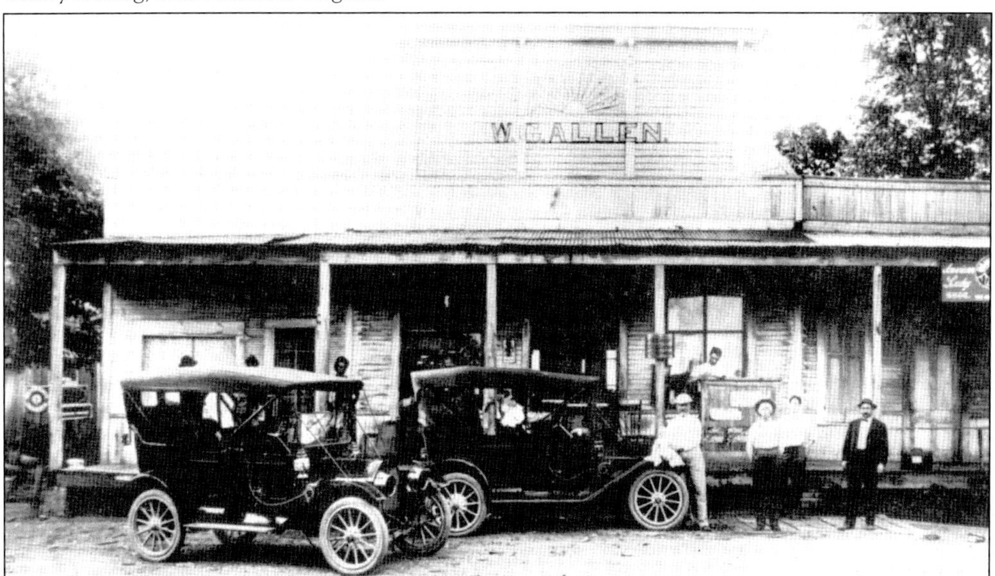

The Allen Store was located on Macon Road in Cordova. This photograph was taken around 1920.

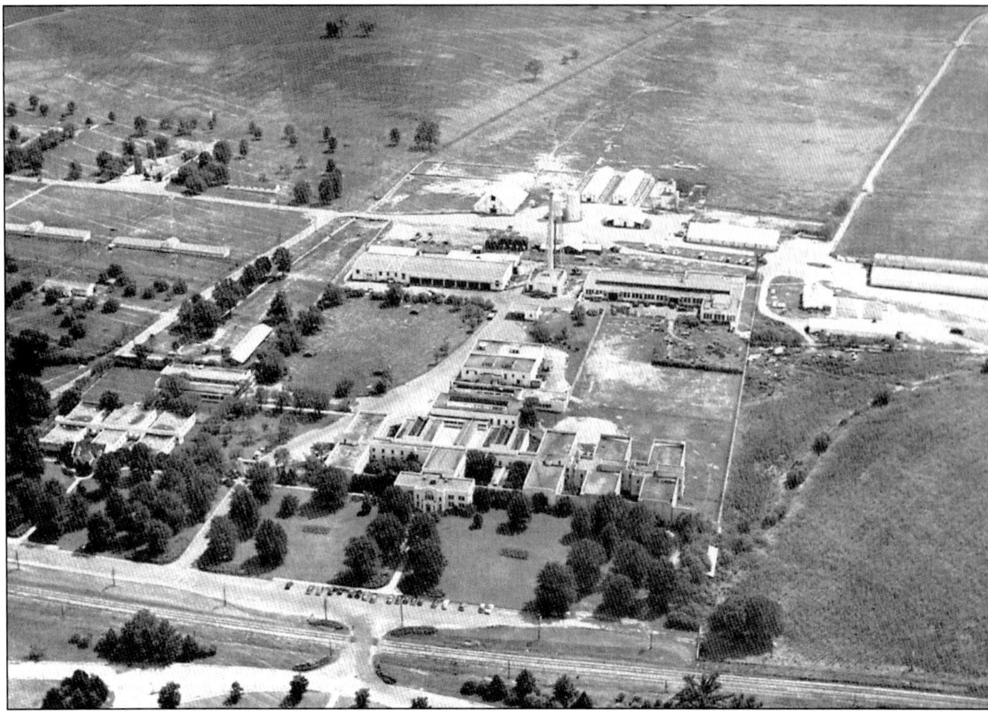

This aerial photograph of the Shelby County Penal Farm in the 1940s shows the immense size of the facility. The facility contained a prison, hospitals, and county government offices.

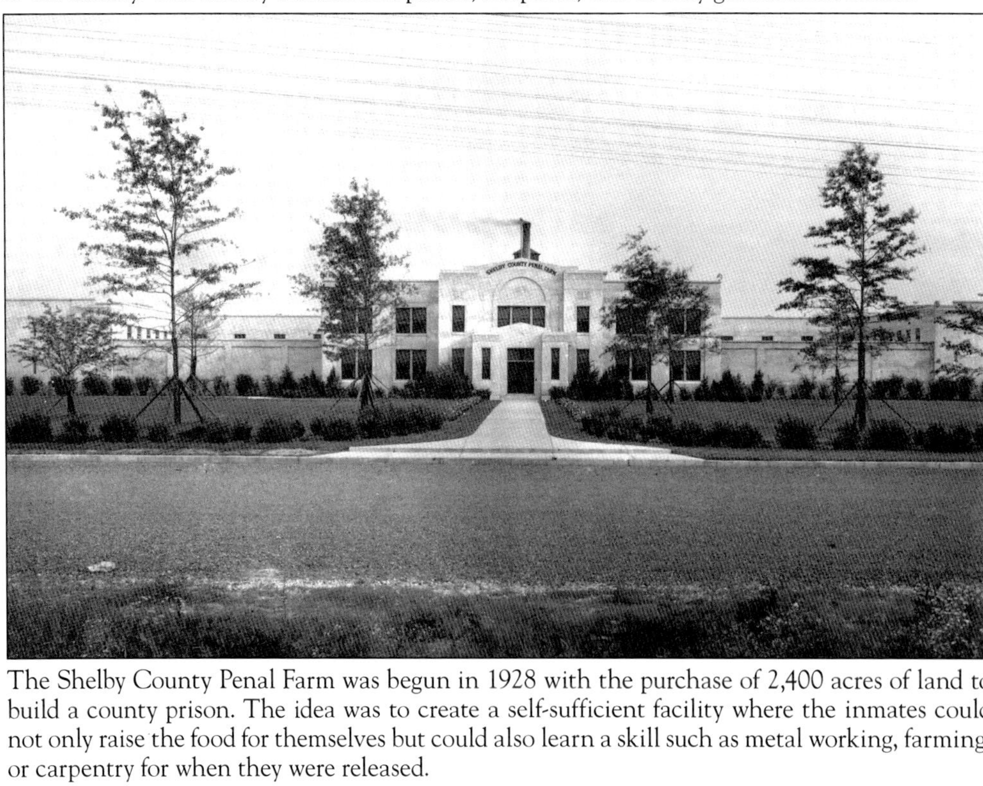

The Shelby County Penal Farm was begun in 1928 with the purchase of 2,400 acres of land to build a county prison. The idea was to create a self-sufficient facility where the inmates could not only raise the food for themselves but could also learn a skill such as metal working, farming, or carpentry for when they were released.

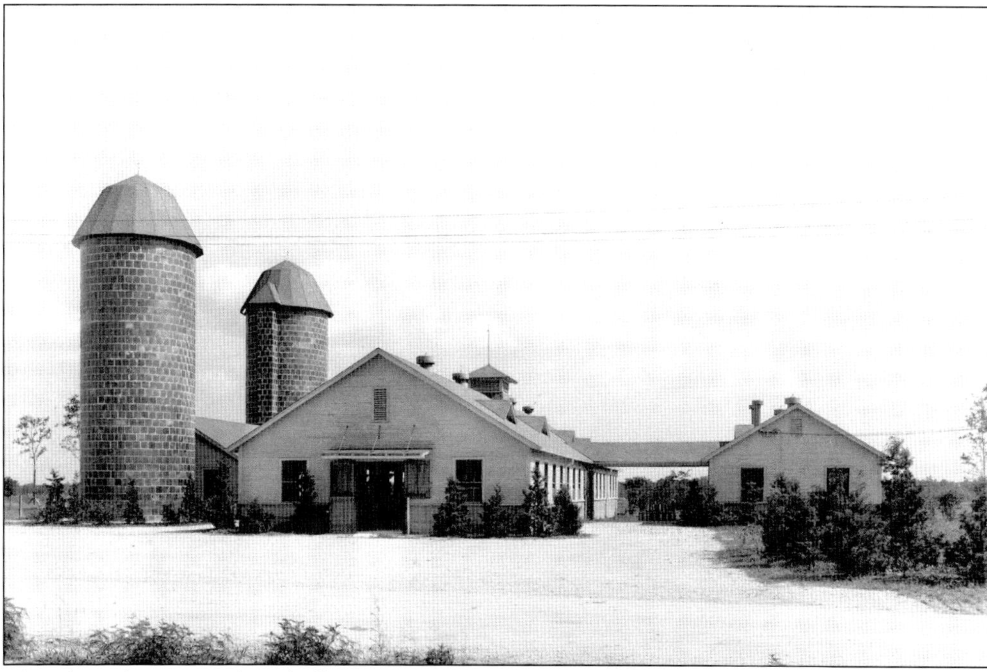

The dairy barns at the Shelby County Penal Farm were some of the cleanest and most productive in the county. The cattle raised here regularly won ribbons at the Mid-South Fair and the state fair.

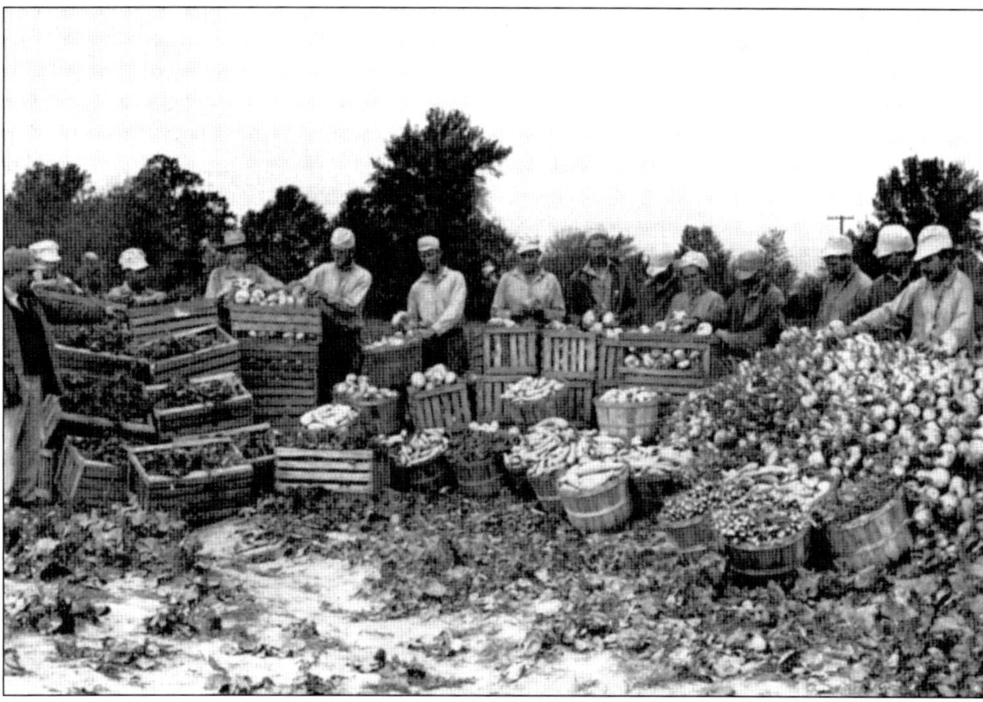

Thirty-nine varieties of vegetables were grown on 300 acres of land at the Shelby County Penal Farm. A canning plant, a dehydrating facility, and a cold storage plant enabled the prisoners to produce and conserve 93 percent of all the food they consumed.

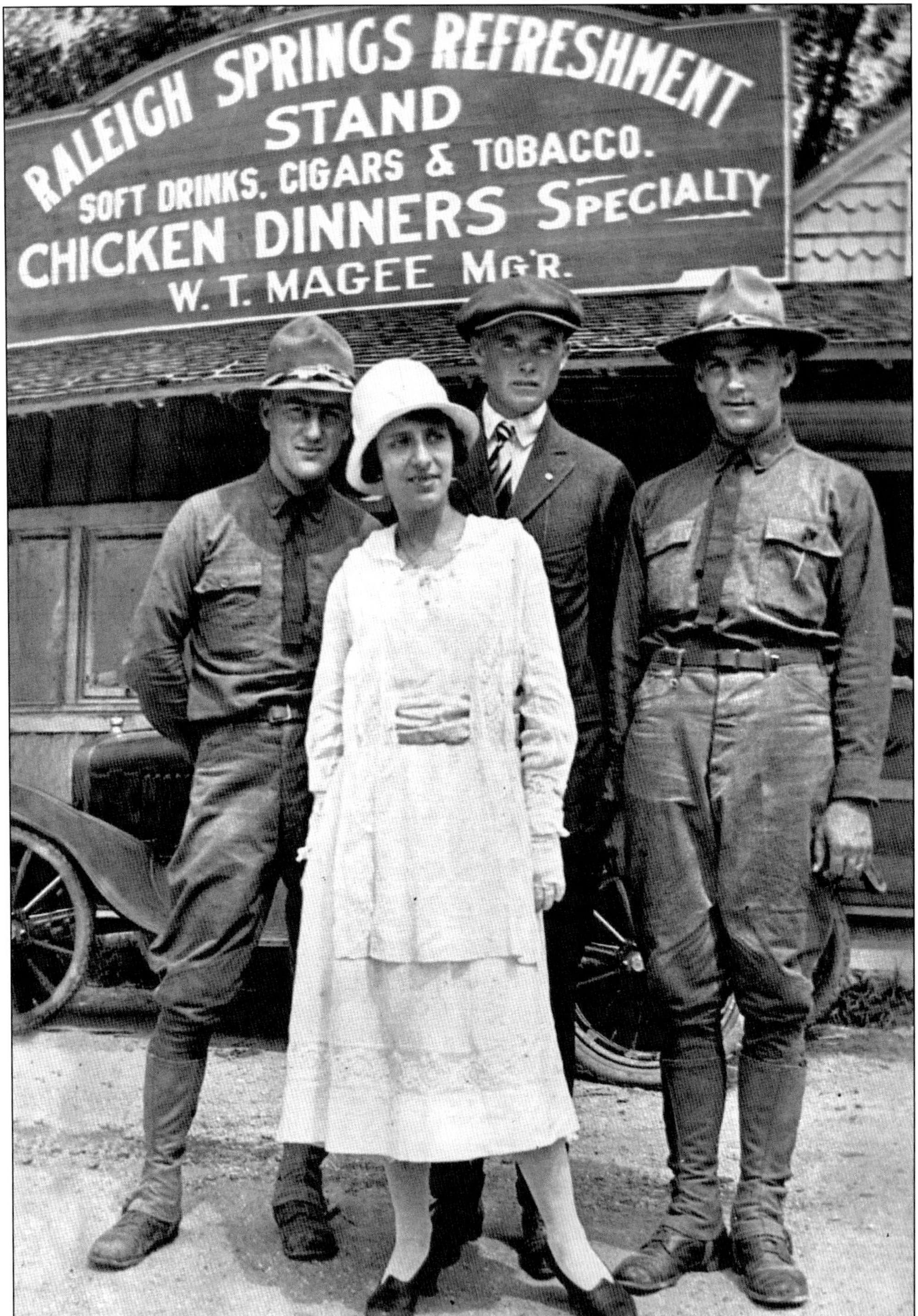

The Raleigh Springs Refreshment Stand was operated by W. T. Magee and was located near the turnaround for the Memphis-to-Raleigh rail line. Shown here in 1918, the stand operated until the late 1920s. The woman is Roberta Weakley.

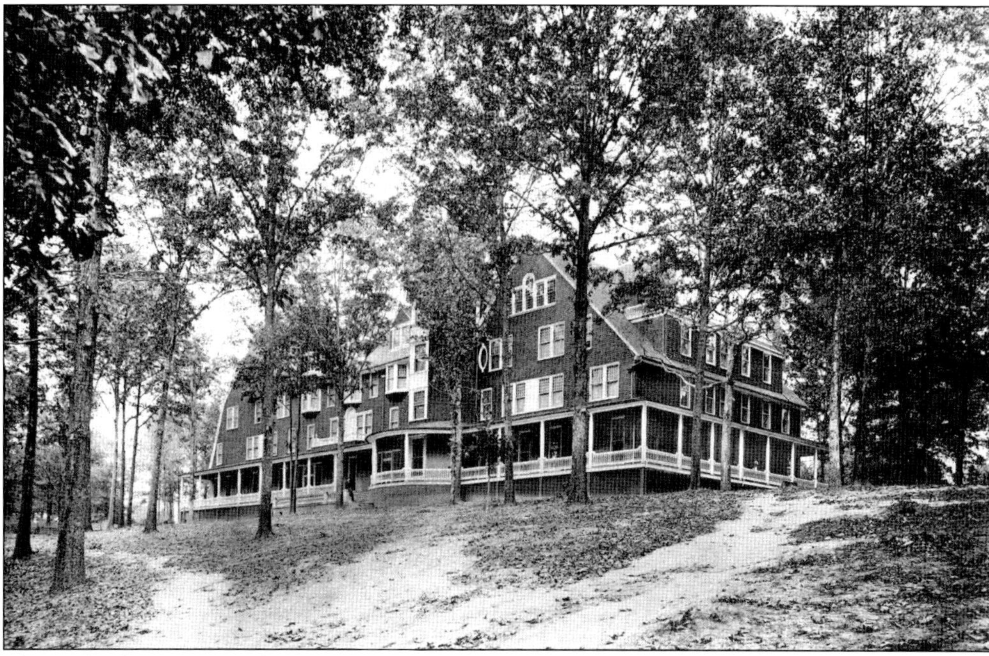

The Raleigh Inn started in 1873 and was updated in 1892 by B. I. Duke of North Carolina. People came for the natural springs, which were reported to have great health benefits. The inn prospered, hosting band concerts, grand balls, and military drills by the Chickasaw Guards until closing in 1903. The inn was briefly a school for girls before becoming the James Sanatorium. The inn burned in 1912.

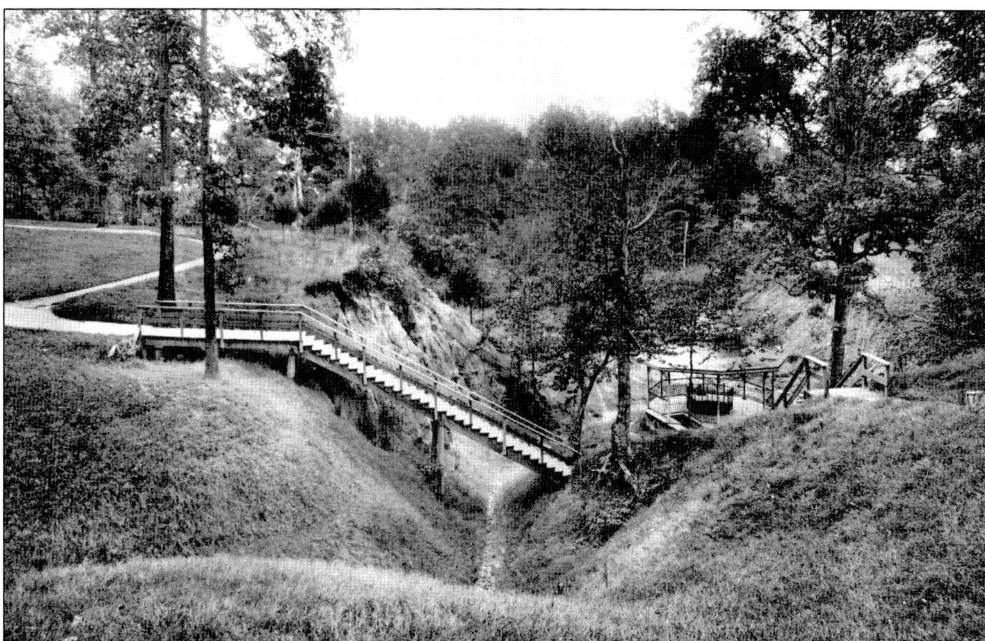

The mineral springs in Raleigh were advertised as far back as 1842. The most famous of the springs was called Baby Spring. It was said that it had cured a sick child who had camped nearby. The water was bottled and sold in Memphis as a cure for colicky babies.

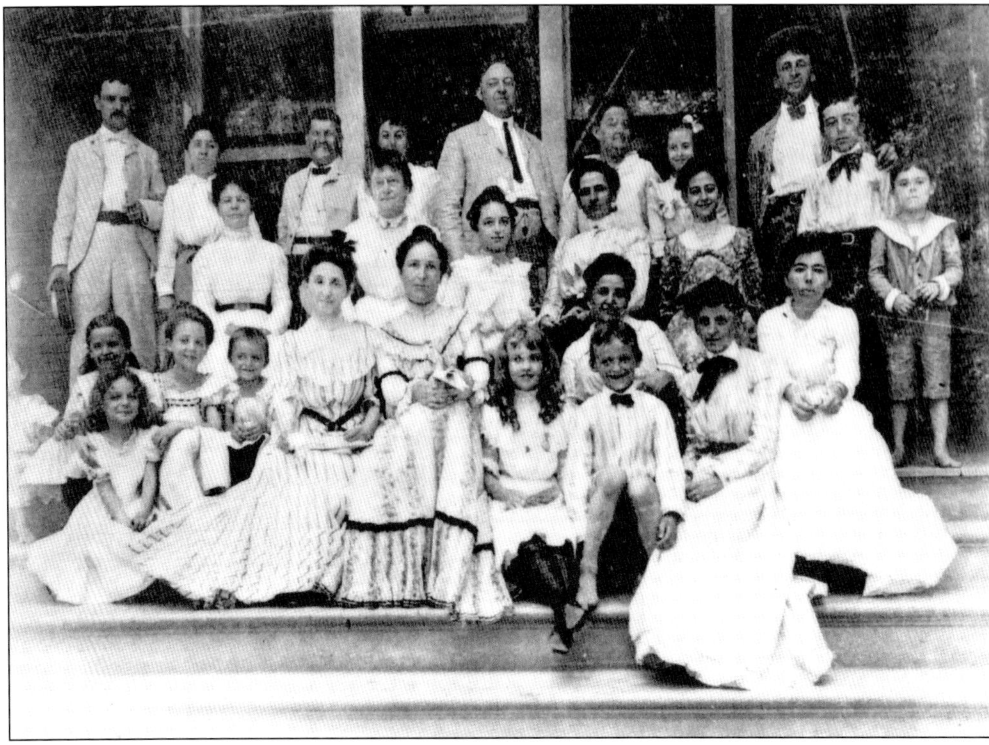

A group of young people pose on the front steps of the Raleigh Inn. This photograph was taken around 1900.

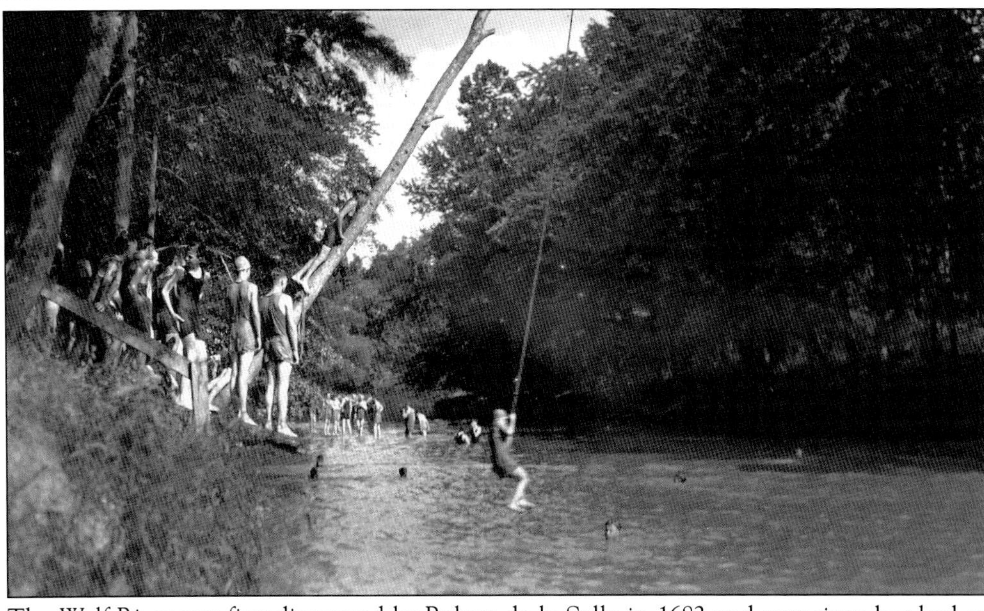

The Wolf River was first discovered by Robert de la Salle in 1682 and ever since has had an important impact on Shelby County. The original layout for the town of Memphis, in 1818, was measured with the Wolf River as the northern boundary. Francis Wright, in 1823, established her Nashoba plantation on the banks of the Wolf River near Germantown. The river was clear in the early days and was a popular swimming hole.

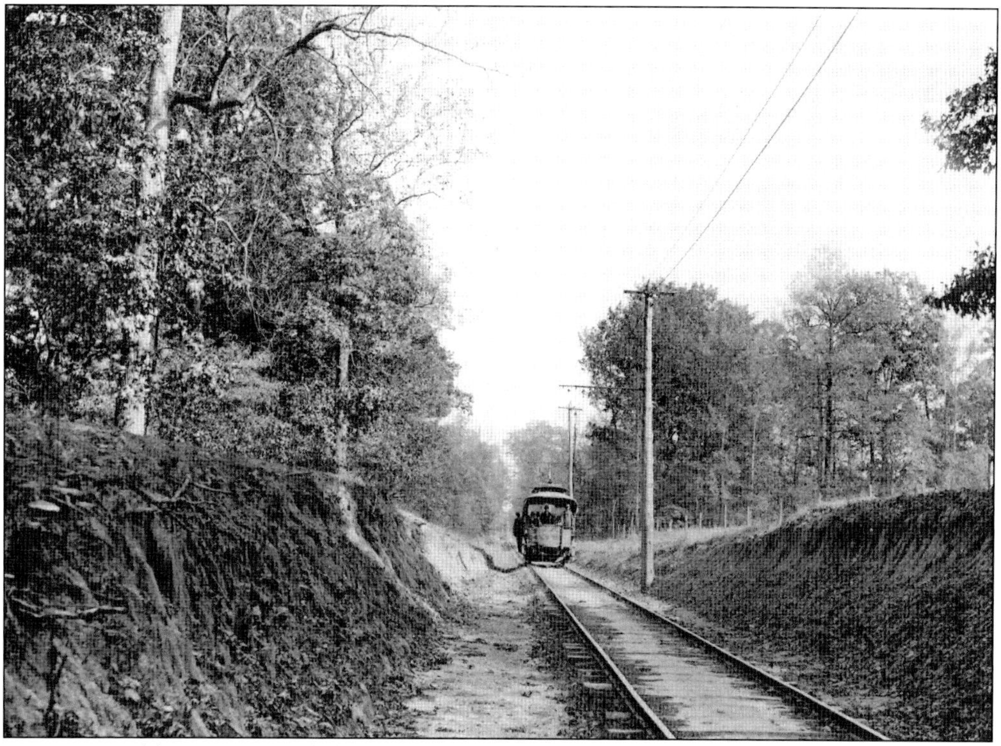

In 1892, a rail line was extended out to Raleigh from downtown Memphis. B. I. Duke of North Carolina invested $50,000 in the new rail line and improvements to the Raleigh Inn.

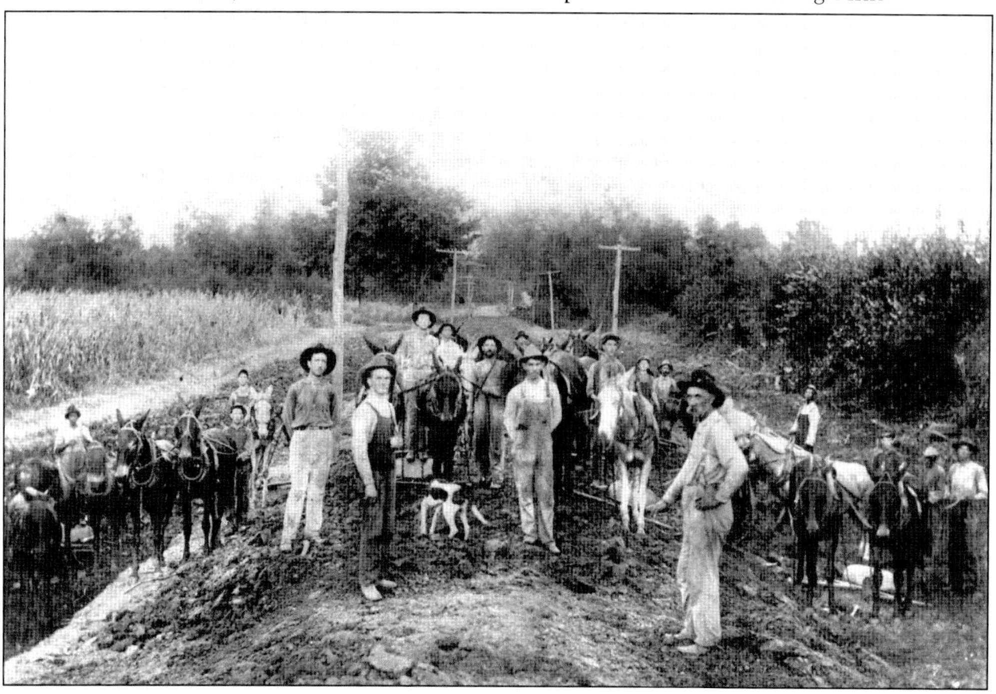

Building roads through the forest and hills of Raleigh was tough work. Workers are shown here in 1910 clearing out stumps on what would eventually become Highway 51.

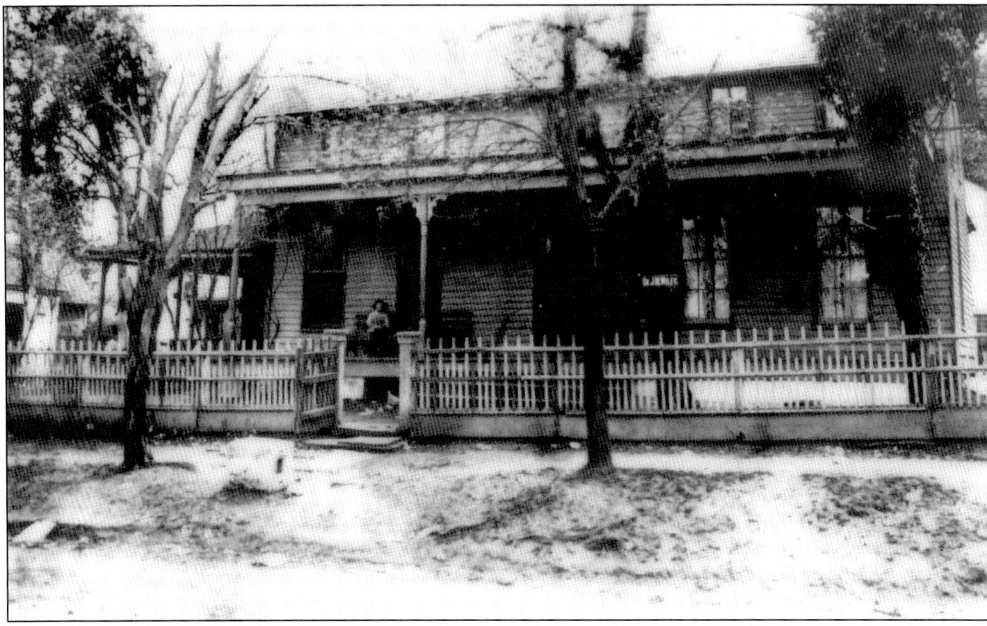

This is the home of Dr. J. M. Wiley. It was located on the east side of Old Raleigh Road, present-day Austin Peay Road, close to Coleman Road. This photograph was taken in 1901.

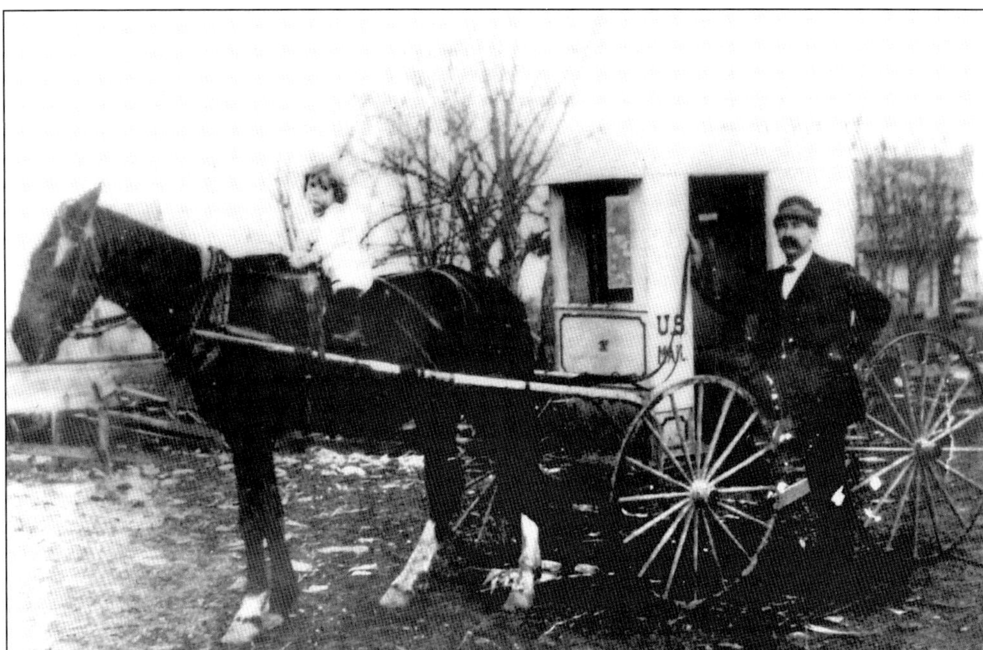

Demps Weakly was the mailman for Raleigh in the early 1900s. His son, Travis, sits on the horse. This photograph was taken on Raleigh Millington Road around 1910.

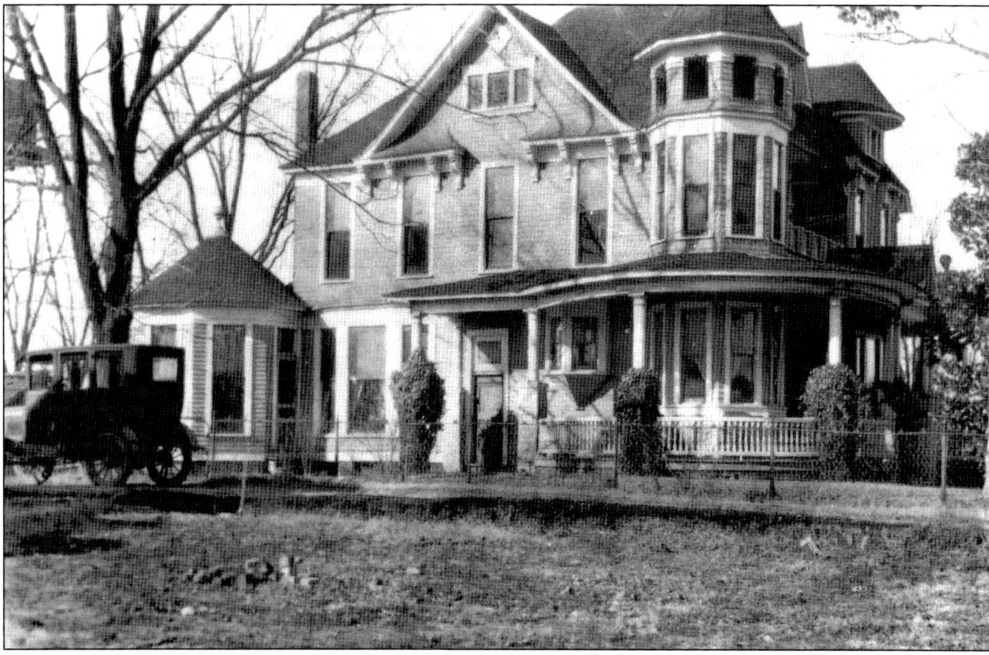

This photograph from 1920 shows the James M. Coleman Home, built in 1895 by James Shivers. Mr. Coleman was the proprietor of the Franklin Inn, located near the famous mineral springs in Raleigh. The home was located on Austin Peay Highway.

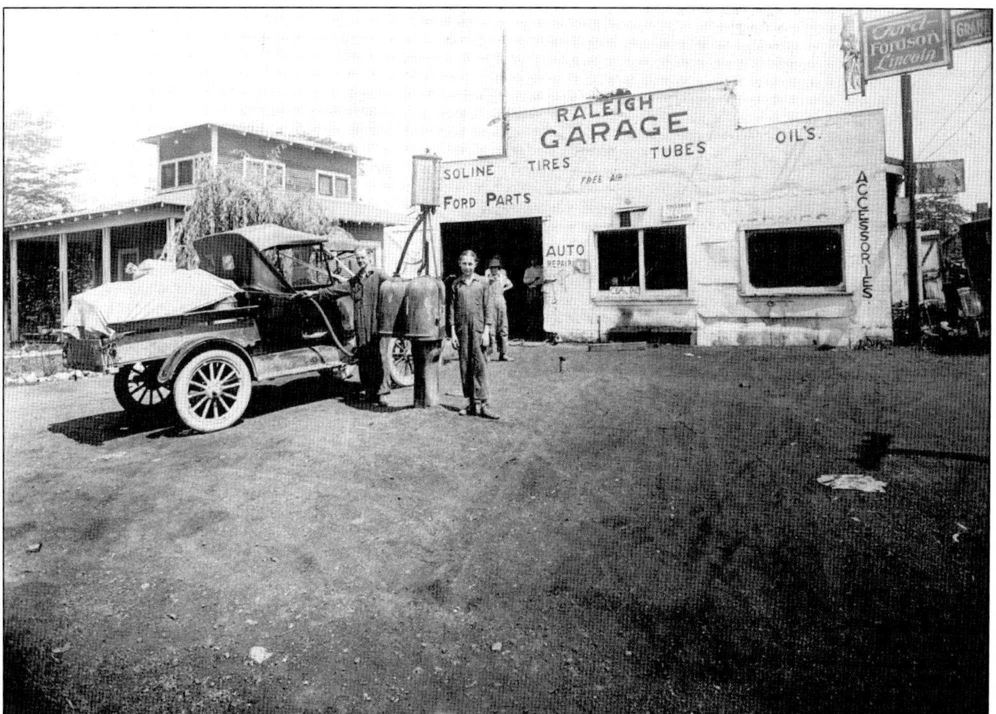

The Raleigh Garage was located on James Road near Stage. This photograph was taken around 1940.

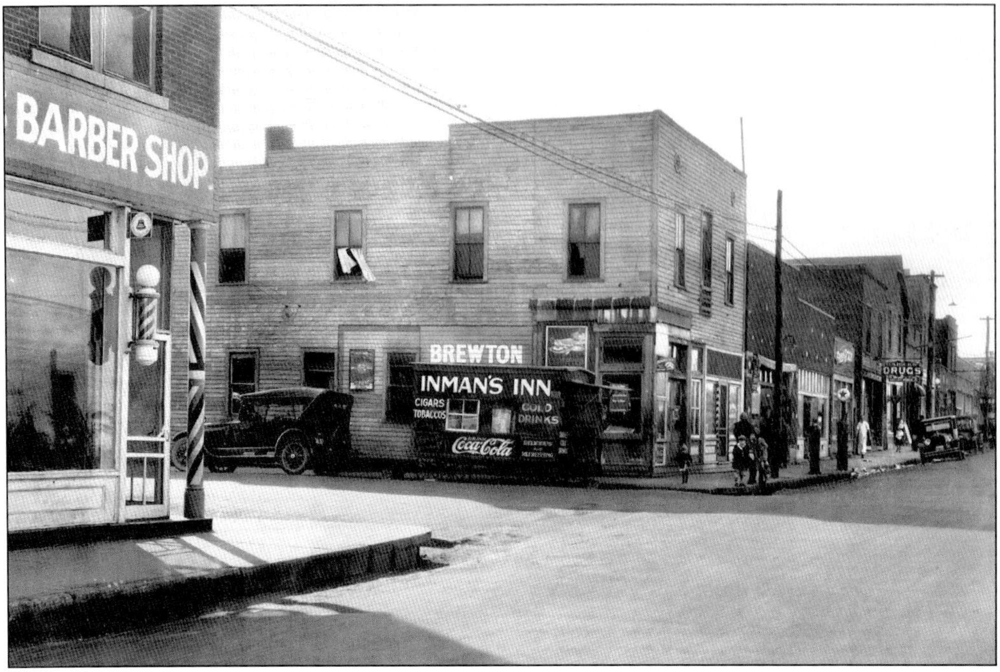

The area known as Binghampton, located just east of Overton Park, was settled by William Bingham in the late 1880s. The area was chartered in 1895, with a population of 1,670 by 1910. The city was annexed into Memphis in 1919. Binghampton's northern boundary was Broad Street, seen above in 1920.

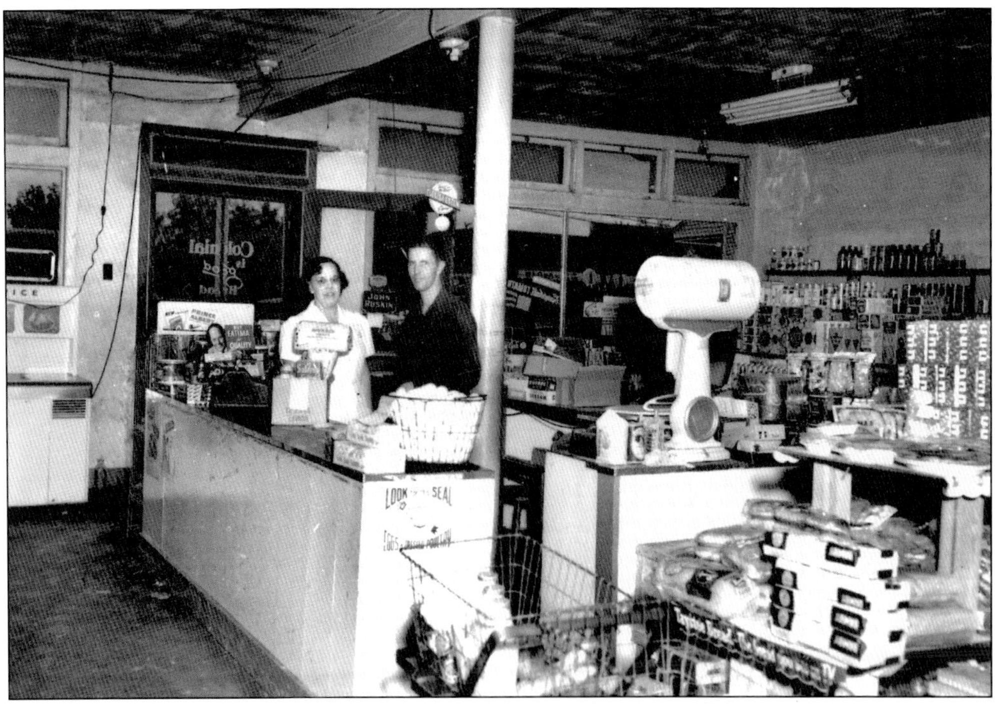

Dunning and Quinn Grocery Store was located in Berclair, east of the city limits on Summer Avenue. Al and Mabel Dunning operated the store, shown here in 1950.

Three

NORTH SHELBY COUNTY

Driving through north Shelby County, one still gets a sense of life from earlier days. One might get behind a tractor pulling a cotton wagon down the road. One might look out the car window and see a plowed field stretching to the horizon. North Shelby County is made up of many smaller towns and communities. Millington is one of the younger cities, whereas communities such as Lucy, Cuba, Arlington, and Rosemark date to the early 1800s. While surveying the area in the second decade of the 1800s, John Ralston found the home of Clem McDaniel located on Big Creek. Ralston married McDaniel's daughter, Lucy Tice McDaniel, in 1822. She is believed to be the source of the community of Lucy's name. Big Creek Baptist Church was formed in 1812 just east of Isaac Bolton's land near Big Creek and Royster Creek. The Presbyterian church was established in the 1820s at its present location at the intersection of Mudville and Miller Roads. The Big Creek Post Office was started in 1824 and was discontinued in 1866. The first major road built out of Memphis was to Randolph, located on the third Chickasaw Bluff. The second road was to the Big Creek community. Located within the Naval Air Station property is the Chamberlayne Cemetery. A tall marker states, "the first settlers in this place 1829." The Chamberlayne plantation covered 5,000 acres and was active for many years until it was sold by descendants in 1942 to the federal government.

Kerrville, originally known as Chester, was a prosperous community founded by a pair of brothers, Rev. Andrew Kerr and Dr. John Kerr. They owned several thousand acres and were instrumental in developing the area into a town with five stores, two steam mills, a cotton gin, a hotel, and a train depot. The Memphis-to-Kerrville plank road was built in the early 1850s. The road was planked with wood boards going into Memphis and dirt heading north. The reason for planks going south was so that the heavy cotton wagons would not sink into the mud while traveling to the Memphis markets. A toll had to be paid to cross the Wolf and Loosahatchie Rivers. It would be some time before bridges were built.

Lucy has the second oldest subdivision in Shelby County, while Raleigh has the oldest. Founded in the early 1820s, Lucy quickly grew to include a cotton gin, five stores, and a school by 1875. The Lucy Baptist Church was organized in 1870 in the Lucy Town Hall. The Methodist church began a few years later in 1889. Both churches are still very active today. The town originally known as Richland was renamed Rosemark in the 1890s as there was another post office by the Richland name. In 1890, the first store, the Richland Farmers and Mercantile

Association, was established in Rosemark by W. L. Thompson and continued in operation for more than 100 years. Some of the earliest families were McCalla, Moffatt, Gragg, McQuiston, and Faulk.

Cuba was part of the 5,000-acre land grant deeded to Thomas Polk in the 1820s. Farmers grew mainly cotton, hauling it to Memphis for bailing and storage. The Union Cumberland Church was organized in the early 1840s, and the first post office was established in 1852. A brick school was built in 1909, but a tornado that same year did extensive damage to the building. Also destroyed by the tornado were the Methodist church at Wilkinville, Fellowship Baptist Church at Quito, West Union School, and the West Union Church. The Cuba school was destroyed by fire in 1922 and never rebuilt. A one-room general store was opened by Anthony and Rebecca Barret in 1850 and continued in operation until 1991, making it the oldest mercantile company in West Tennessee. J. H. Barret and Sons also operated general stores in Kerrville, Millington, and Idaville. The general store building today, built in 1930, is the third one built on the site, the others having burned. The Barretville Bank and Trust was established in 1920 by Paul W. Barret. The bank was connected to the general store, which was burned in a burglary attempt in 1930. Thieves tried to use blow torches at night to break into the vault. The attempt was unsuccessful, as no money was taken, but the building was totally destroyed. The bank continued to grow and eventually merged with Trustmark Bank, making it part of one of the largest banks in the South. Lakeland is the youngest of the incorporated cities in Shelby County. Chartered in 1977, Lakeland was the first city in Shelby County to have a female mayor, Beverly Rivera, who was elected in 1977. The concept for the Lakeland Amusement Park dates back to 1959, when Louis Garner purchased several hundred acres for a family summer home. After visiting Winniepaiuka, an amusement park in Chattanooga, he returned and worked to create the same type of park here. The park prospered for several years, but a gas crisis and competition from Libertyland amusement park in Memphis caused the theme park to close in 1977. Today all that remains is the lake, surrounded by large estate homes.

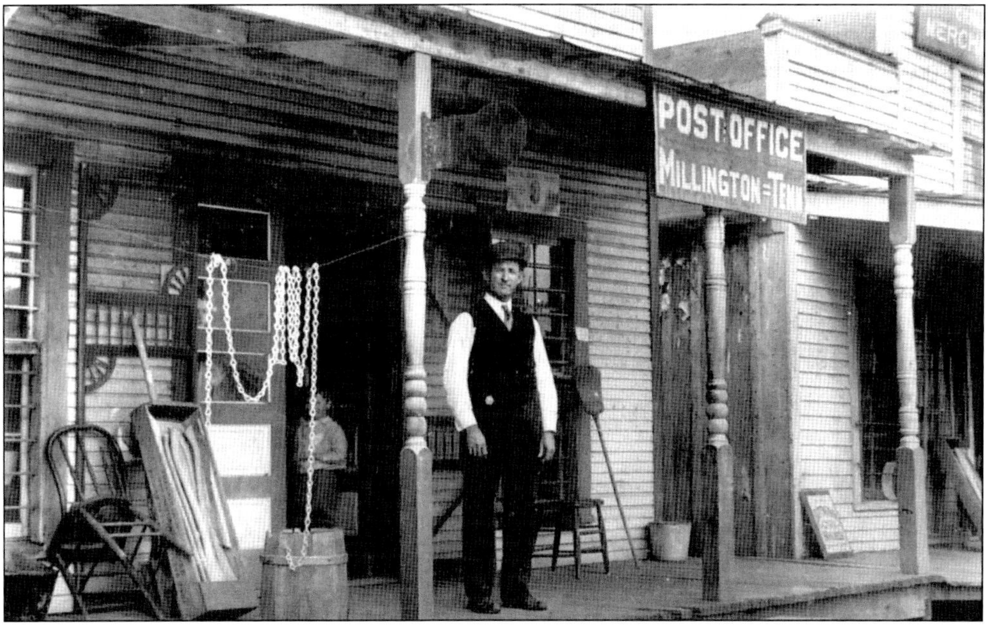

Ed Adkins, shown here in 1902, served as postmaster for the fourth-class post office located in his grocery store.

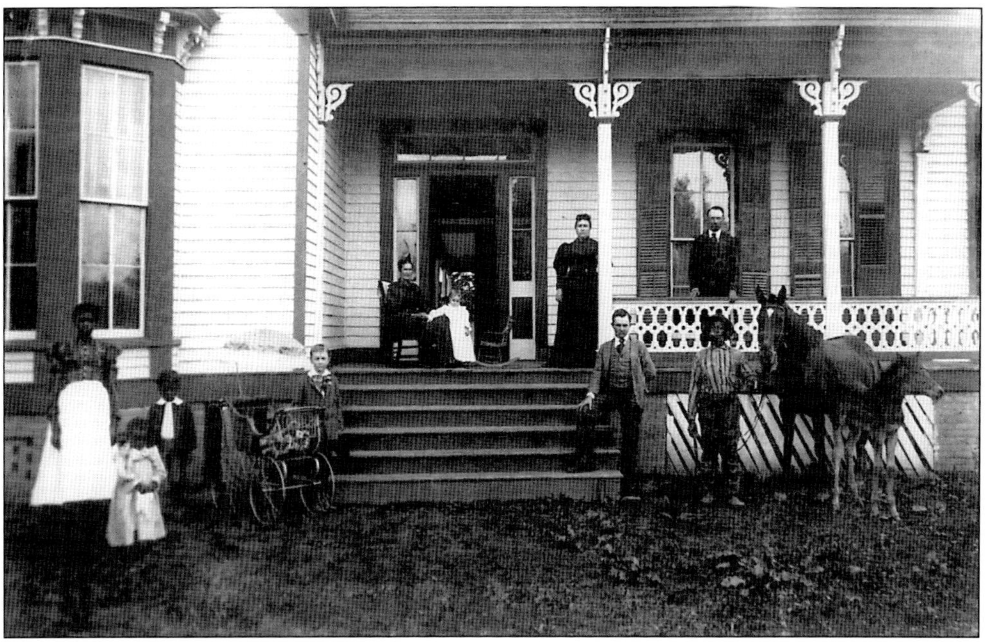

W. E. Polk, standing on the porch far right, was the first mayor of Millington, serving from 1903 to 1912. This photograph from 1890 was taken at his residence, which was located on Wilkerson Road. His wife, Lena, stands to his right with her mother and daughter, Evie, beside her. On the left step is Lewie Polk and on the right is Charlie Polk.

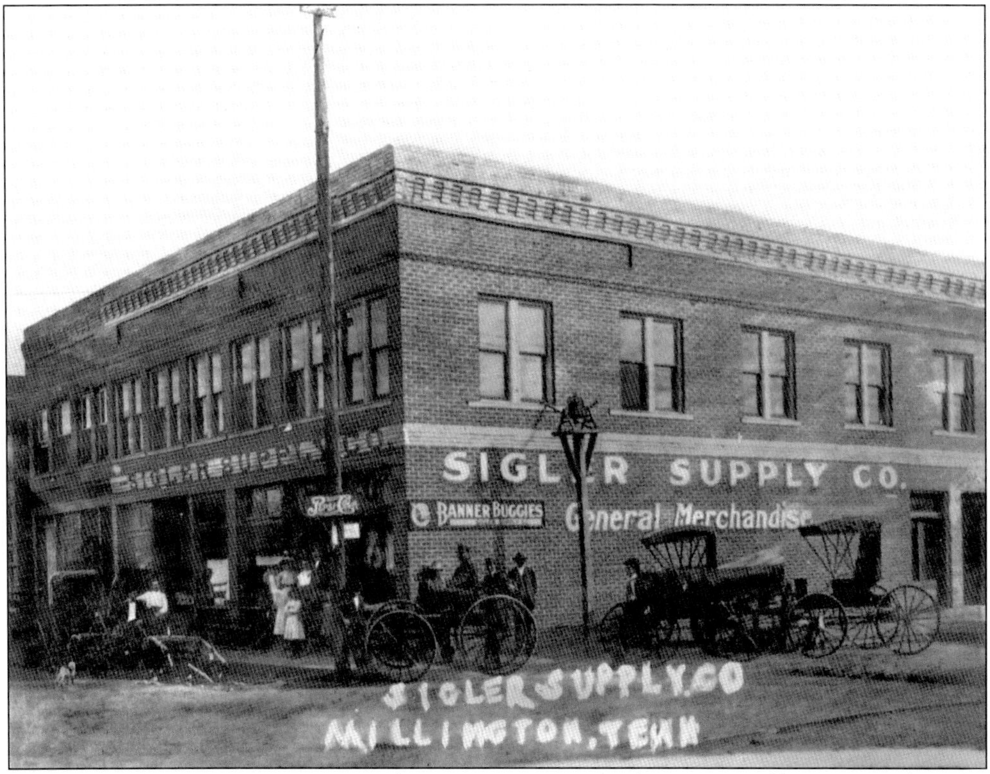

Sigler's Supply Company store, seen here in 1907, was the largest in Millington. Buck Sigler also built Harold's store and owned what is now Maxwell's hardware store. The vehicle in the center is driven by Lum Ward, who was a master carpenter and built the one-cylinder car, one of Millington's first automobiles.

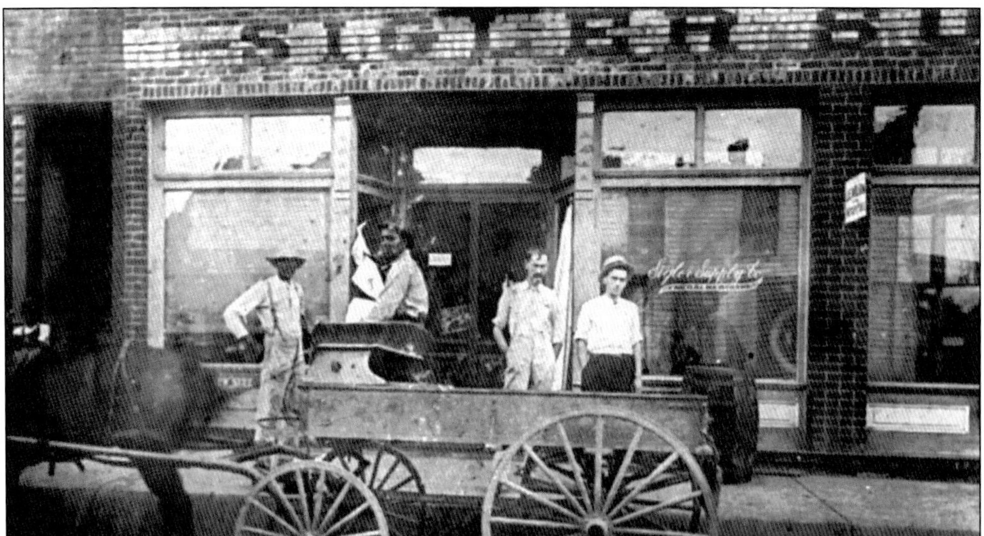

Sigler's Supply store, shown here in 1912, was located on Main Street, now known as Easley Street, in Millington. Lee Jackson, Sigler's delivery man, sits on his delivery wagon with, from left to right, an unidentified man, Ed Black, and Johnnie Corbitt behind him.

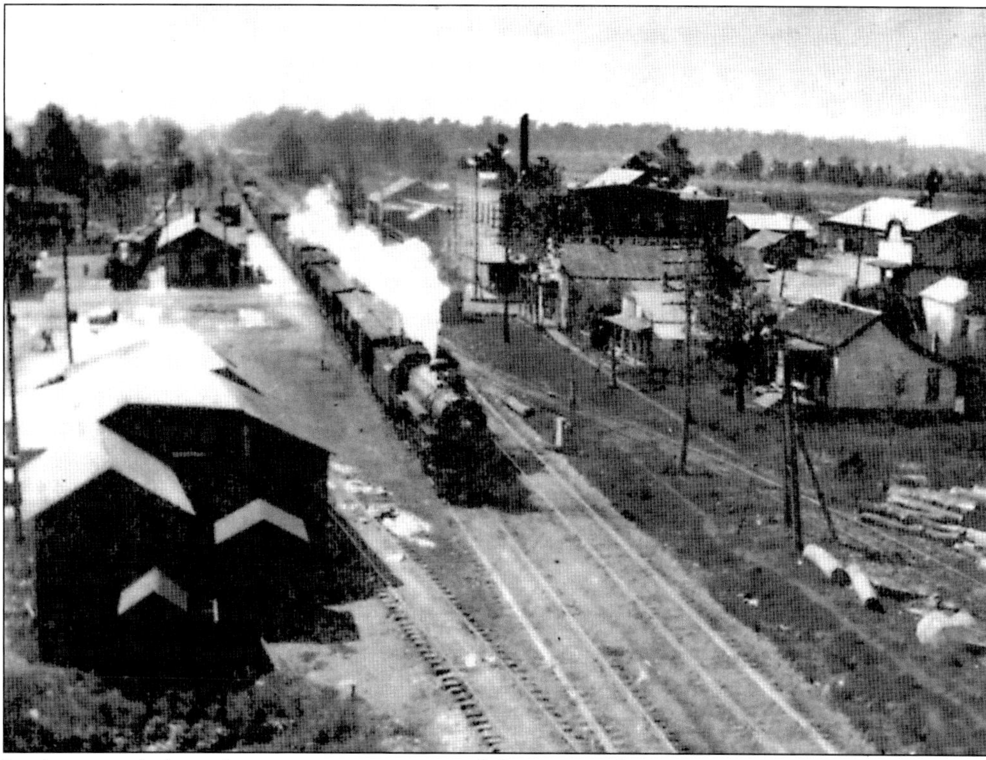

Looking south from the water tower, a train glides into Millington during the 1920s. The train depot is located in the background to the left, with Harold's store across the tracks.

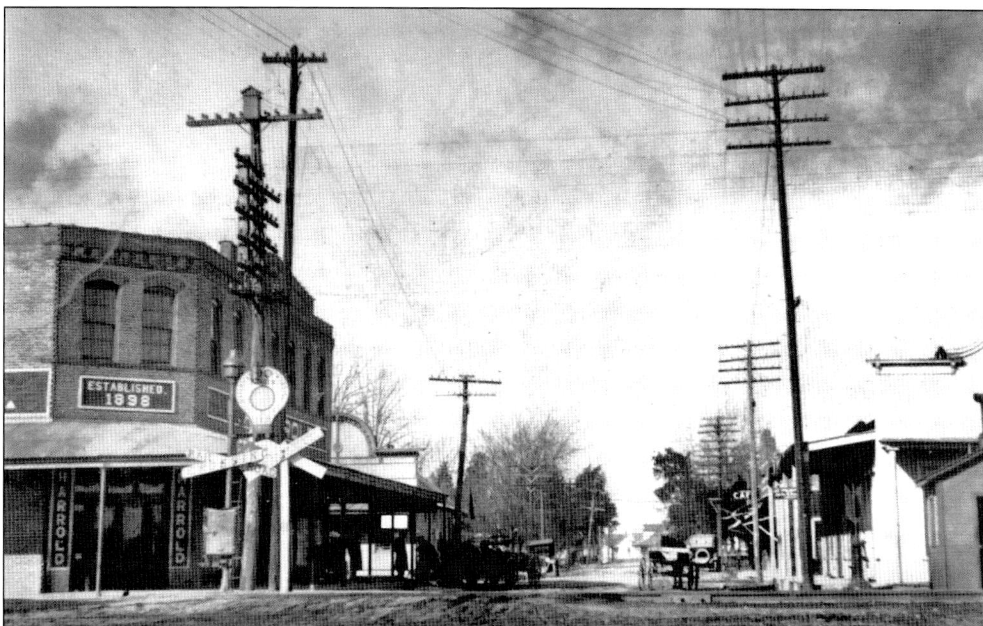

This view looks west down Main Street in Millington around 1918. Main Street was renamed Easley after the 1930s. On the left is Harold's store, built in 1898 by Buck Sigler. Harold's store is today home to the Millington Cable Company.

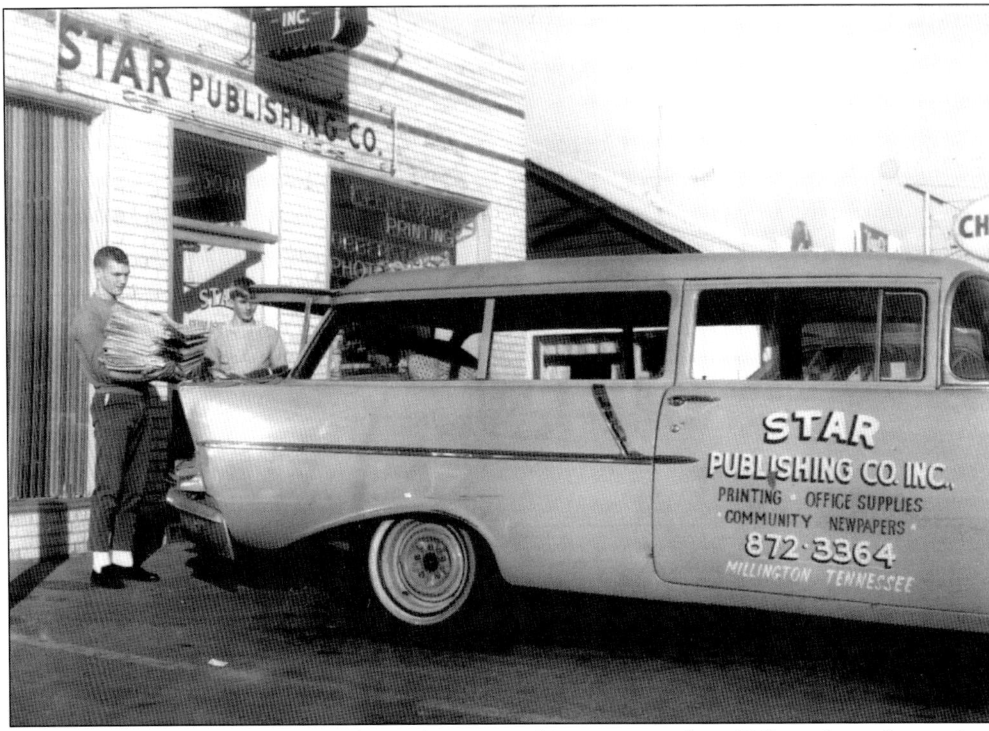

The *Millington Star* newspaper, shown here in 1958, was started in 1951 and was located on Navy Road. Today the newspaper is located on Easley Street and has a circulation of more than 20,000.

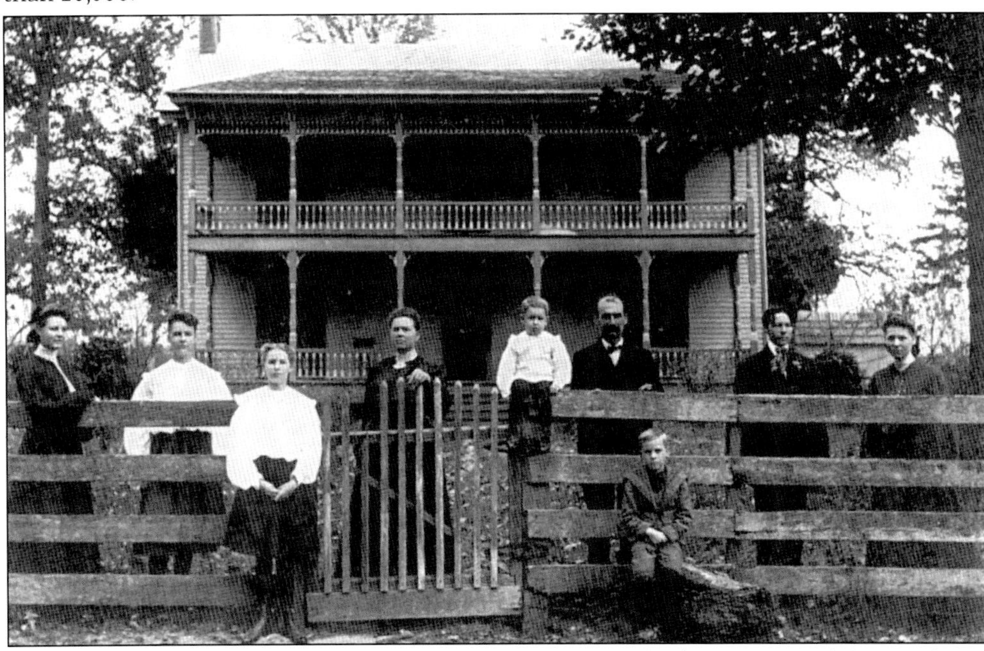

George Smith purchased this home and 100 acres in 1903 for $5,000. From left to right are Margaret Smith, Mary Smith, Lucy Smith, Louanna Smith, Otis Smith, George Smith, Hoyt Smith, John Smith, and Ethel Martin Smith.

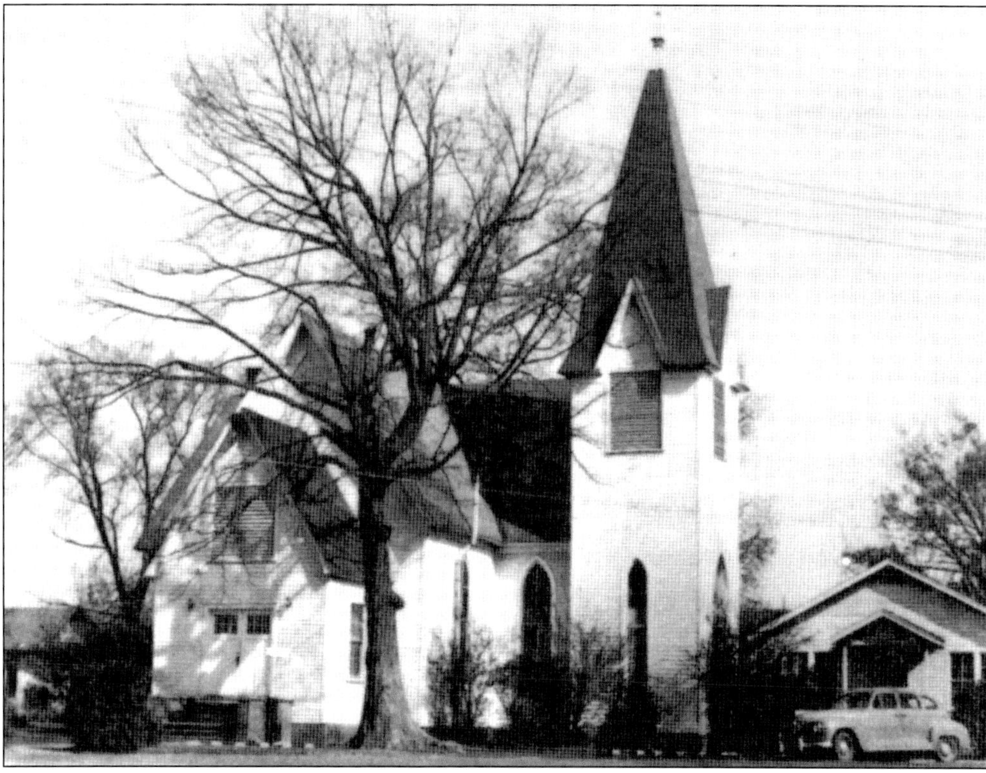

Millington Baptist Church is the oldest church structure in Millington. Organized in 1888, the church was built in 1890 with help from W. E. Polk and Will McCaughn. The members of the church did much of the construction. The first pastor was Rev. Jeffrey Anderson. The church moved in 1953 and is today located on the north side of Millington High School.

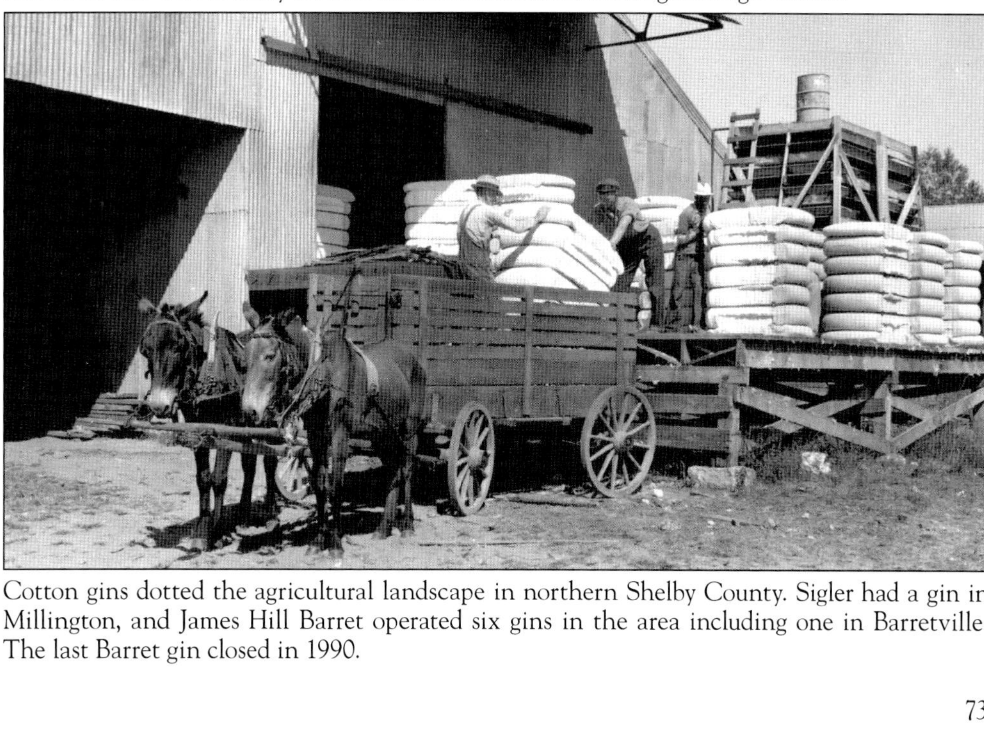

Cotton gins dotted the agricultural landscape in northern Shelby County. Sigler had a gin in Millington, and James Hill Barret operated six gins in the area including one in Barretville. The last Barret gin closed in 1990.

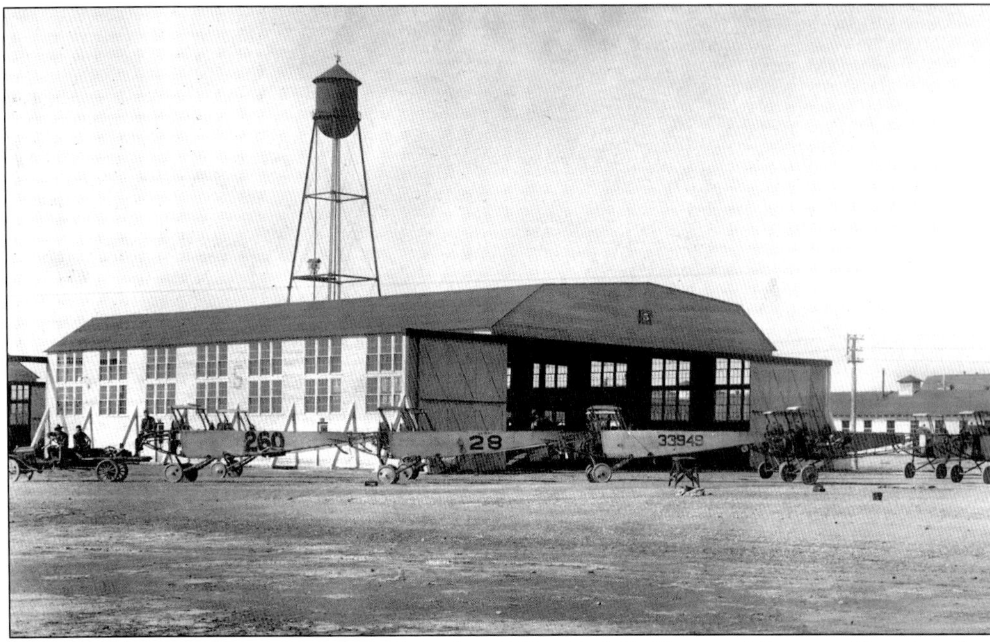

Shelby County's first airport was established in 1917 at Park Field near Millington. Nine hundred acres of land were purchased for $87,000 from local farmers, and a training school for military pilots was established. The field was named for Lt. Joseph D. Park, who was killed in a plane crash in California.

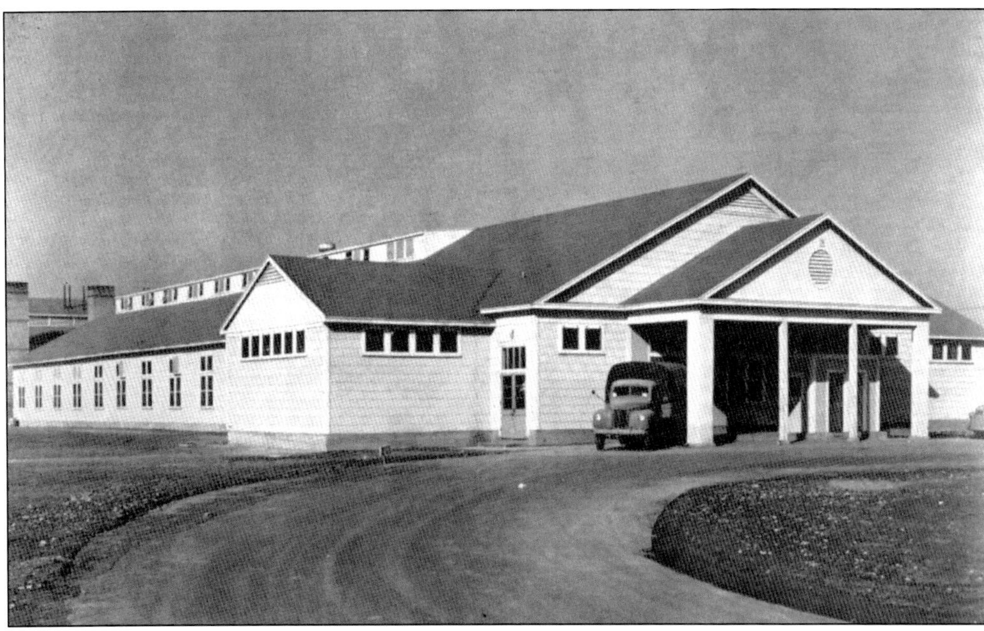

Once the site of Park Field in 1917, the Naval Reserve Aviation Base was built during World War II on a grand scale. There were 8,700 construction workers who daily unloaded materials from 80 train cars. The new base was completed in 1942 and covered more than 2,200 acres and employed more than 5,000 personnel. The population of Millington jumped from 730 in 1940 to more than 4,600 in 1950.

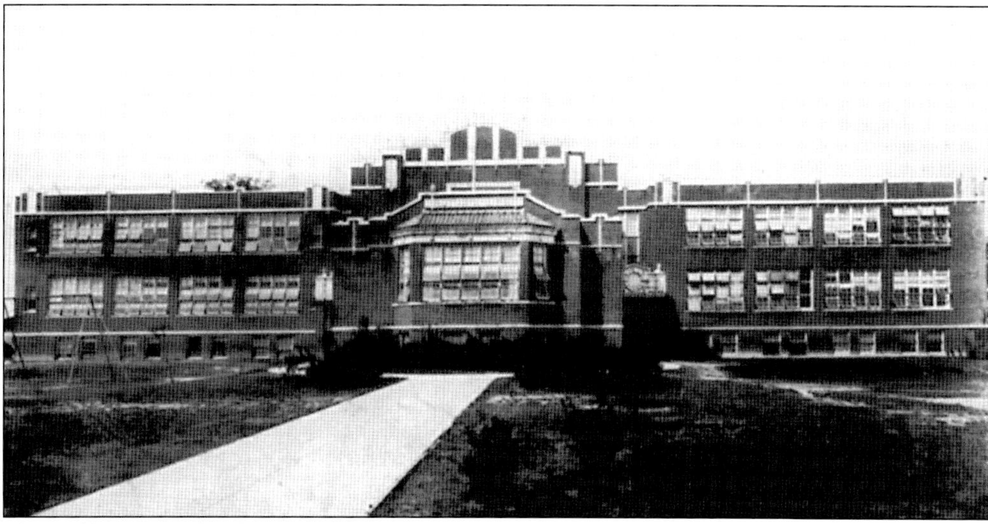

The Millington School was torn down in 1916 to make way for Millington Central High School, seen above. Built in 1917, the school would eventually incorporate students from all over north Shelby County. Millington had West Tennessee's first lighted football field in 1947. William Osteen was principal of the school from 1940 until 1971 and was responsible for many of the improvements to the school over the years.

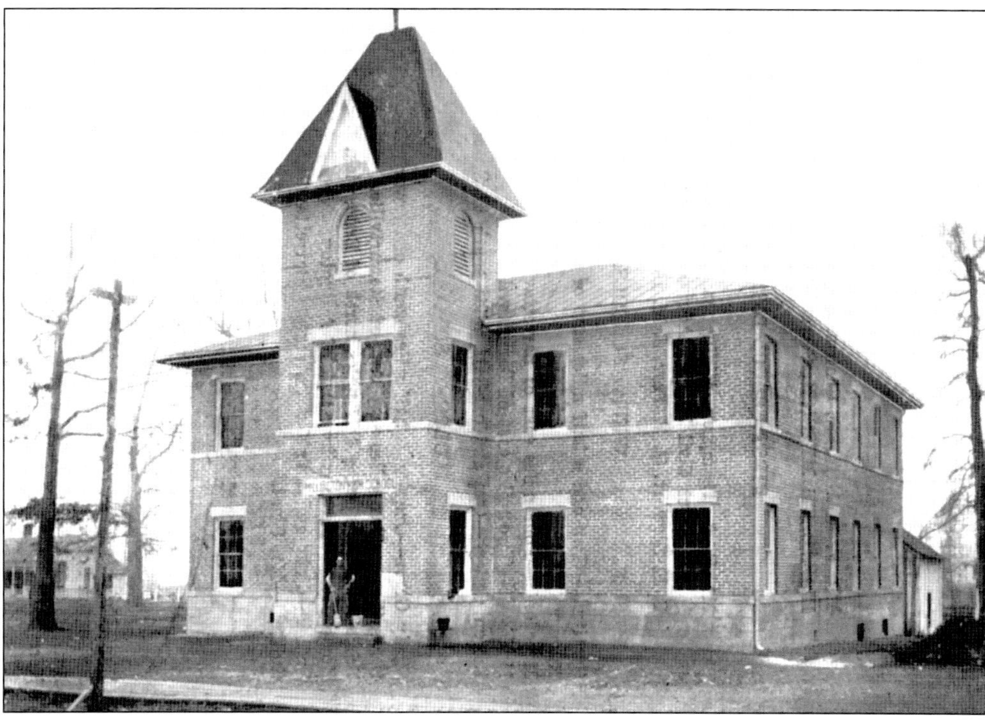

The Millington School, shown above, was built in 1907 at the site of the present-day Millington High School. The property was donated by George Millington in the 1880s, and a small frame school was originally built on the site.

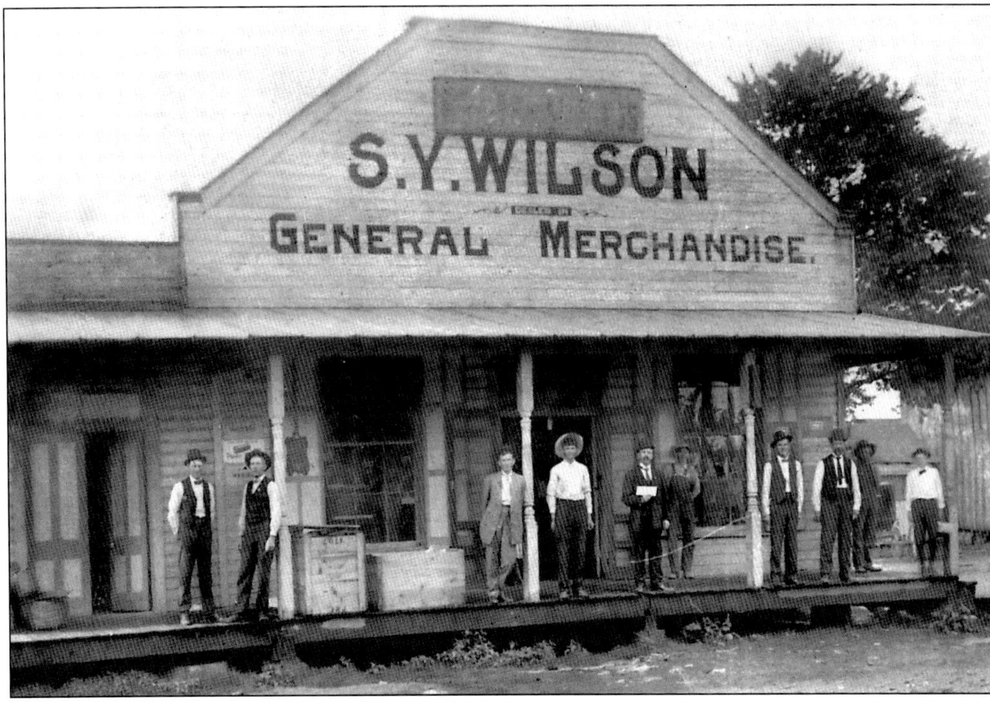

Established in 1893 in Arlington, the S. Y. Wilson store is still in operation and run by the Wilson family. Samuel Young Wilson was born in 1865 and moved to Arlington around 1885, working in the A. R. Armistad Store for several years before opening his own general store.

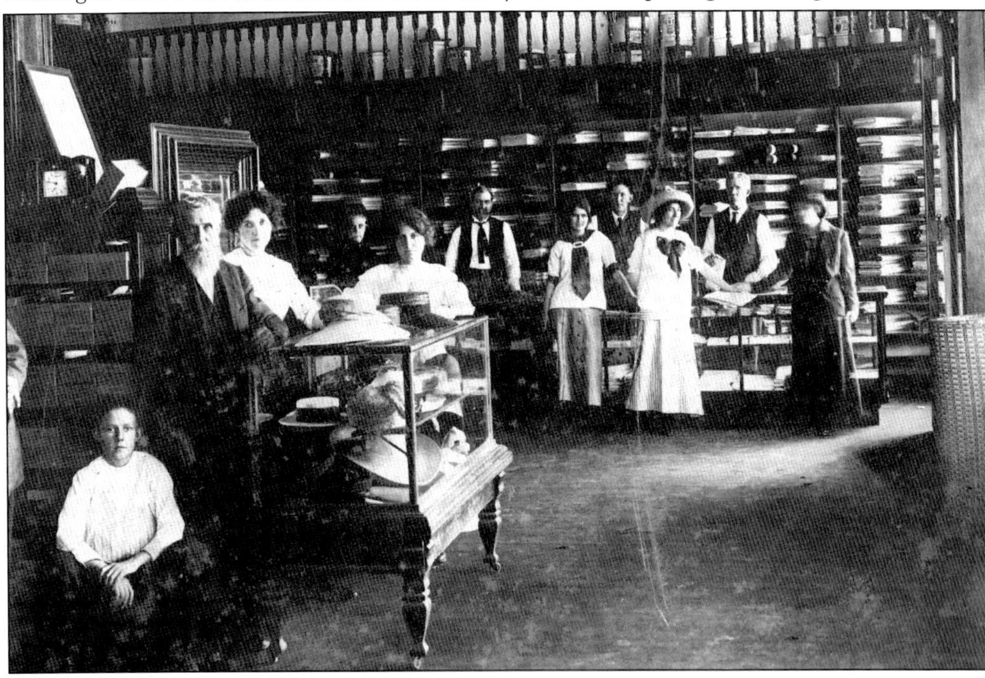

The S. Y. Wilson store, shown here in 1900, is one of the oldest general stores still in existence in Shelby County. In 1892, Samuel Wilson married Emma Elizabeth Gragg. The couple was married for 57 years, and they were very active in the community of Arlington.

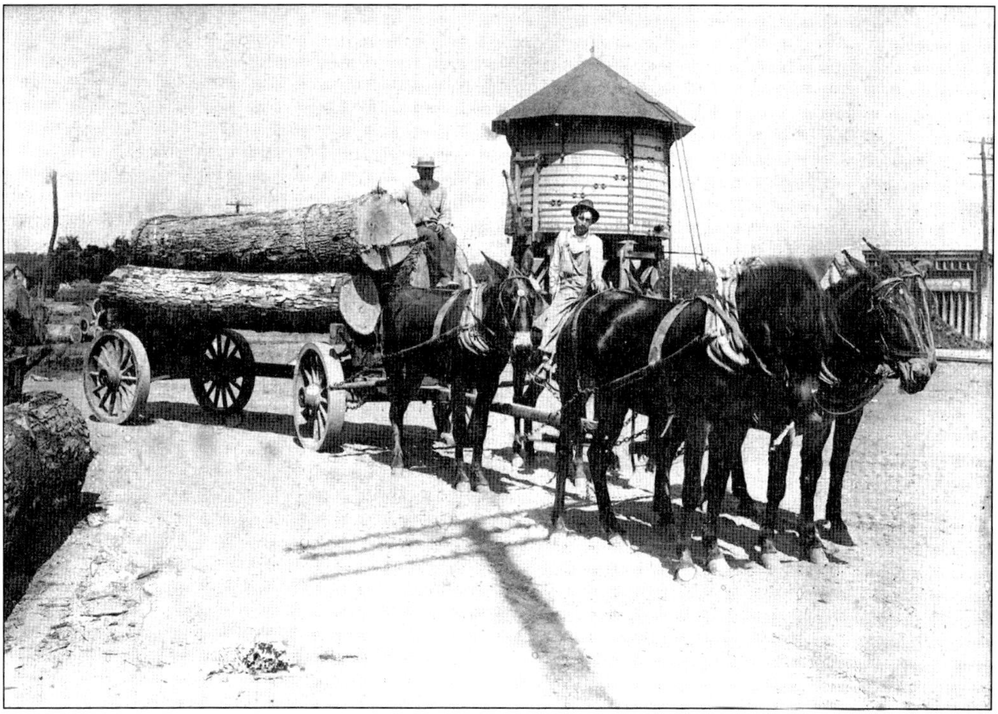

Memphis is known as the "Hardwood Capital of the World." The great forests of oak and poplar had to be cleared for fields and roads. Many sawmills were located throughout the county. Here is a mule-drawn team pulling logs to the mill near Arlington.

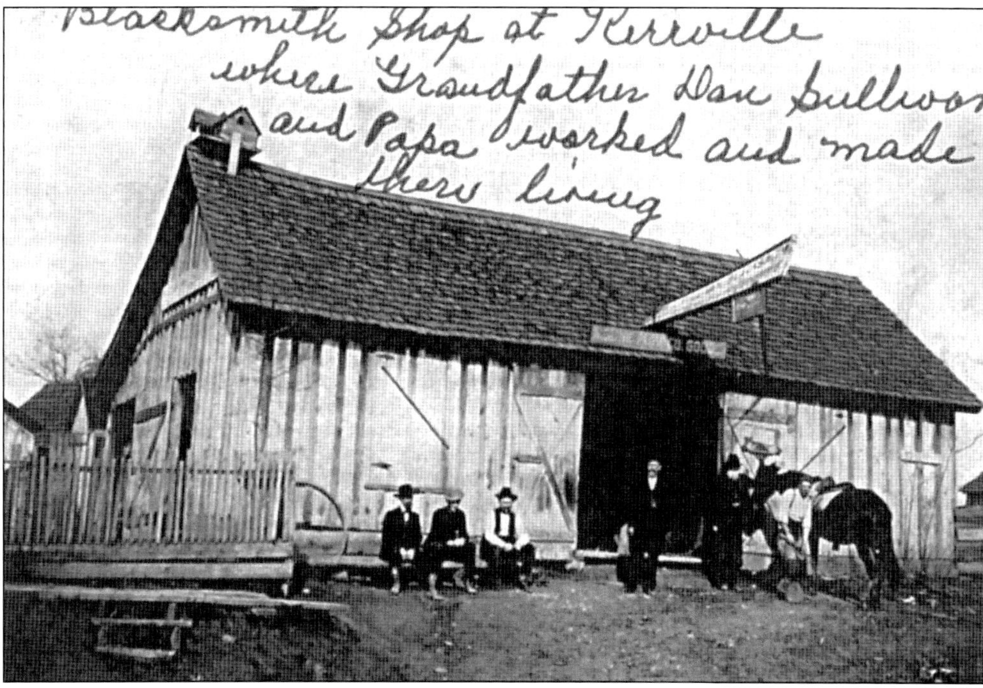

This photograph shows Sullivan Blacksmith shop in 1902. The business was run by Daniel and Michael Sullivan and located on the corner of Sullivan Street and Kerrville Rosemark Road.

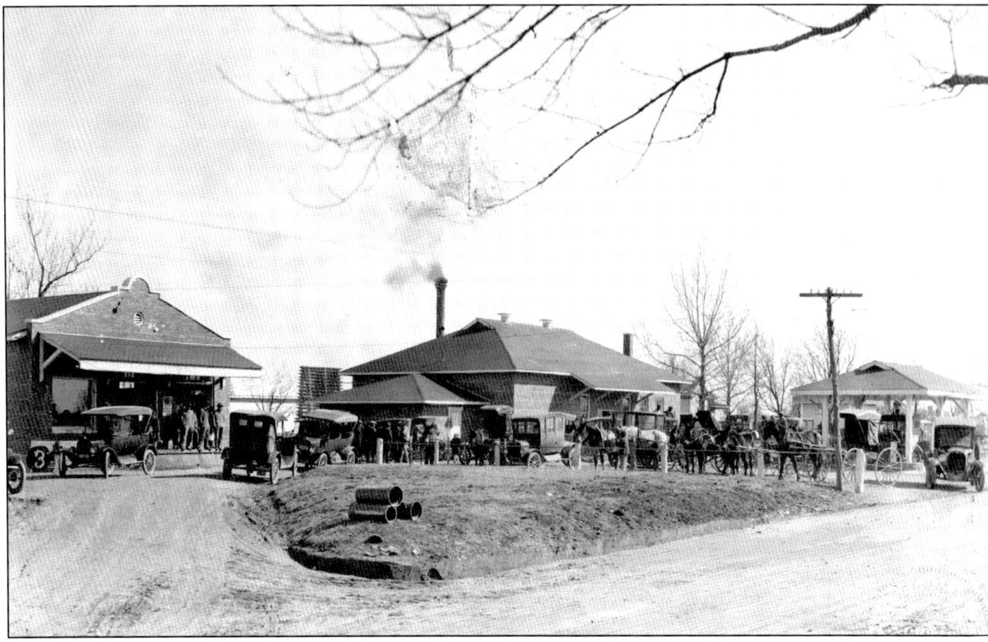

The Hansonhurst community was started by C. C. Hanson as a model town with large estates, a large dairy plant, a refrigeration plant, an electric gin, a large public swimming pool, and a small amusement park. The community was located near Rosemark but was sold in the late 1930s for $30,000 at an auction.

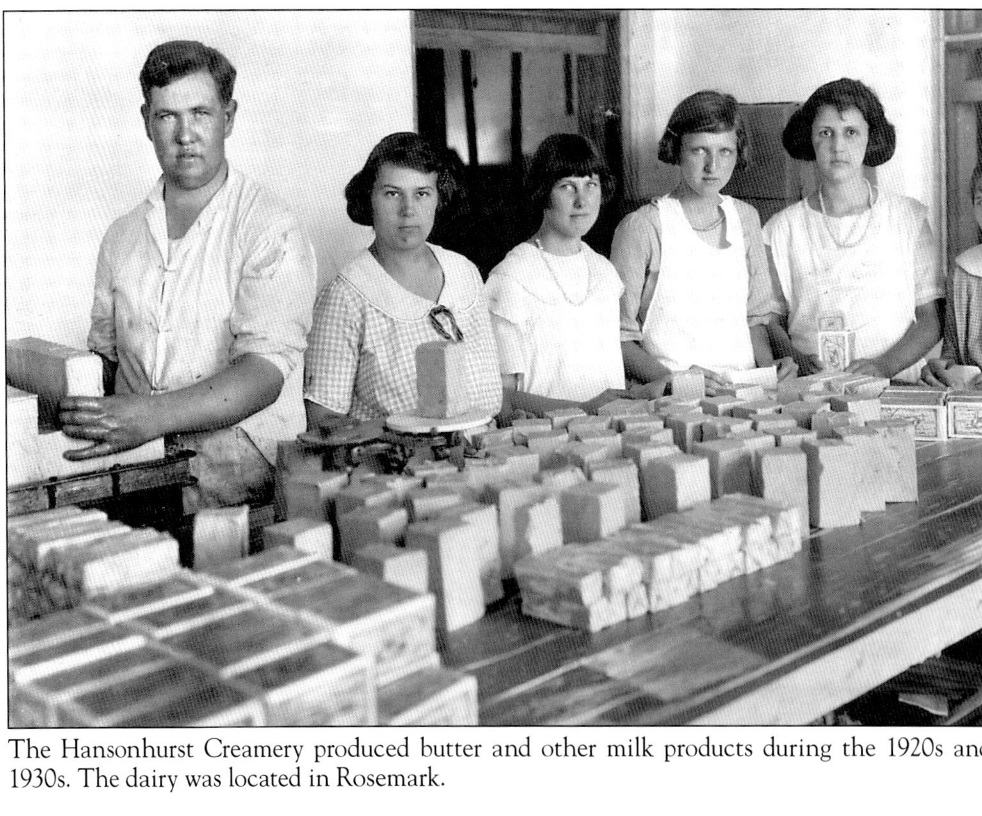

The Hansonhurst Creamery produced butter and other milk products during the 1920s and 1930s. The dairy was located in Rosemark.

Rev. Andrew Hart Kerr arrived in West Tennessee in 1854, purchasing several thousand acres. In 1872, the town of Kerrville was established in his name, and in 1887, he donated land and supplies for a brick depot to be built. It was said that, at the time, it was the only brick depot between Memphis and Chicago.

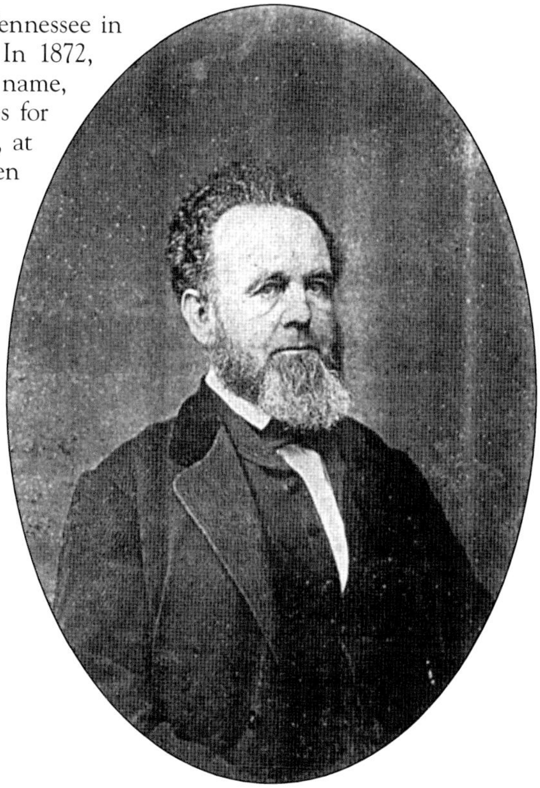

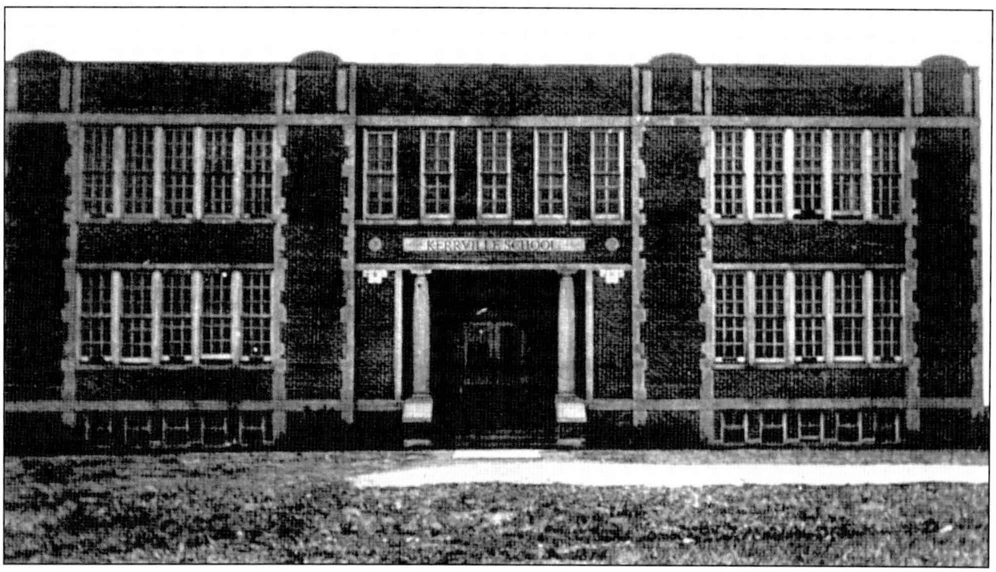

Kerrville School, shown here in 1923, was built in 1916. The school, located on Kerrville Rosemark Road, was in operation until 1935, when it was consolidated with Millington High School. The building was demolished in 1937 to make way for the Kerrville United Methodist Church.

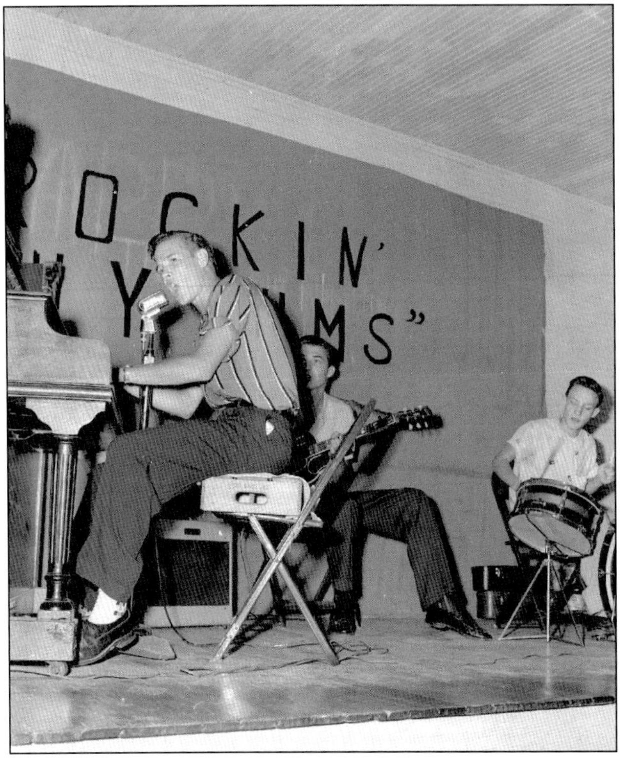

Bartlett High School students Jimmy Dye (on piano), Paul Miller (on guitar), and Gene Acre (on drums) play in a converted church on Seed Tick Road in Lakeland. The band, formed in 1954, was known as the Rockin' Rhythms and even auditioned for Sun Records producer Sam Phillips.

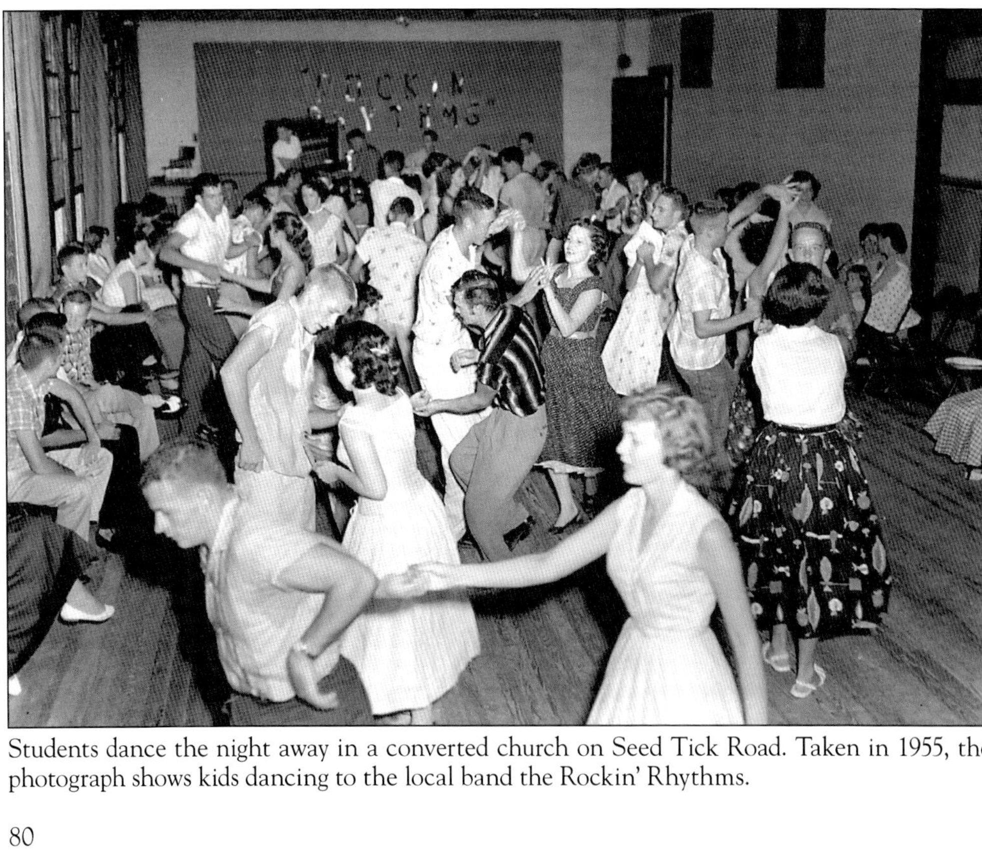

Students dance the night away in a converted church on Seed Tick Road. Taken in 1955, the photograph shows kids dancing to the local band the Rockin' Rhythms.

Four

Bartlett

Situated in the geographical center of Shelby County, Bartlett is one of the county's fastest-growing communities. Chartered in 1866, the city of Bartlett has a rich and colorful history. The area that encompasses Bartlett today covers more than 17 square miles. Gabrial Maston Bartlett, for whom the city is named, first arrived in the area in 1847. Born in Robertson County, Tennessee, Major Bartlett, as he became known, was a politician and planter. He purchased a large tract of land from his cousin John Blackwell, who had settled in the area a few years earlier. His home was on Stage Road in an area called Greenbottom, located east of Highway 70. Major Bartlett was a tall man, standing six-feet-four-inches tall, with dark hair. He was elected justice of the peace and a member of the county quarterly court in 1848. He purchased large areas of land in the area, and in 1860, he had more than $40,000 worth of land and personal property worth $30,000. He moved to a new home between Court and Shelby on Stage Road in 1853. This home was the headquarters for Gen. Lew Wallace during the Civil War. The Northern general has become best known as the author of *Ben Hur*. In 1859, Major Bartlett had the 300 acres surrounding his home surveyed for a community. He donated land for a school, church, and a Masonic lodge. Following the Civil War, Union Station, as it had become known, decided to incorporate, and in 1866, the town was named in honor of Gabrial Bartlett, who was elected as the city's first mayor.

Financial misfortune caused Major Bartlett to sell off much of his land including his home and the remaining lots in Bartlett. He sold his land to a second cousin, Dr. Nicholas Blackwell, and his business partner, Dr. William Pryor, for $24,000. Blackwell and Pryor continued to develop the 300 acres. Some of the early residents included Williford, Pruden, Priddy, Alexander, Bond, and Ward. Gabrial Bartlett continued to live in the city named in his honor until his death in 1876. In 1875, the county decided to build a courthouse in Bartlett, due to its centralized location in Shelby County. Blackwell and Pryor donated land for the courthouse located at the present-day intersection of Court and Woodlawn, which was a wheat field in their day. Court was held in Bartlett until 1885 when it was moved back to Memphis. The two-story building was converted into a school and eventually demolished in 1919. The Blackwell family donated additional land adjoining the courthouse property, and Nicholas Blackwell High School was built in 1917.

Cotton was the chief agricultural export for many Shelby County towns, and Bartlett was no exception. At one time, there were three cotton gins located in the area, each producing

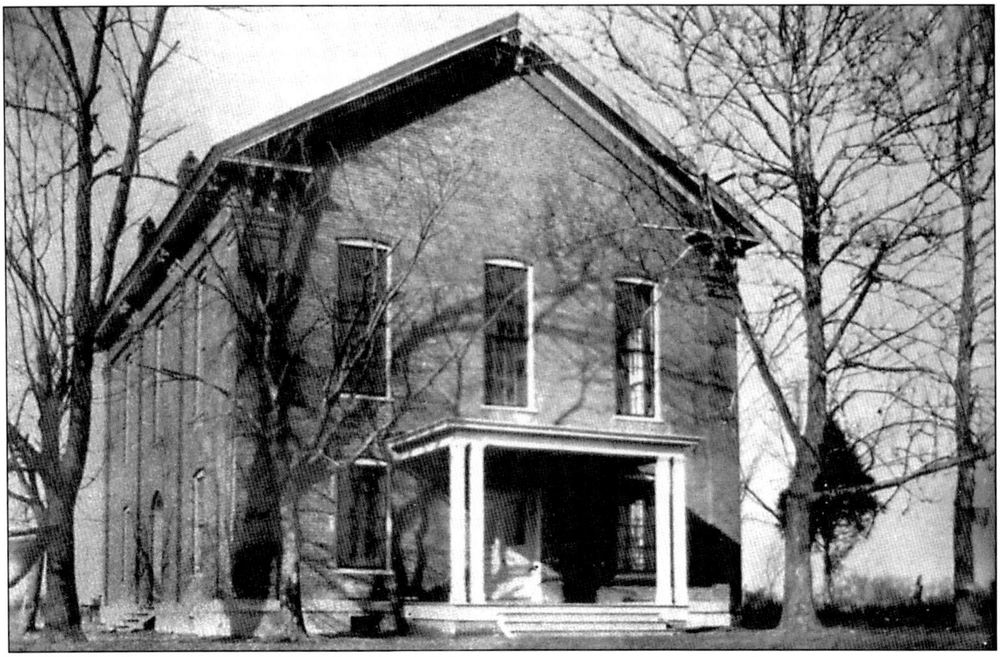

As Shelby County grew after the Civil War, citizens found the need for a circuit courthouse that was more centrally located than Memphis. Bartlett was chosen as it was centrally located within the county. In 1875, James Oglesby built the Bartlett Courthouse, costing $12,449. The courthouse operated from 1875 until 1885, when the courts were moved back to Memphis. After the courts left, the property was used as a school until 1917.

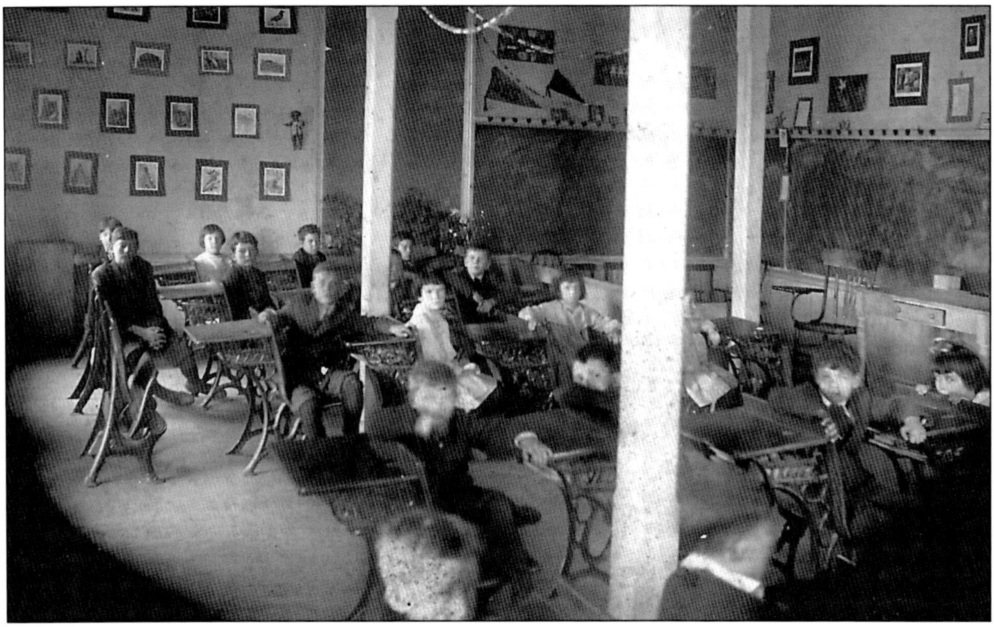

This was the last class to attend the Bartlett Courthouse School. A new school, Nicholas Blackwell High School, was built next door and opened in 1917. The student fourth from the left is W. J. Freeman, who was the city's alderman for 35 years. The Freeman family arrived in Bartlett in 1853.

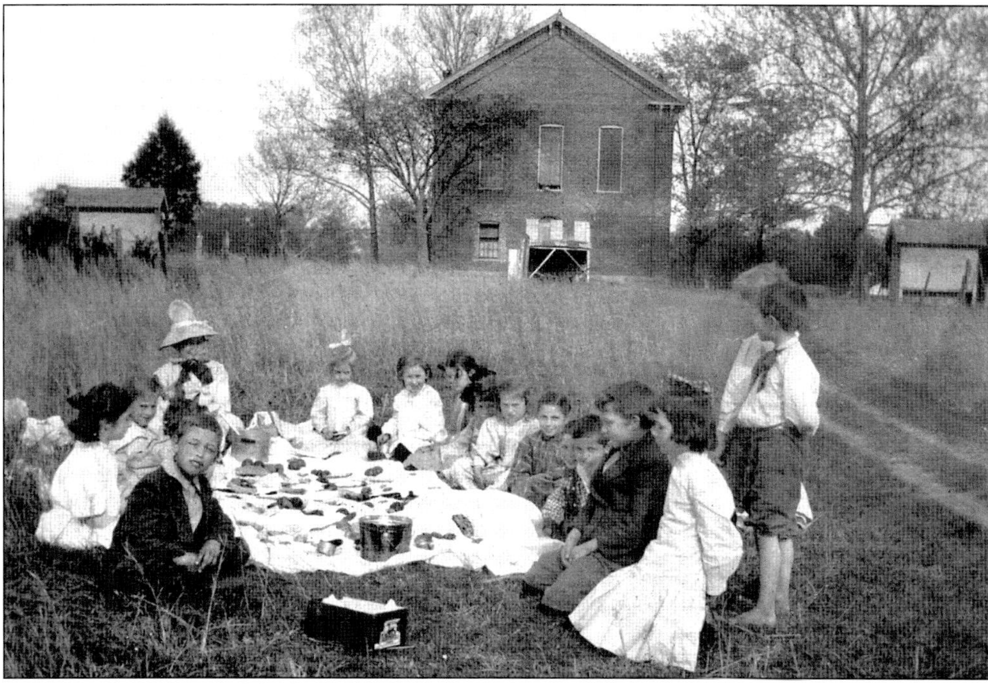

Students spread out a blanket for a picnic behind the Bartlett Courthouse School. After the courts left Bartlett, Nicholas Blackwell allowed the building to be used as a school. The Bartlett Training Institute, as it was known, operated until 1917, when Nicholas Blackwell High School was built just west of the courthouse.

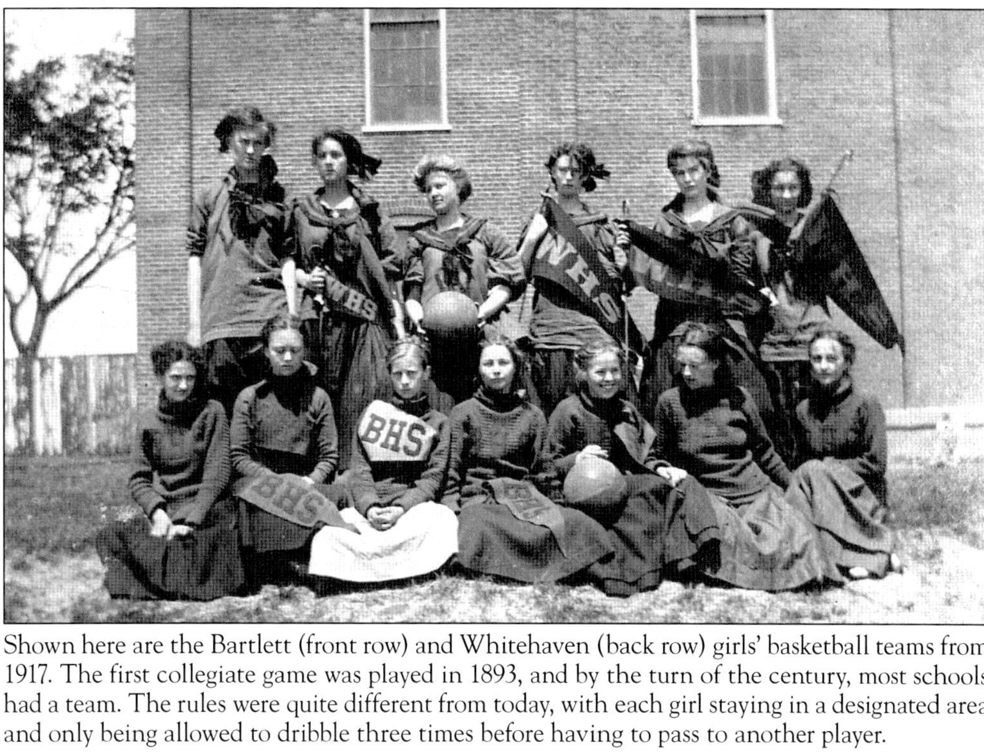

Shown here are the Bartlett (front row) and Whitehaven (back row) girls' basketball teams from 1917. The first collegiate game was played in 1893, and by the turn of the century, most schools had a team. The rules were quite different from today, with each girl staying in a designated area and only being allowed to dribble three times before having to pass to another player.

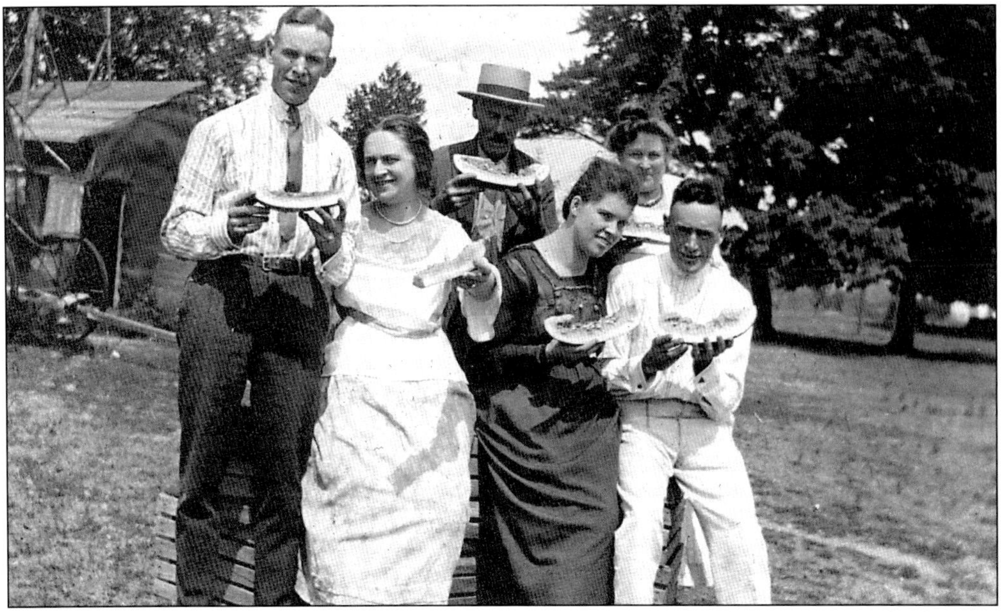

Bartlett was home to many festivals and celebrations. The Old Folks Society, today known as the West Tennessee Historical Society, held several celebrations there in the 1870s, some attracting as many as 3,500 people. Politicians would give long speeches, tables would be set up with food and drink, and dances were held under a canopy of trees. The festivals took place on Sycamore Road, just north of Stage Road. Fairgoers, shown above, enjoy watermelon in the early 1900s.

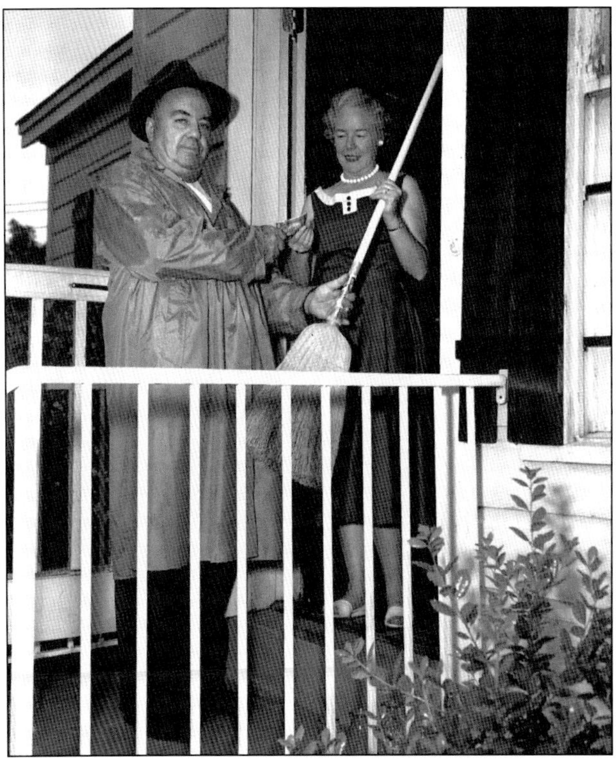

John George, principal of Nicholas Blackwell High School, sells a broom to Mary Ann Freeman of Bartlett during a fund-raiser for the Lions Club in 1953.

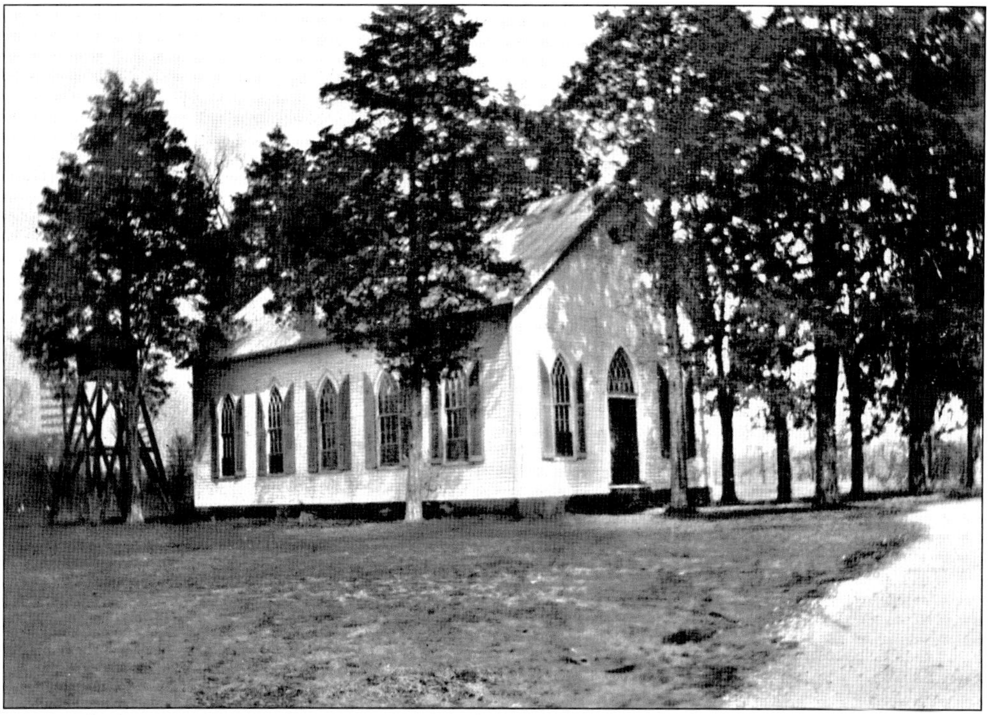

Originally known as Prosperity Baptist, Bartlett Baptist Church was organized in 1849. The congregation moved to Bartlett in 1871 and built a small frame church. The chapel was bricked over in 1935 and today is the oldest public building in Bartlett.

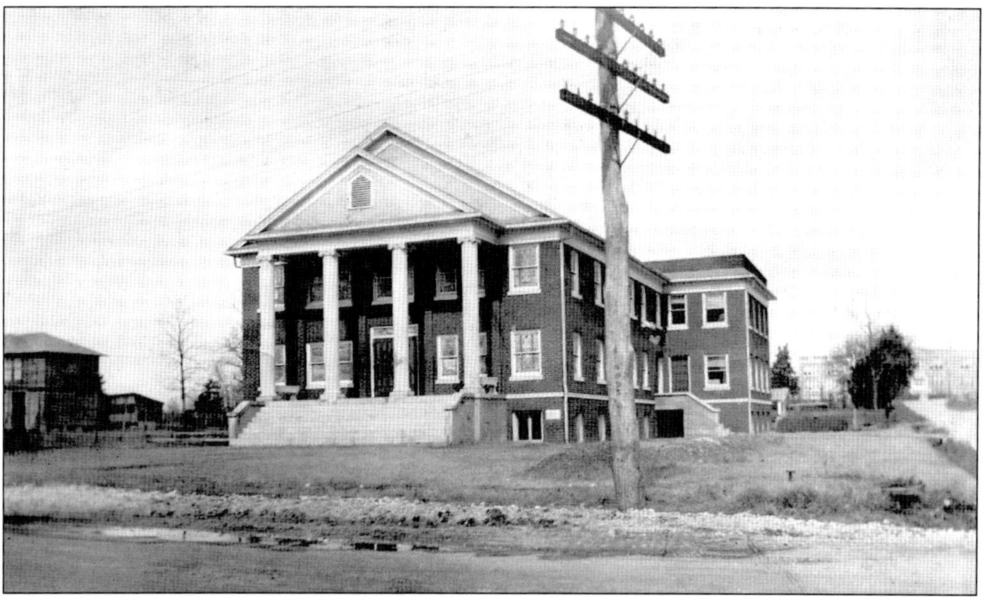

In 1871, the local Methodist congregation built a Gothic chapel on the corner of Court Street and Stage Road. This building tragically burned in 1923, and within a few years, the members rebuilt it just down the street at Shelby and Stage Road, where they are located today. In 2004, a new, larger sanctuary was built just west of the old sanctuary.

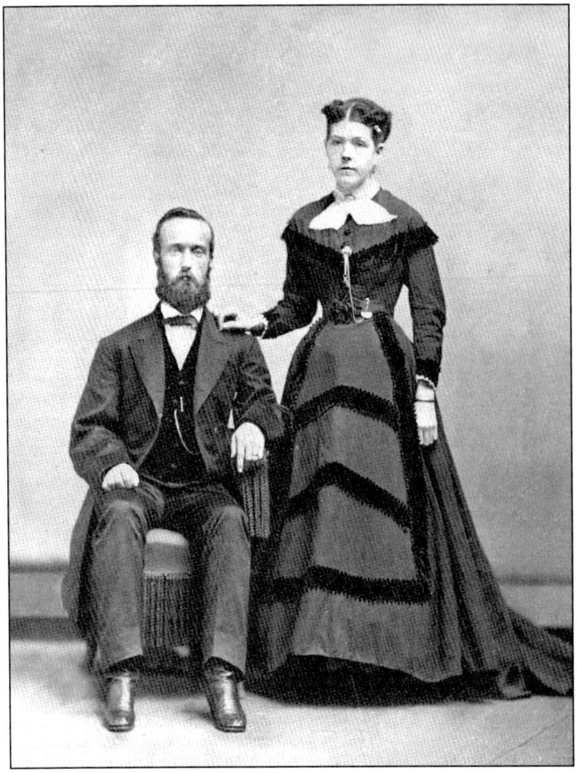

Nicholas Blackwell moved to Bartlett just after the Civil War and became a leading physician and land developer in the area. In 1866, he married Lucy Virginia Ward, whose family owned a large farm on Stage Road. Virginia was the granddaughter of Col. Adam Alexander, a political rival of Davy Crockett. Sadly, Virginia died in 1872, leaving Nicholas with their only child, Willie Bugg Blackwell.

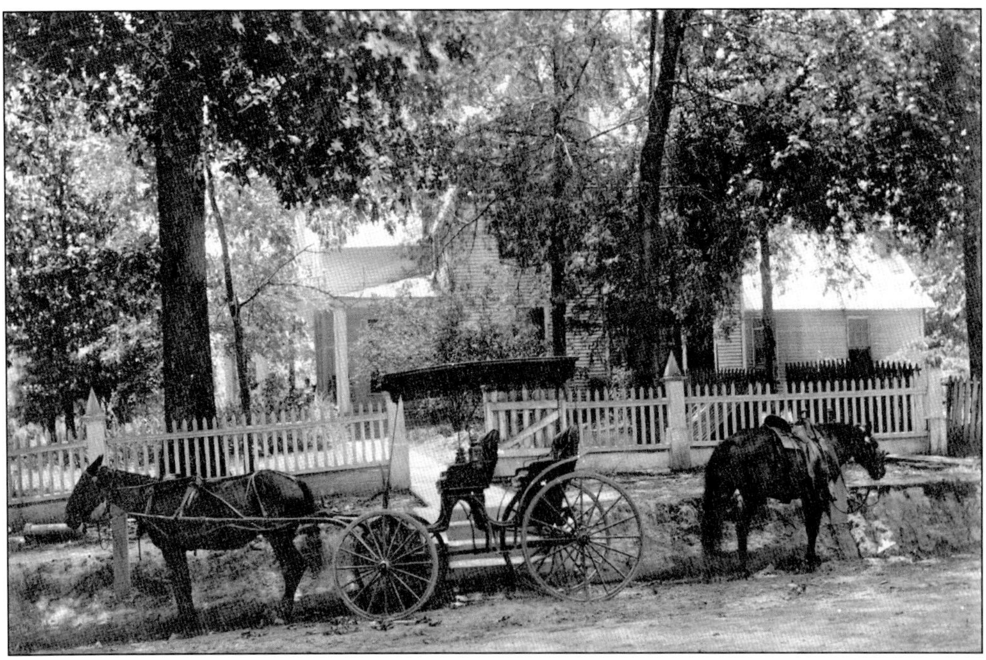

The Blackwell House, which is located at the corner of Sycamore and Blackwell Street, was constructed by James Oglesby in 1869. Dr. Nicholas Blackwell lived in the home until his death in 1910. Dr. Blackwell was noted for his selfless work during the yellow fever epidemic of the late 1870s.

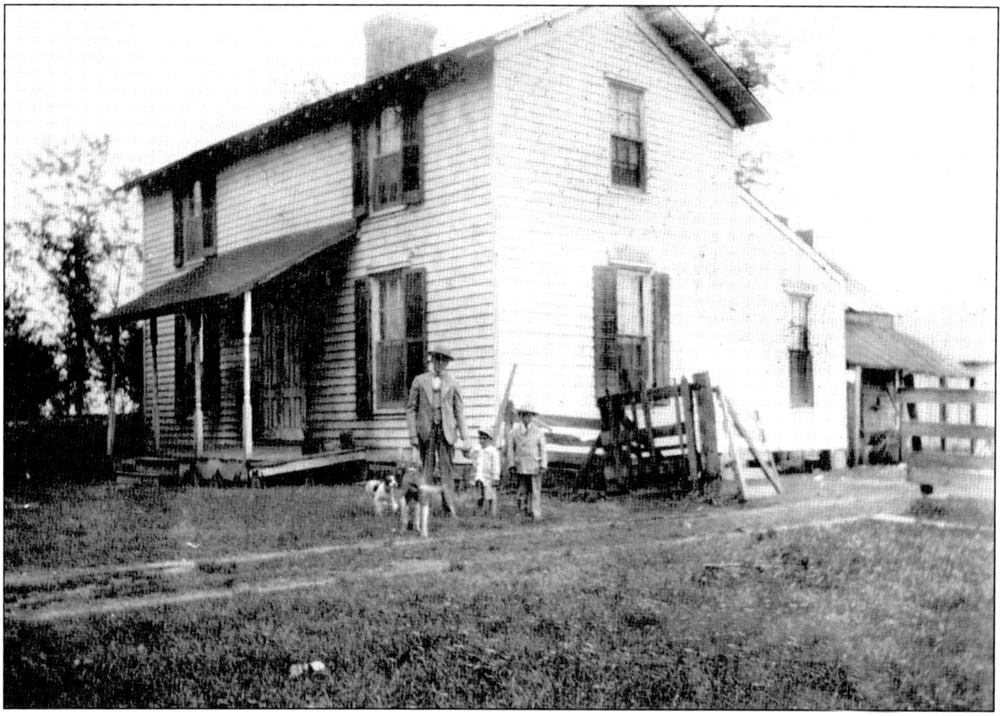

One of the earliest settlers in the area was Benjamin Williamson, who moved to Raleigh LaGrange Road in 1829. His son, W. W. Williamson, built the house shown above in 1870 on Bartlett Road. In 1925, the house was purchased by Jesse Dye, shown here with his two sons, Lorell (center) and Robert. The house burned on Christmas Eve 1927.

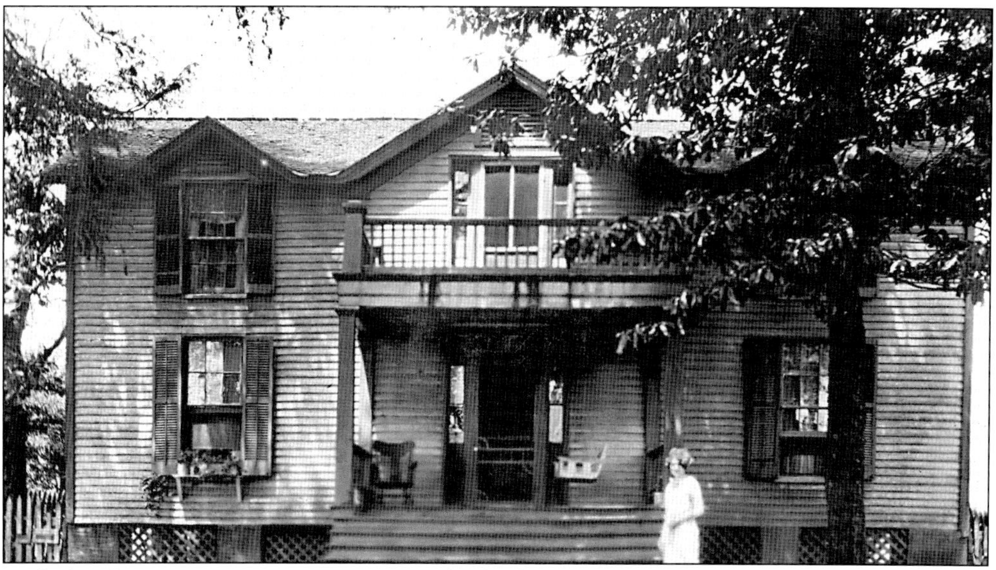

Nicholas Gotten, a Prussian immigrant who had fought with Nathan Bedford Forrest in the Civil War, moved to Bartlett in 1860. Gotten was the city's first alderman and also a blacksmith and ginner. He was granted a patent for an improved cotton feeder in 1879. The house today, located on Court Street, is home to the Bartlett Historical Society and is listed on the National Register of Historic Places.

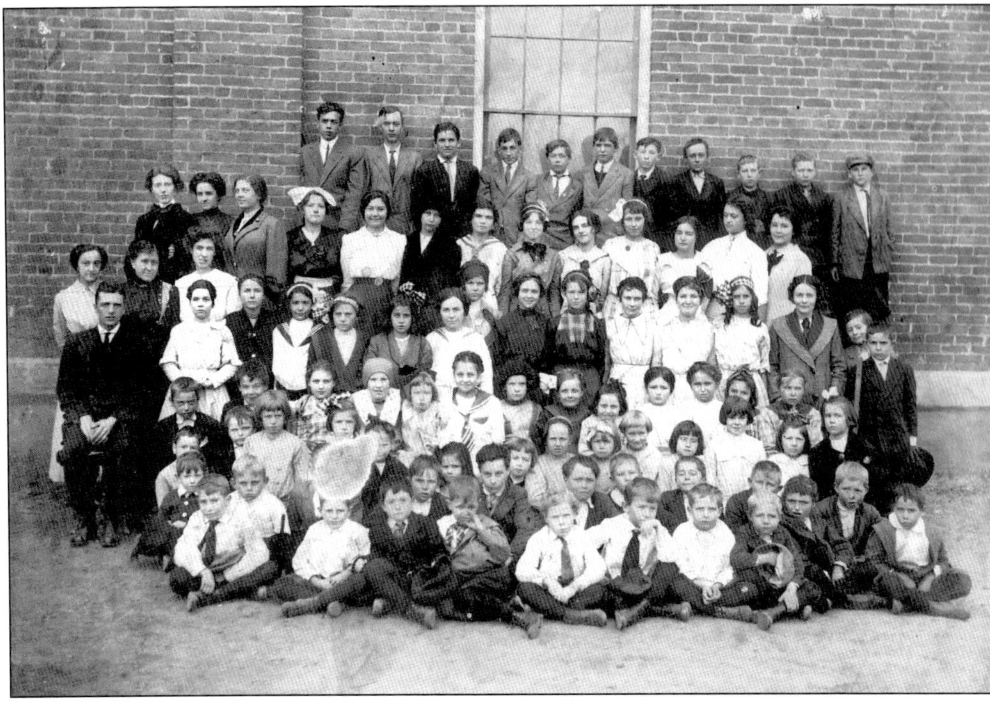

Here is an early class photograph from the Bartlett Courthouse School around 1912.

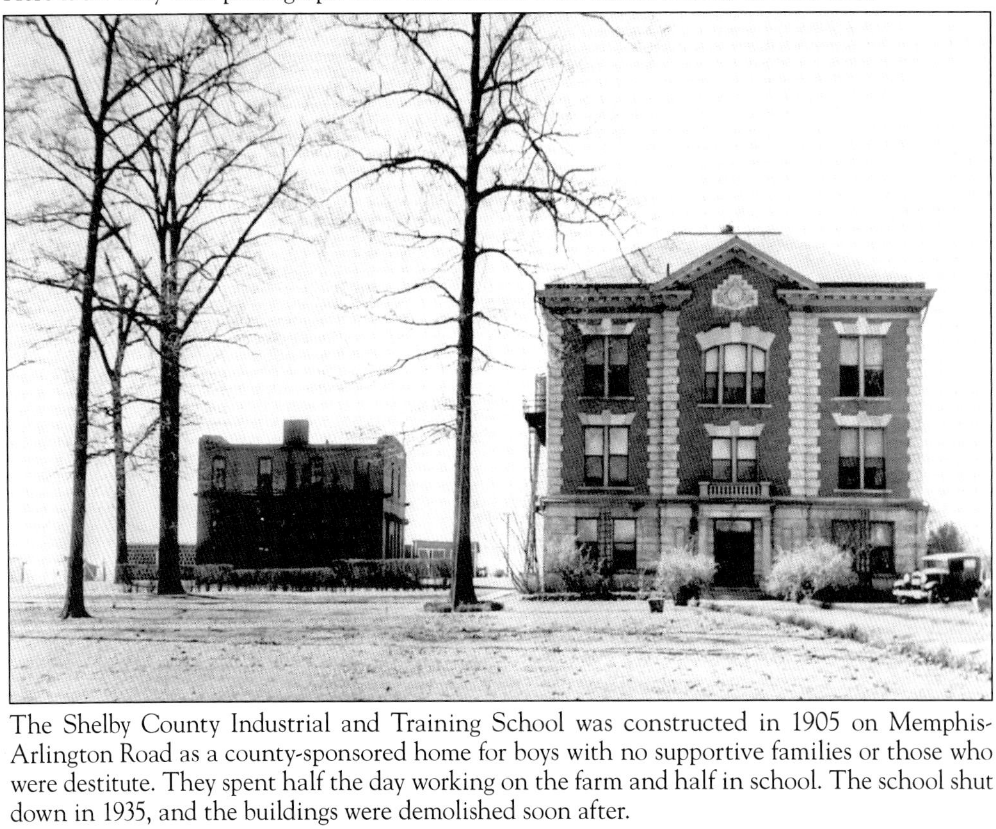

The Shelby County Industrial and Training School was constructed in 1905 on Memphis-Arlington Road as a county-sponsored home for boys with no supportive families or those who were destitute. They spent half the day working on the farm and half in school. The school shut down in 1935, and the buildings were demolished soon after.

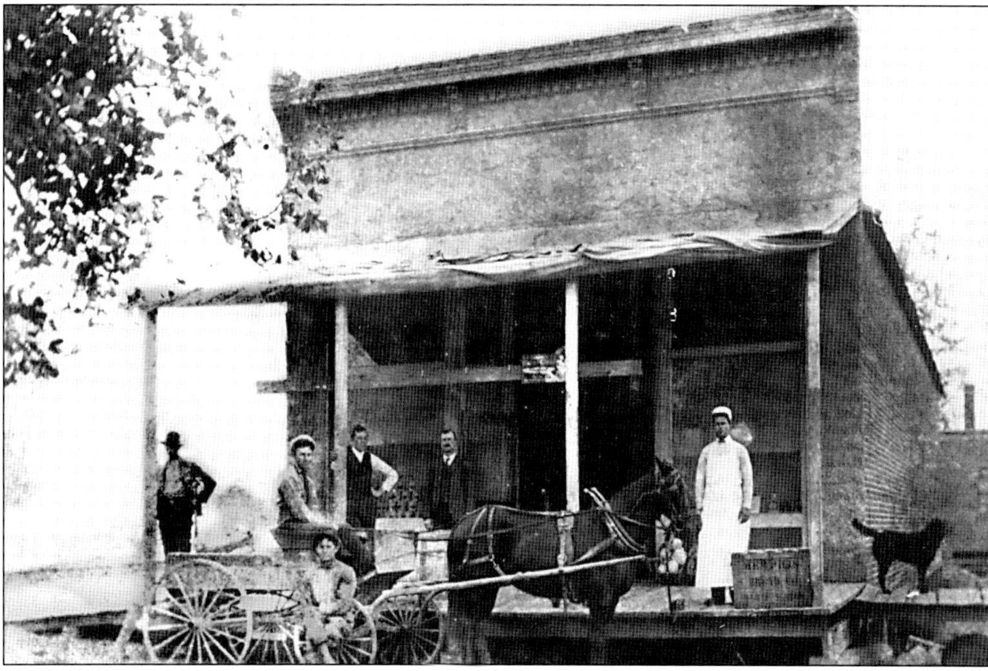

Operated by Hood Tatum, the general store shown here in 1920 was located just east of the railroad tracks on Stage Road.

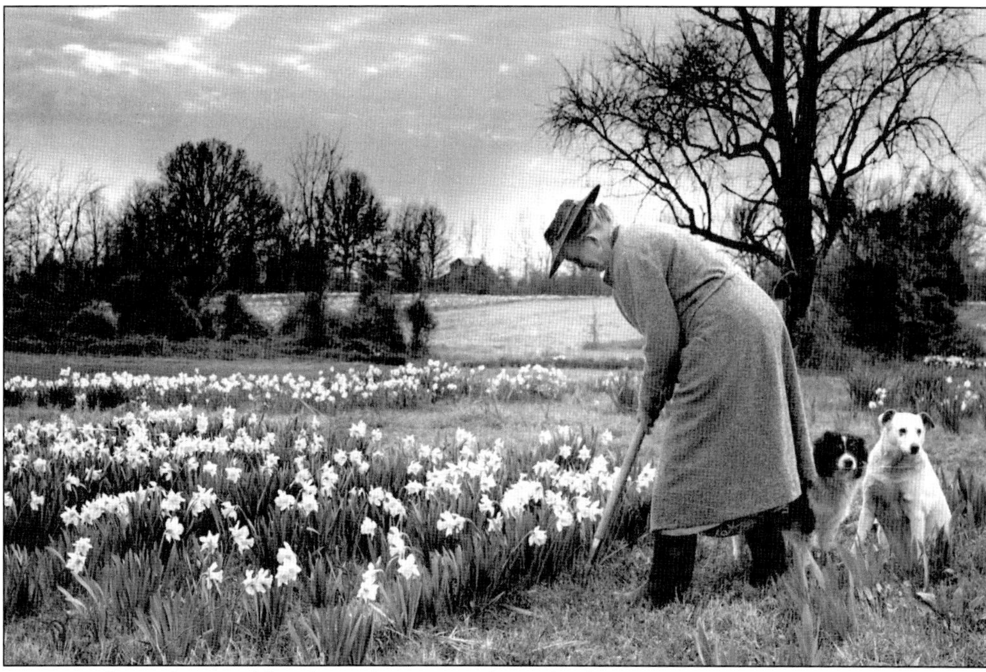

Kate Bond was the granddaughter of Dr. Samuel Bond, who settled in Ellendale in the 1830s. She inherited her parents' homestead located on Stage Road and became one of the county's leading horticulturists. She provided the flowers for the opening of the Claridge and Peabody Hotels in the 1920s and filled the local hospitals with her beautiful arrangements. Kate Bond Elementary School was named in her honor and is today one of the leading schools in the county.

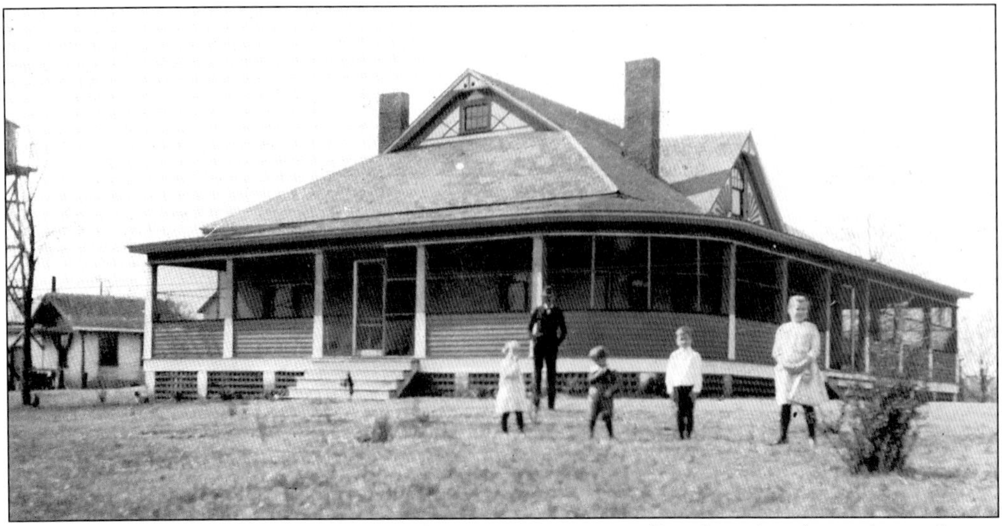

Built in 1905, the Wilfong House at Cedar Grove was originally a boarding house located next to the L&N train platform on Raleigh LaGrange Road. In 1916, the Wilfong family purchased the house and established Cedar Grove Dairy, one of the area's largest processing dairies.

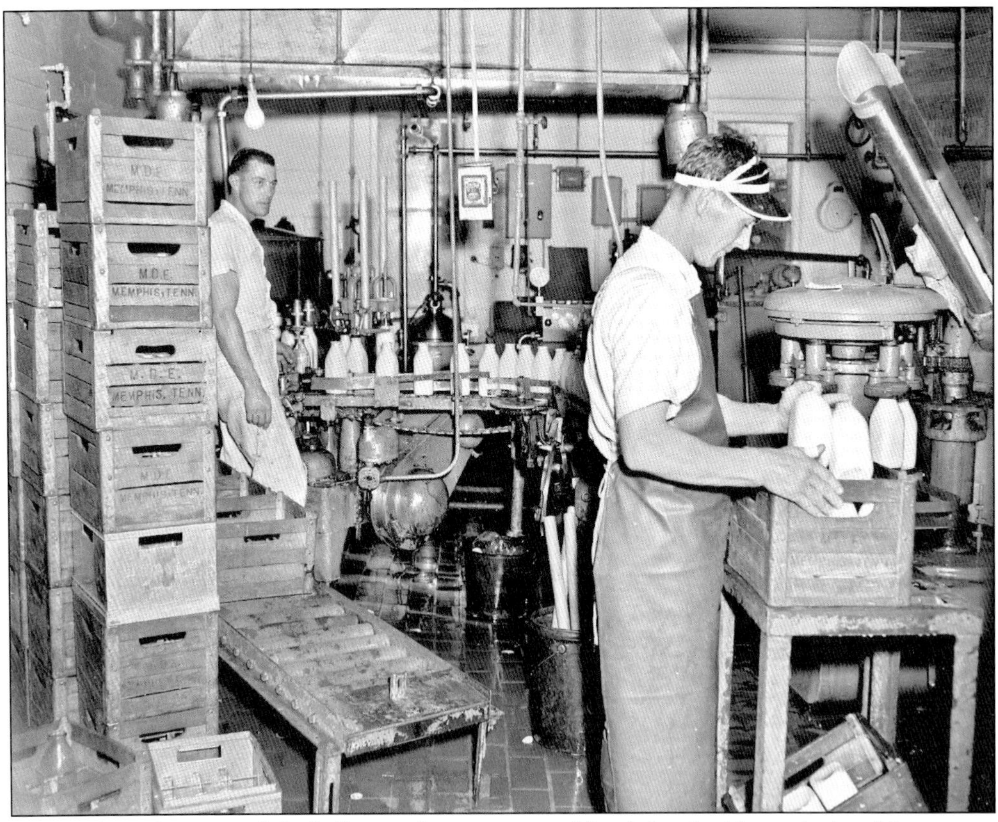

Due to the infestation of the boll weevil on cotton and land that had been depleted from years of farming, cattle dairies saw a dramatic upswing beginning in the 1920s. By the 1950s, there were as many as 20 dairies in the Bartlett area. The largest were Cedar Grove (shown above), Norwood Brothers, and the Klinke Dairy.

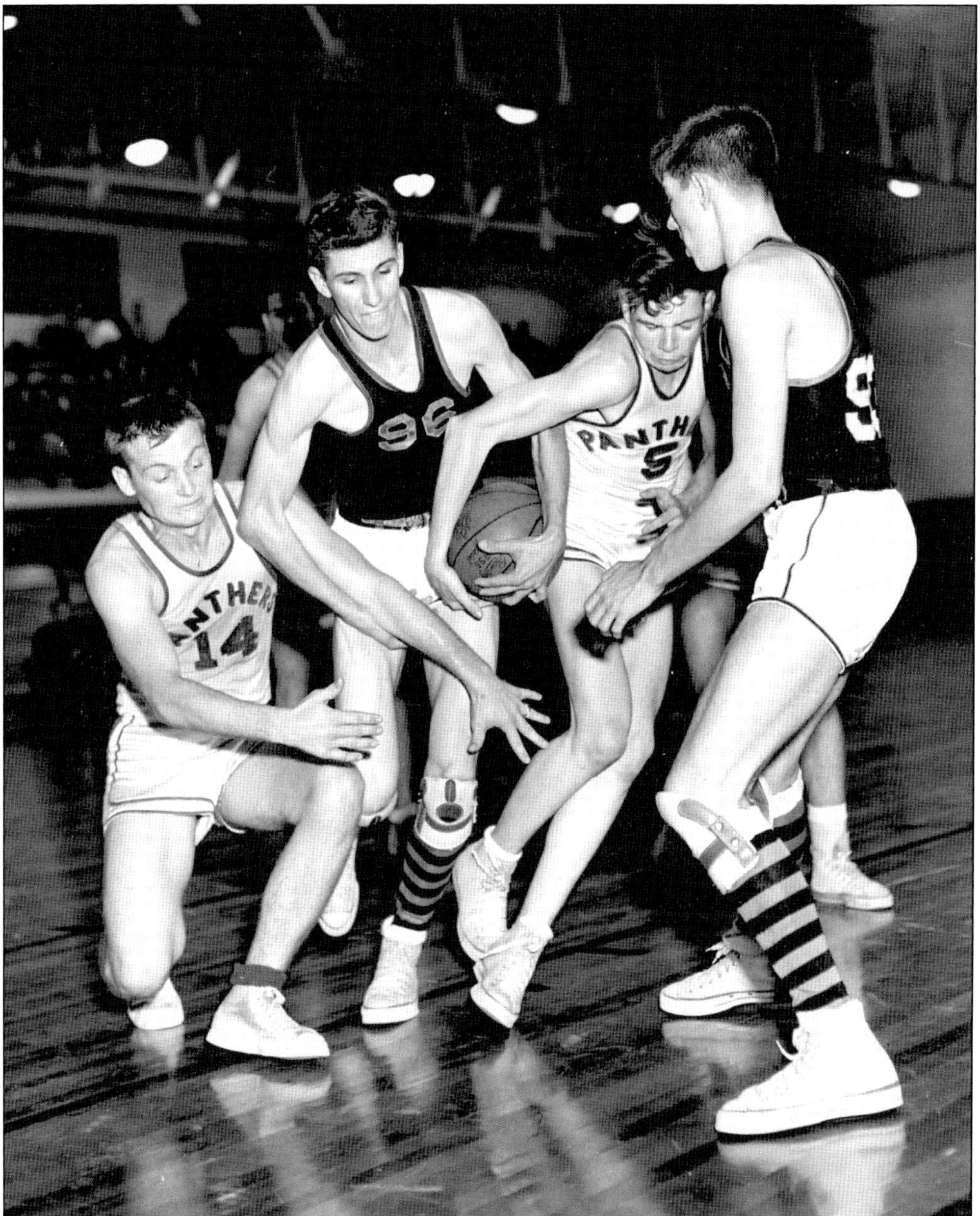

One of the biggest basketball rivalries was between Bartlett and Whitehaven. In this national award-winning photograph from 1951, the players fight over a loose ball. The players, from left to right, are Tom Brown, Billy Joe Jones, Eugene Sanders, and John McGee.

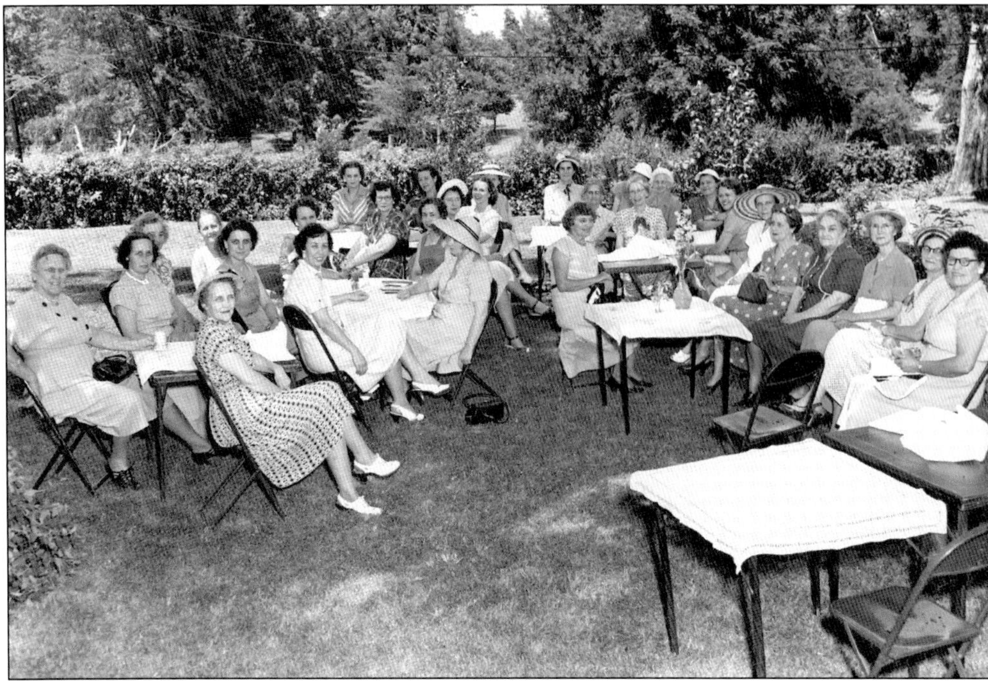

Organized in 1931, the Bartlett Garden Club is one of Bartlett's oldest civic organizations. Shown here at the 25th anniversary in 1956, the club is still active today.

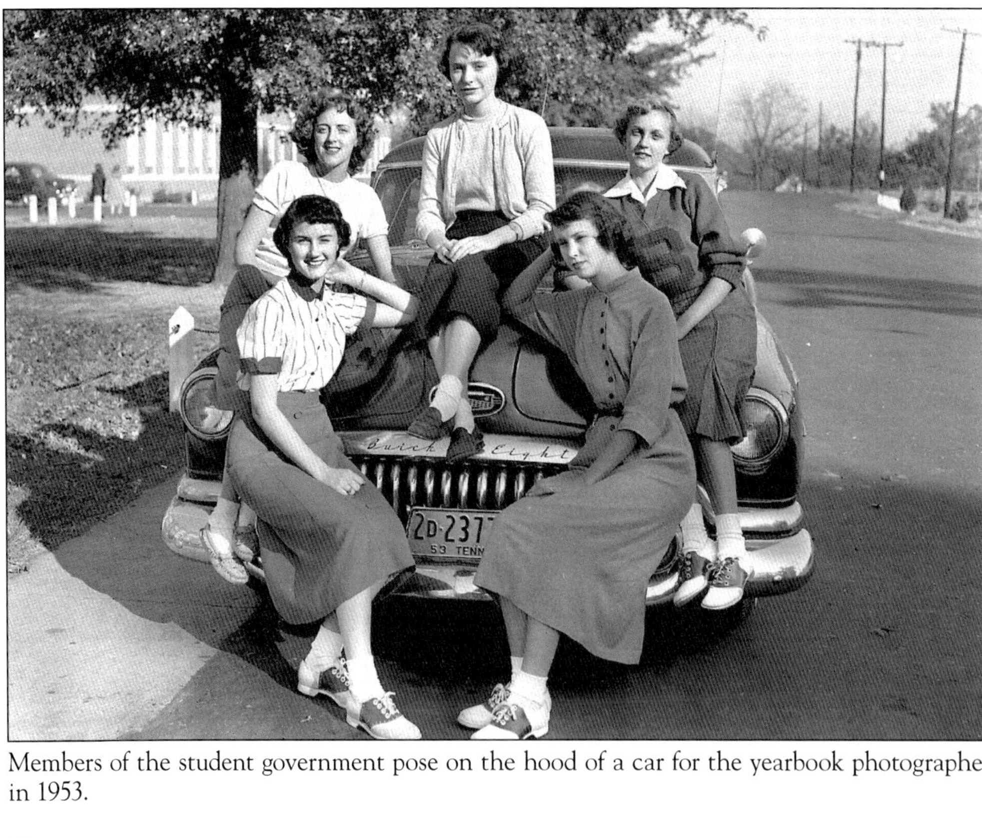

Members of the student government pose on the hood of a car for the yearbook photographer in 1953.

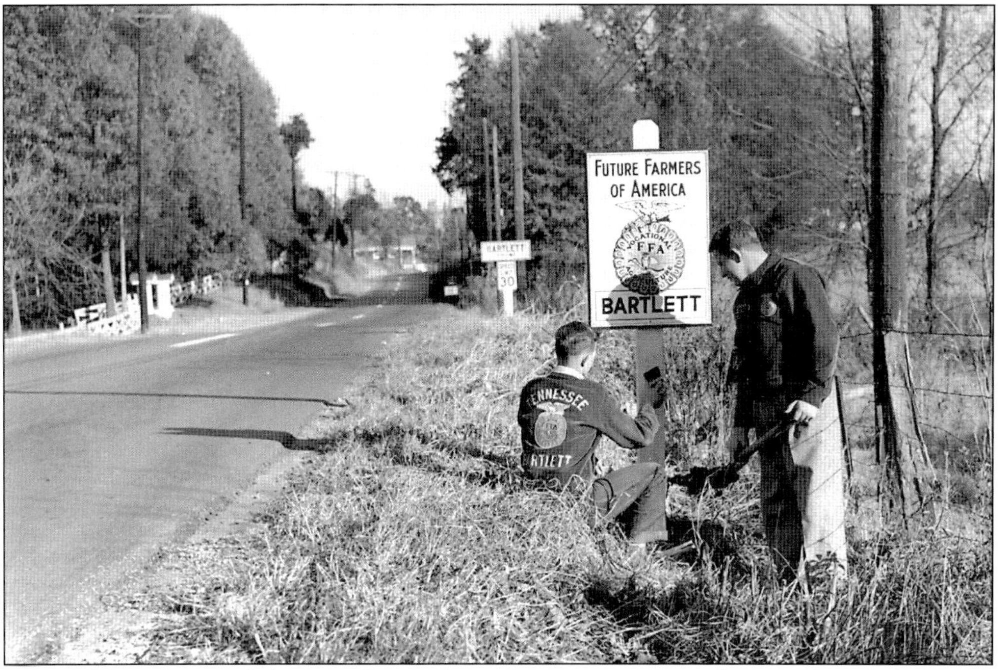

Under the guidance of their teacher and mentor, Mr. David McPherson, the Bartlett High School Future Farmers of America was one of the leading chapters in Shelby County. Shown here installing a welcome sign on Stage Road just west of Bartlett are Billy Klemm (left) and Otto Rahm.

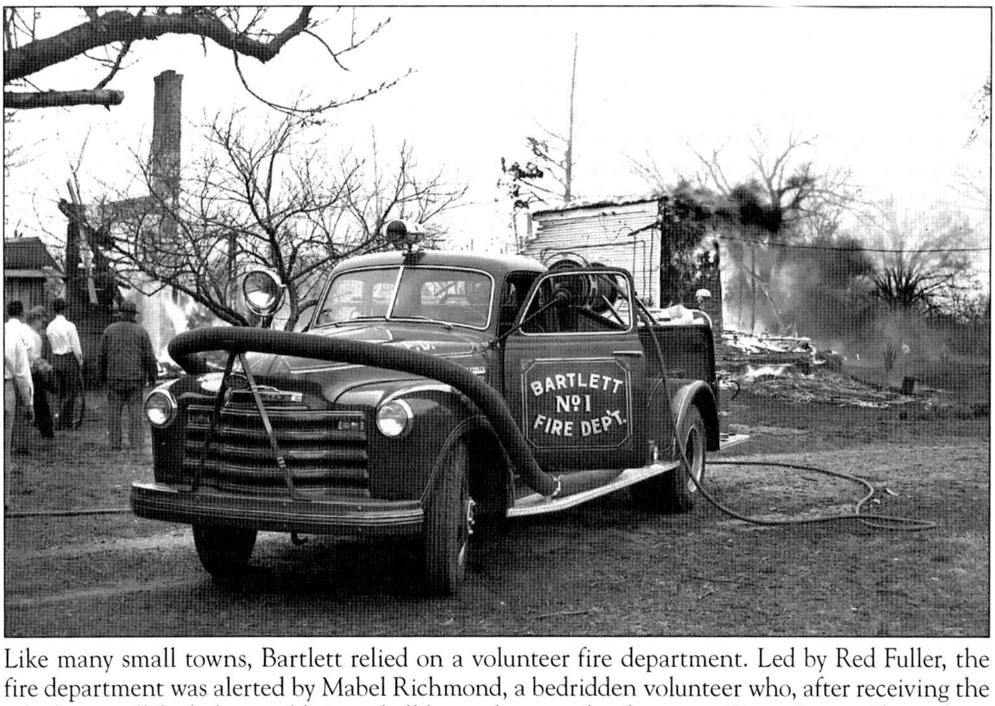

Like many small towns, Bartlett relied on a volunteer fire department. Led by Red Fuller, the fire department was alerted by Mabel Richmond, a bedridden volunteer who, after receiving the telephone call for help, would ring a bell located next to her home on Court Street. Shown here is the first fire truck for Bartlett in 1949.

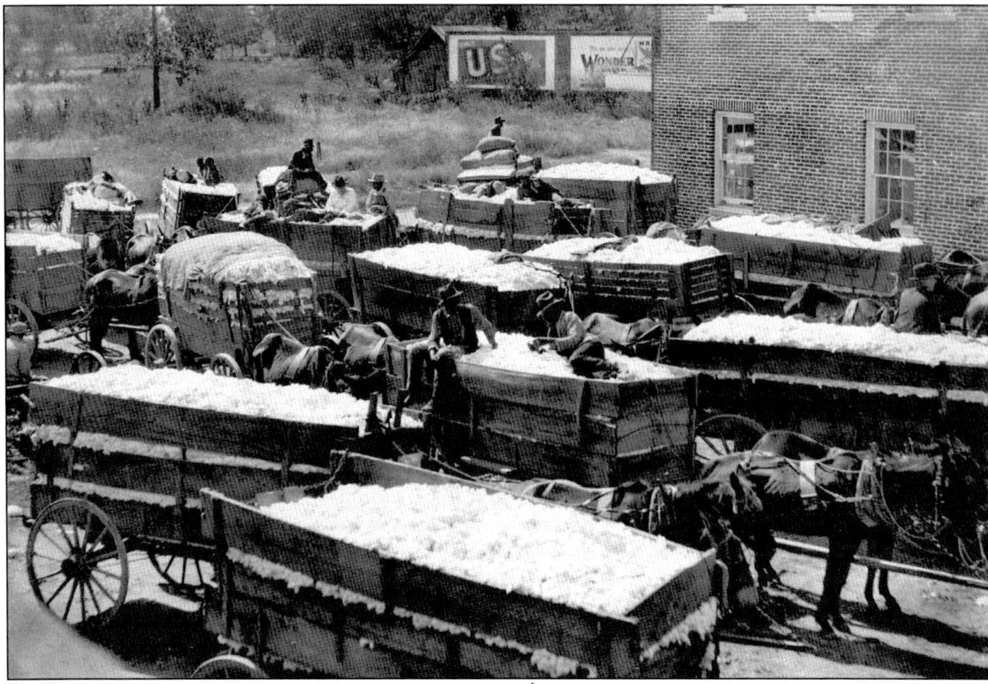

Cotton wagons line up at the Bartlett cotton gin in the early 1930s. Cotton was the predominant crop for farmers in Shelby County, with each community having several gins. The Bartlett Gin was first operated by Nicholas Gotten in the 1870s, then by the Albright family during the mid-1900s. The Bartlett cotton gin was located on Stage Road between Court and Sycamore.

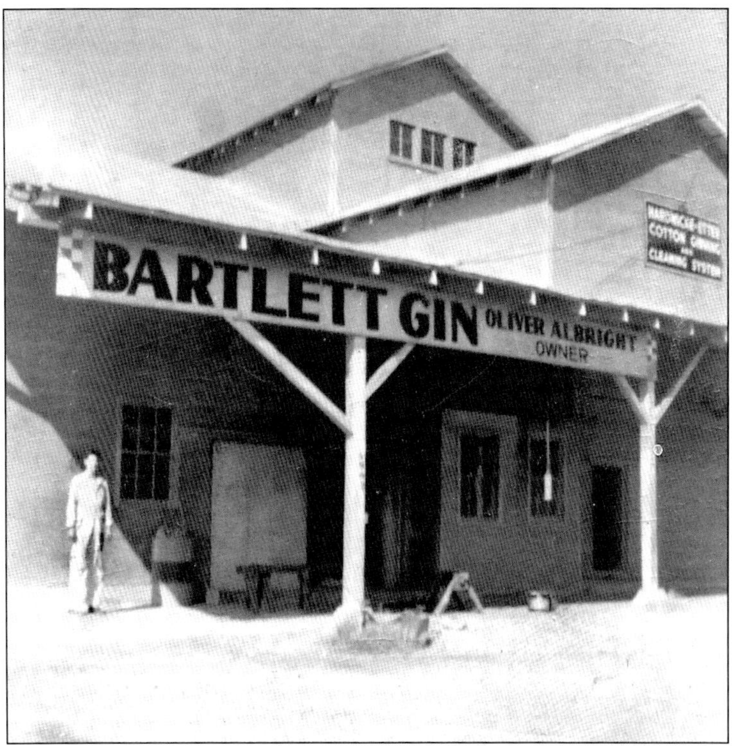

The Bartlett cotton gin is shown here in 1952 when it was owned by the Albright family. The gin was torn down in the 1970s and is today a parking lot.

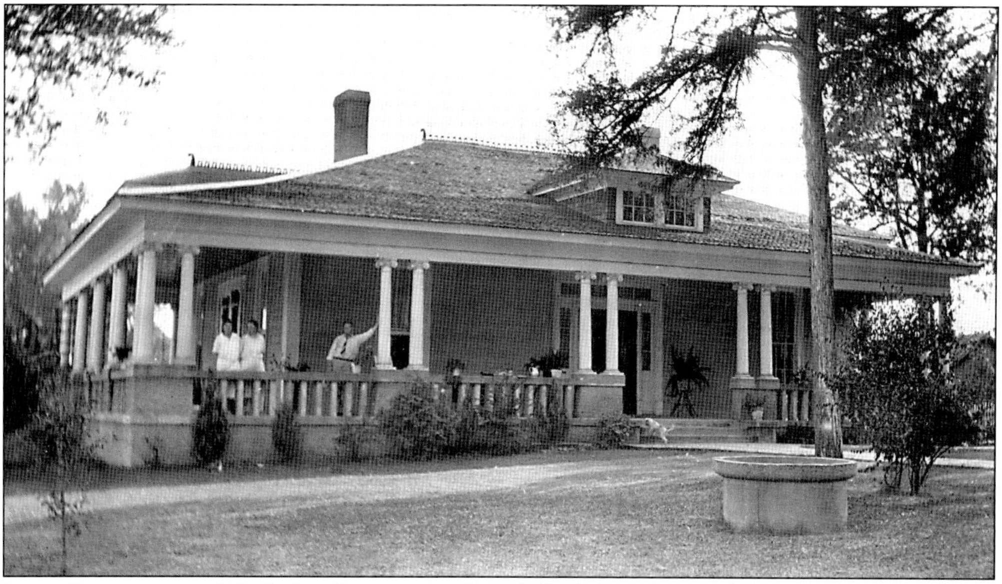

Dave Gotten, son of Nicholas Gotten, purchased the home shown above in 1910. The home, located on Stage Road across from Court Street, was built in the 1880s for the Elmore family.

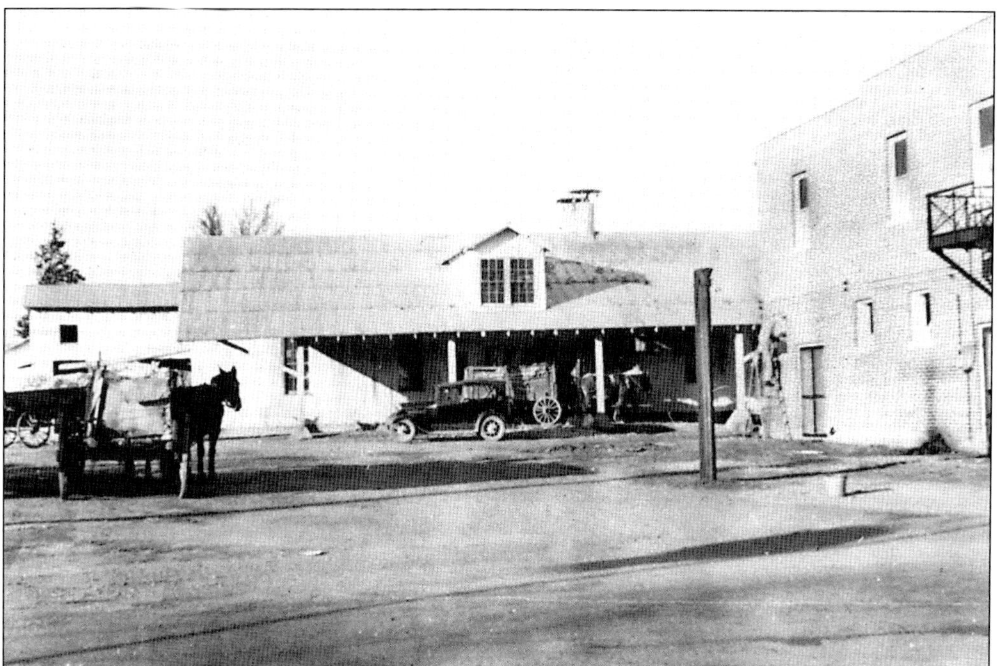

The first cotton gin was established in Bartlett just after the Civil War and operated by Nicholas Gotten. The gin, shown here in the 1930s, served an area of more than 10 miles around Bartlett.

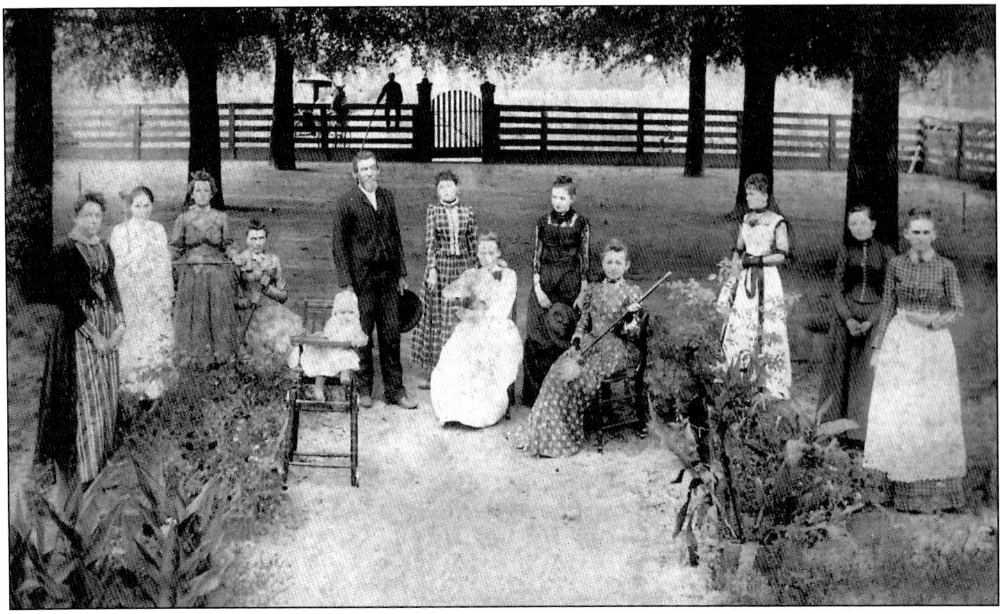

The Bond family, shown here around 1900, arrived in the Bartlett area around 1830, settling in the Ellendale community northeast of Bartlett. Among the first Bonds were Dr. Washington Bond, Dr. Samuel Bond, John Bond, and Newton Bond; all were brothers who moved from Alabama around 1830. The home of Dr. Samuel Bond, built in 1845, still stands in Ellendale today and is listed on the National Register of Historic Places.

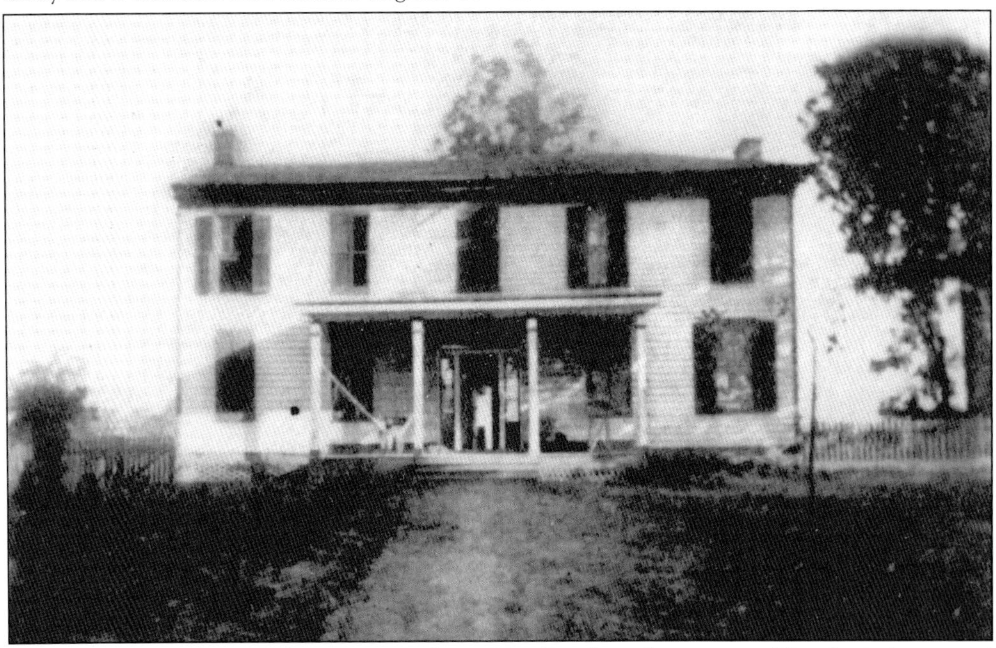

Originally owned by Joseph Cotton in the 1830s, Goodwood was one of Bartlett's few actual plantations. The 960-acre plantation was sold to John Blackwell in the 1840s for $16,000. Consisting of a main house, 12 slave houses containing 72 slaves, and vast fields of cotton and corn, Goodwood prospered until the death of John Blackwell in 1860, after which it was divided and sold at auction.

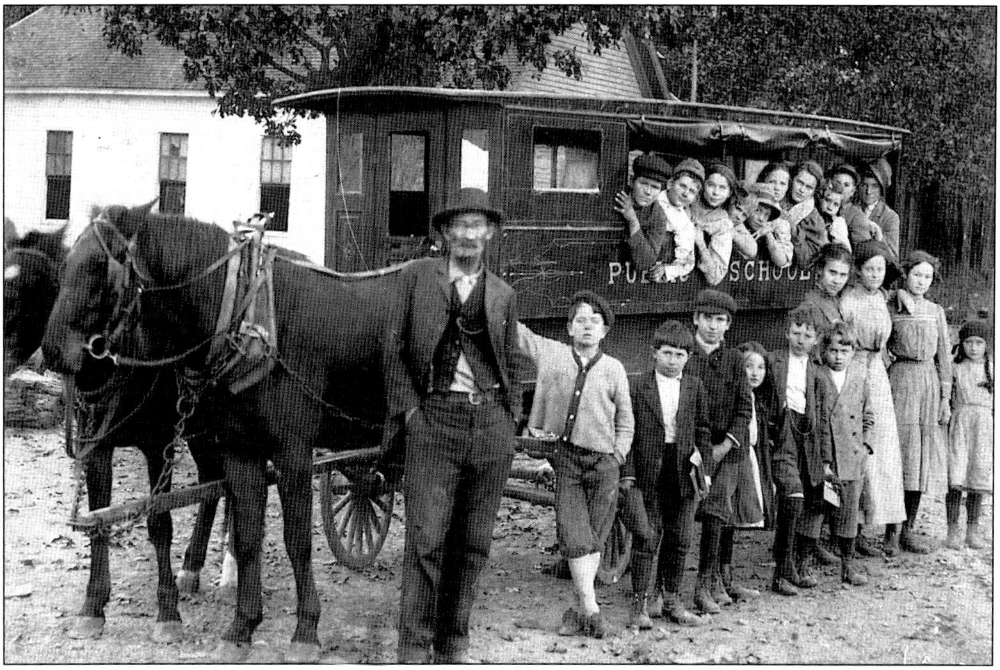

Before the advent of the modern school bus, children rode a wagonette pulled by either mules or horses. During the cold winter months, the wagons were enclosed, and heated bricks were kept on the floor. The first wagonettes were introduced in 1908 and eventually were replaced by motorized buses in the 1920s.

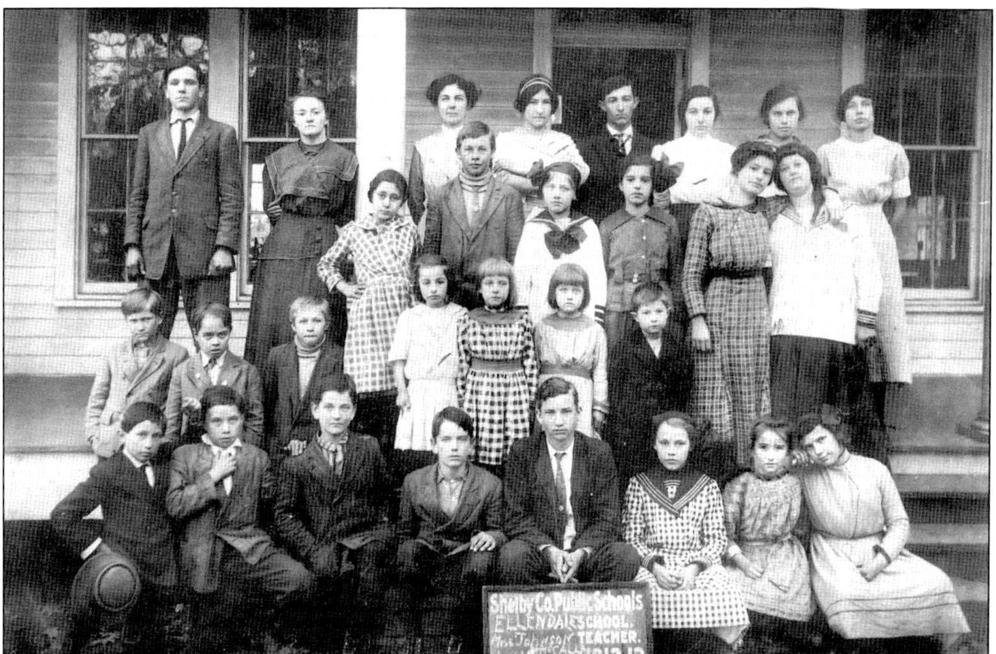

This photograph from 1913 shows the Ellendale School, which consisted of just 28 students for grades 1 through 11. Miss Johnson and Miss McCalla were teachers. Teachers, who had to be single and of good standing, typically earned $30 to $50 per month during the early 1900s.

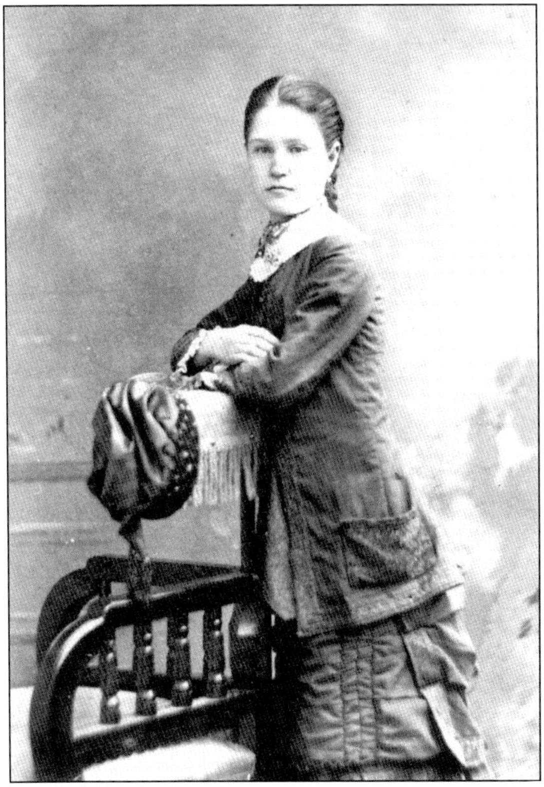

Amanda Duncan arrived in Bartlett in 1872 to care for the daughter of her uncle, Nicholas Blackwell. Amanda helped raise Willie Bugg, whose mother had died suddenly the same year. Nicholas often took Amanda to Memphis to have her portrait made in one of the photography studios located on Main Street.

James and Emma Blackwell lived on Stage Road near the present-day intersection of Stage Road and Highway 70. James was the brother of Nicholas Blackwell and a veteran of the Civil War. Their only daughter, Mamie Blackwell Rock, donated the land for the Baptist Children's Home, located across the street from their home.

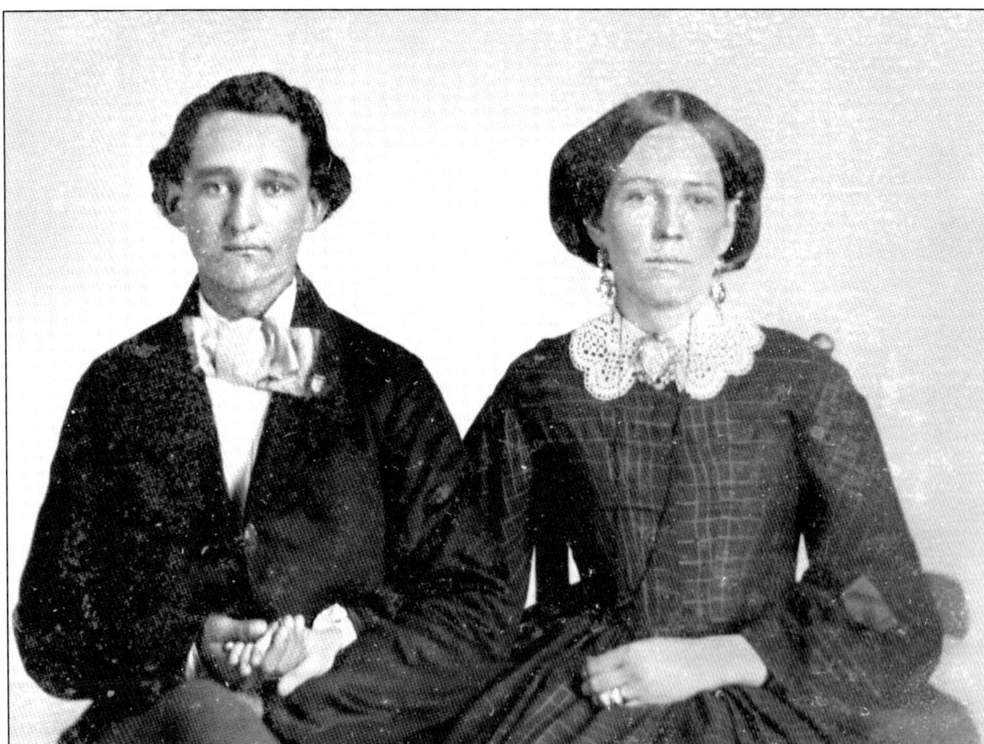

Five

GERMANTOWN

One of the earliest settlements in the Germantown area was Francis Wright's Nashoba Plantation. In 1824, Lafayette, accompanied by Scottish philanthropist Francis Wright, stopped at the fourth Chickasaw Bluff on his way to Nashville. While here, Wright spoke with various citizens about farming and purchasing land. She was an imposing figure, standing 5-feet-10-inches tall, and seen on the Memphis streets as quite eccentric, often wearing a man's hat and walking with a rather masculine stride. The next year, she returned and began to acquire large amounts of real estate. Established in 1825 along the Wolf River, the project was to provide slaves a way to earn their freedom through education and work on the plantation. She was advised by Andrew Jackson about a possible location for her utopian experiment. She eventually purchased 2,000 acres along the Wolf River just west of Germantown Road. The name Nashoba came from the Chickasaw word for wolf. The community failed in just a few years, and the remaining slaves were sent to Haiti. The land stayed in the family until the early 1900s, when it was sold to the former overseer, Thomas Payne. The house stood until 1947 when it was torn down to build a new residence on the same foundation.

William Twyford came to the area from Kentucky in 1825. He was said to have assisted in building the first storehouse in Memphis. Other settlers including the Massey, Robbins, Eppy, and White families all came to the area before 1835. An early settlement known as Pea Ridge grew up on a Native American trail that ran along the present-day Poplar Avenue. A post office was opened in 1833, and soon a town was laid out by Col. G. P. Shepard. It is not known exactly how Germantown received its name. The surveyor who surveyed the land for Shepard was named N. T. German. Two of the earliest settlers were Germans named Lucken and Schieley. Lucken was the first postmaster and innkeeper.

The town grew with the addition of several churches. The Presbyterians established a church in 1838 with Rev. A. G. McNutt as pastor. A few years later, the Methodists built a small frame church on Church Street. In 1840, the New Hope Baptist Church was established on Bridge Street, today called Germantown Road. The Presbyterian church was the only one to escape the effects of the Civil War; the others were burned or destroyed by the Union army. In 1841, the town was incorporated and a Masonic lodge built. In 1852, the Memphis and Charleston Railroad was completed through Germantown, which at that time had a population of 245. A pamphlet distributed by the railroad described the citizens of Germantown as "generally moral, intelligent, and a reading people." Many citizens of Memphis, trying to distance themselves from the ravages of the yellow fever epidemic, traveled to the small towns outside of the city. Many people moved to Germantown during the worst part of the epidemic of 1878. Even Germantown was not safe from the ravages of the fever. According to Goodspeed's *History of Shelby County*, nearly 50 percent of all persons infected in Germantown died within days.

Germantown overcame the epidemics of the late 1800s and kept a low profile over the next half century. During the late 1940s, the Germantown Charity Horse Show was begun as a way to showcase many of the area's finest horses. The first shows were held on the football field of Germantown High School. In the 1950s, a permanent facility was built just south of the school. "Sonny" Foster, the owner of the Germantown Gin, was one of the founders of the show and a leading promoter of the Oak Grove Hunt Club. During this time, fox hunting became very popular also, with rides being held on nearby farms such as Cotton Plant Plantation and Wildwood Farms.

Since 1970, Germantown has seen a 1,000-percent growth in population. The city covers over 18 square miles and has a population of over 40,000. Events such as the Germantown Festival, Germantown Charity Horse Show, and FedEx–St. Jude Classic at Southwind draw national attention to a city that, just a few decades earlier, was a small rural community.

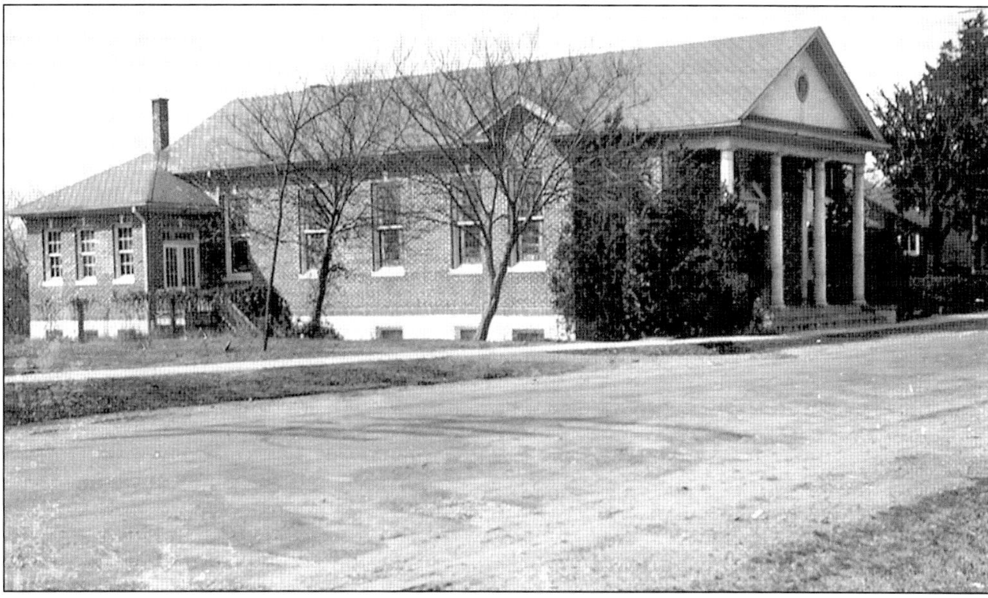

The Germantown Methodist Church was established in 1840 with the sanctuary shown above being built in 1929 on Germantown Road. The first building was burned during the Civil War, and the second was struck by lightning.

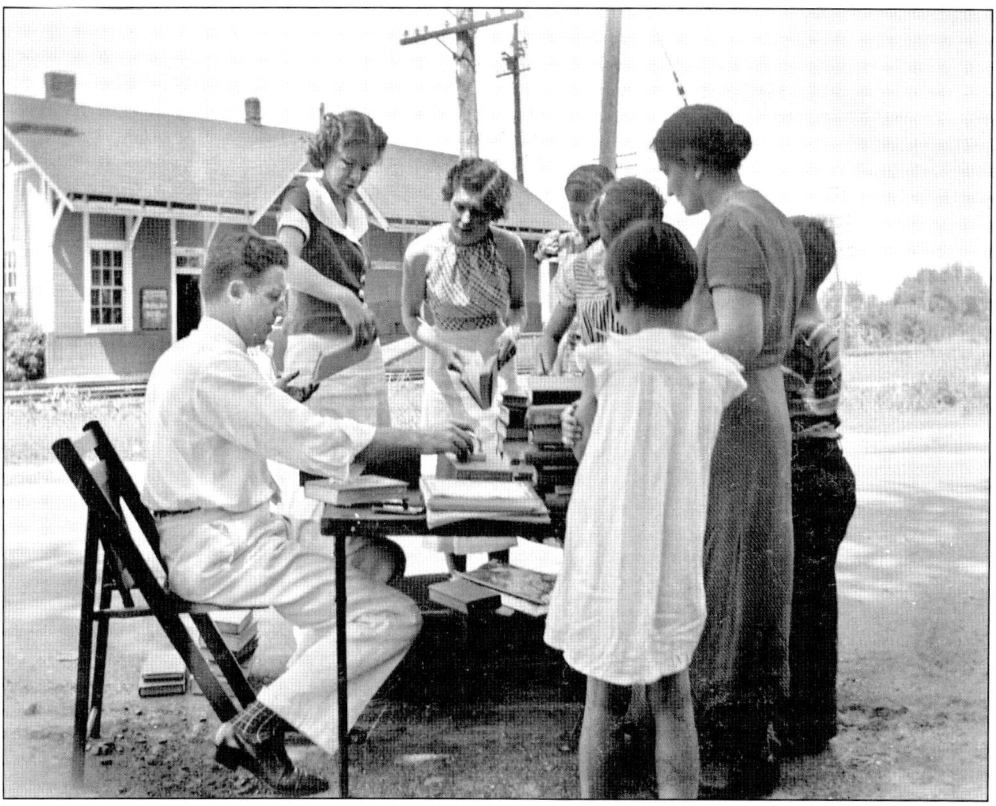

The bookmobile was a common sight in rural towns in Shelby County during the 1930s and 1940s. The main library at the time was the Cossitt Library on Front Street.

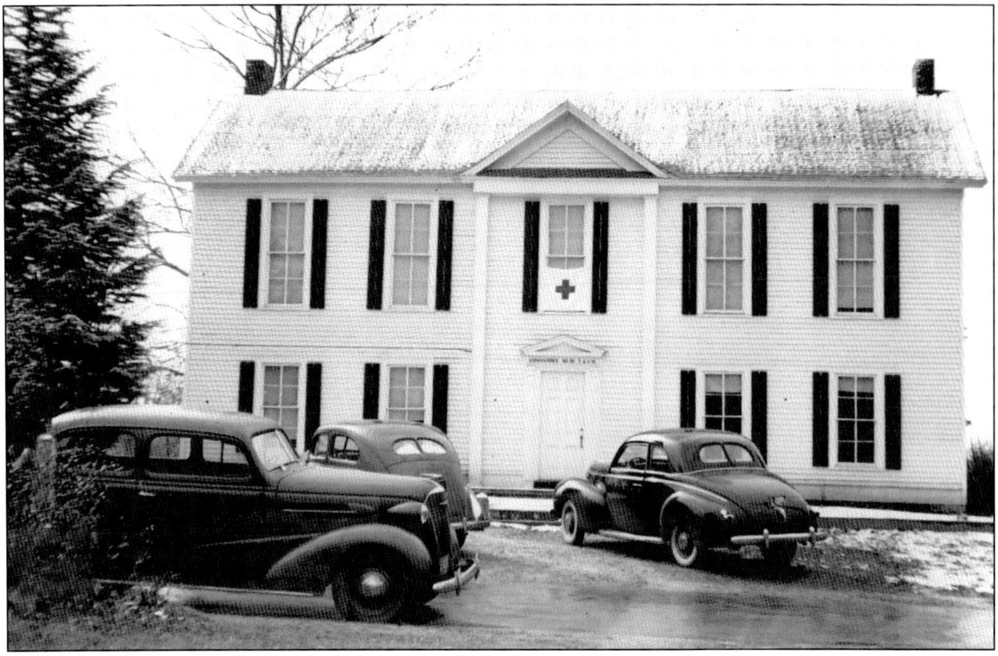

The Masonic lodge was built in 1841 and was the oldest building in Germantown when it was demolished in 1985. During the Civil War, it served as a hospital, and during World War I, it was a Red Cross office. The first public school in Germantown was held in the lodge, located west of the Presbyterian church on Germantown Road.

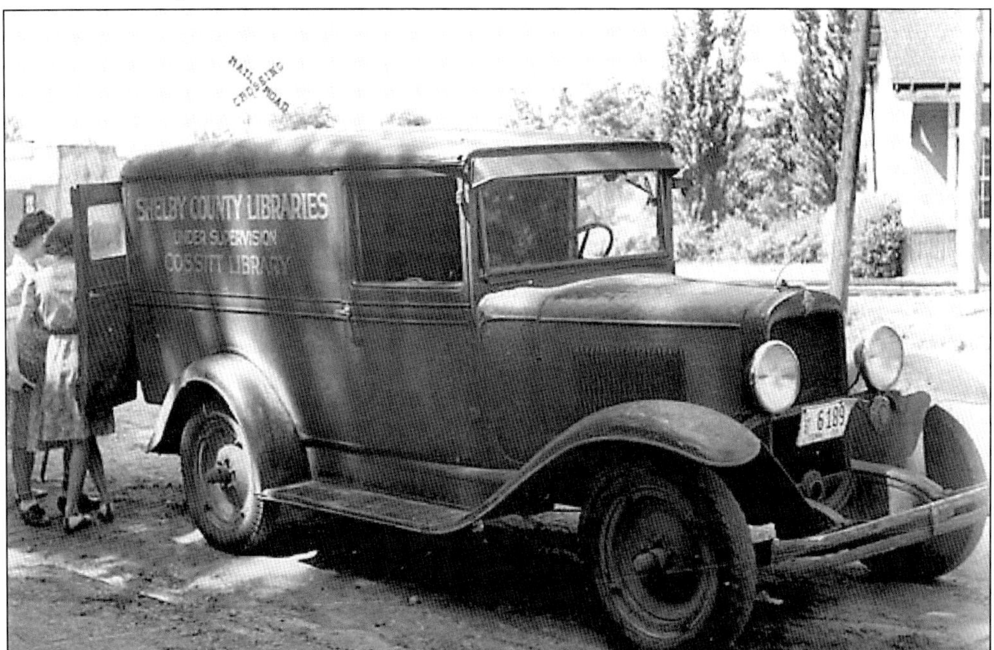

Books were brought out by truck and signed out to citizens who would return them the next time the bookmobile passed through. The bookmobile made the rounds of most towns in Shelby County.

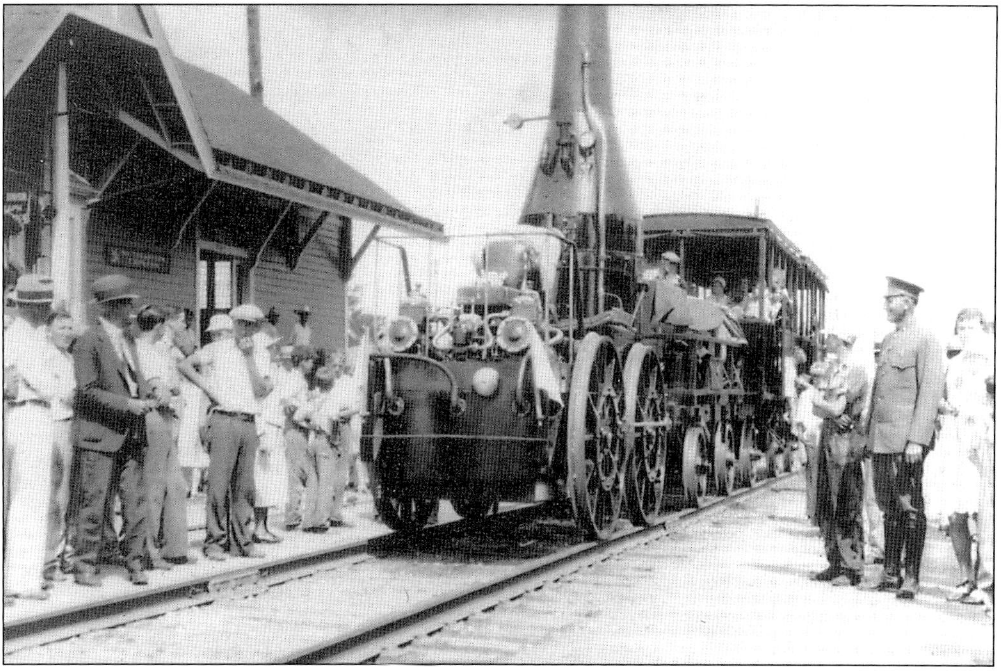

On July 10, 1829, a reenactment was held of the first Memphis and Charleston Railroad train to pass through Germantown. Crowds gathered at each small town to celebrate the building of the rail line in the 1850s. The train line ran from Memphis to Corinth and on to Charleston, South Carolina. The tracks were highly prized during the Civil War, and both sides fought for their control.

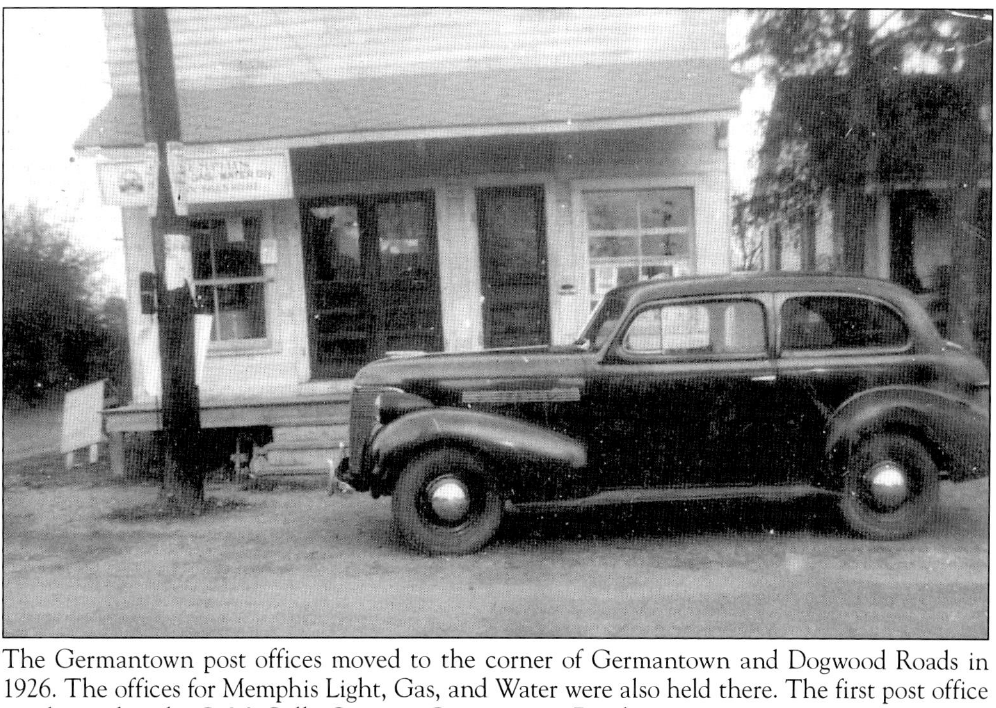

The Germantown post offices moved to the corner of Germantown and Dogwood Roads in 1926. The offices for Memphis Light, Gas, and Water were also held there. The first post office was located in the C. M. Callis Store on Germantown Road.

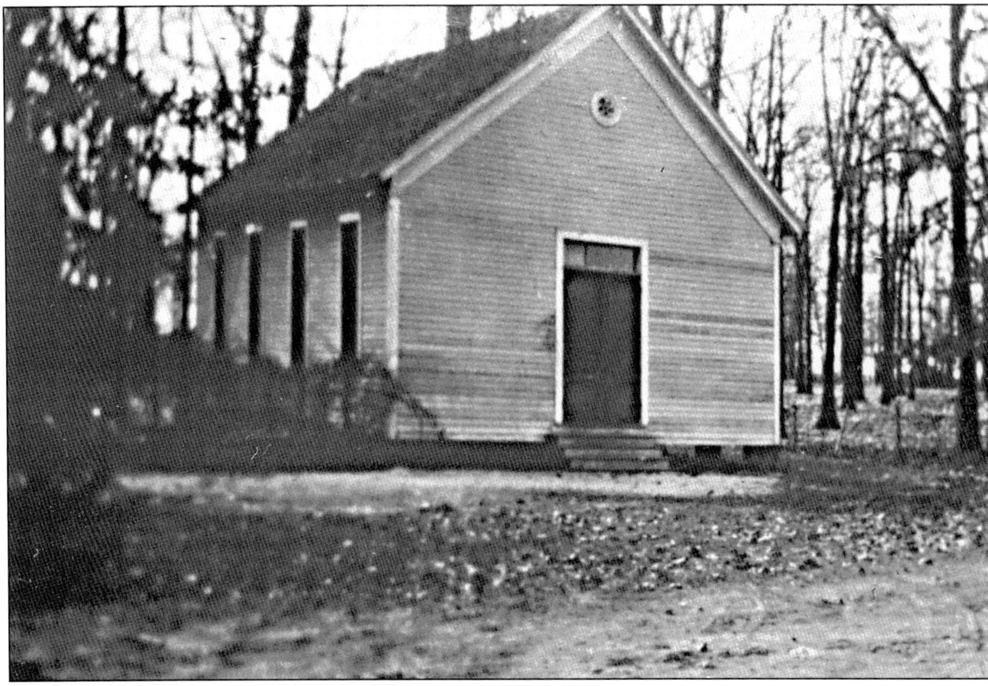

The Forrest Hill Baptist Church was built in the mid-1800s. The building also served as a school until being replaced in 1913 with a new Forrest Hill school. The church continued to use the building until 1925, when the congregation moved to a new location.

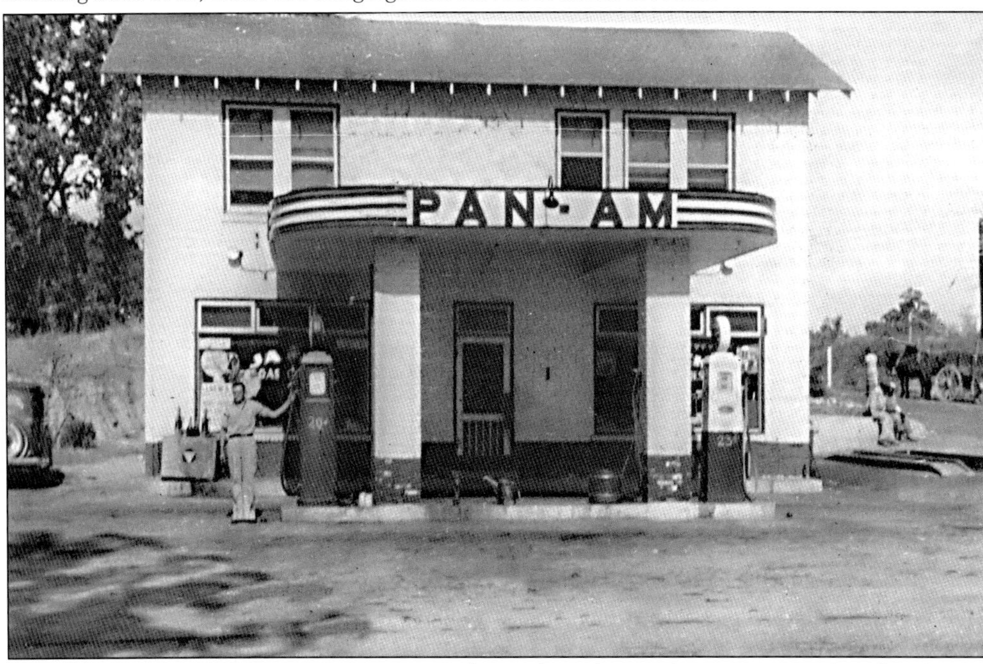

James Burd ran the Pan Am service station, located on the northwest corner of Poplar Avenue and Germantown Road. This photograph from 1938 shows the distinctive station with twin pumps. The station was sold to the Hopper family in the late 1950s and operated as Hopper's Grocery for many years.

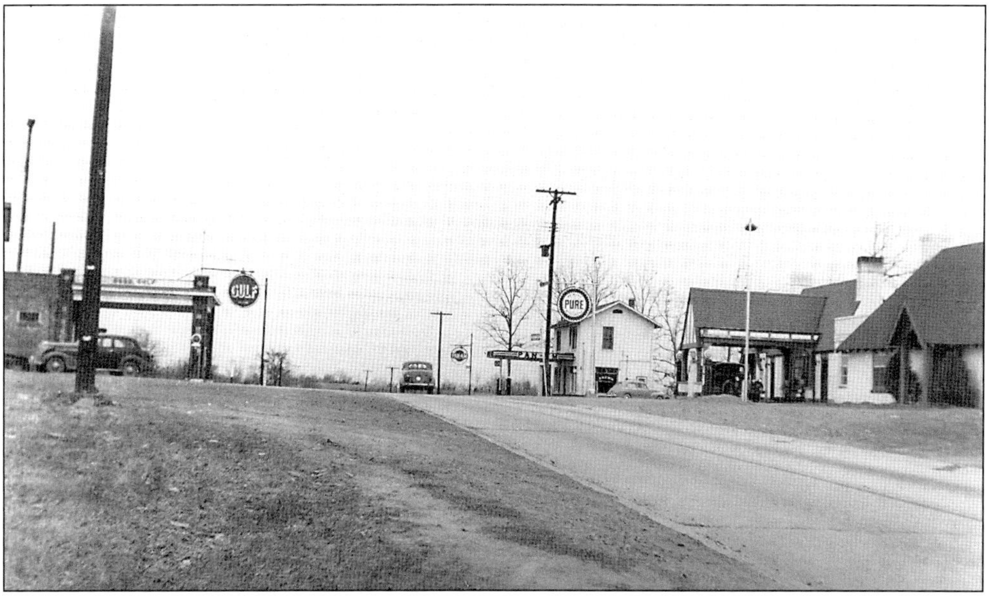

The intersection of Poplar Avenue and Germantown Road, shown here in 1940, has changed dramatically over the years. Looking west down Poplar Avenue toward Germantown Road, we see James Burd's Pan Am gas station on the right with the Gulf station on the left.

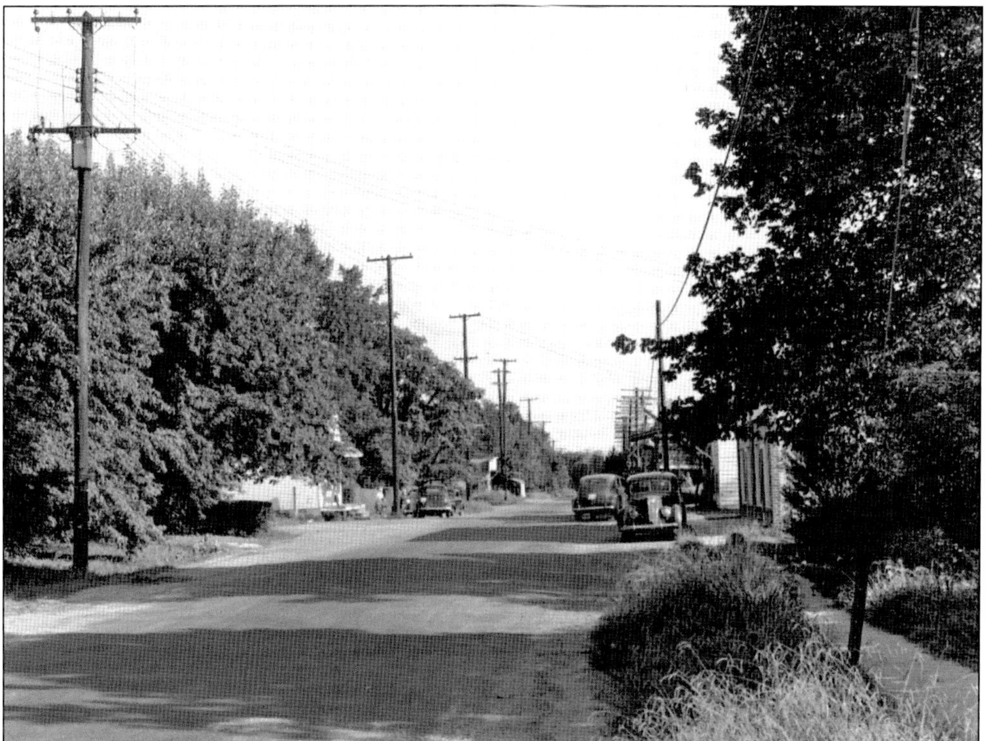

This photograph looks south down Germantown Road from North Street in the early 1940s. Germantown Road was originally named Bridge Street and later known as Germantown and Olive Branch Road.

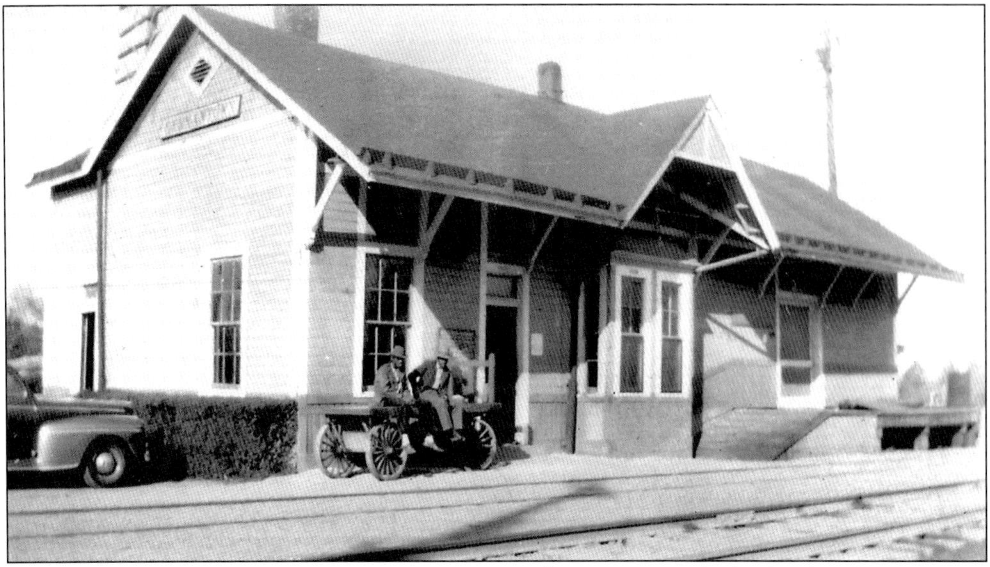

The original Germantown Depot, shown here in the 1940s, was built shortly after the Civil War. The building stood until a fire destroyed it in 1948. The new depot was rebuilt with some of the original timbers. The depot ceased to be used as an official train stop in 1986 and is today part of Depot Square.

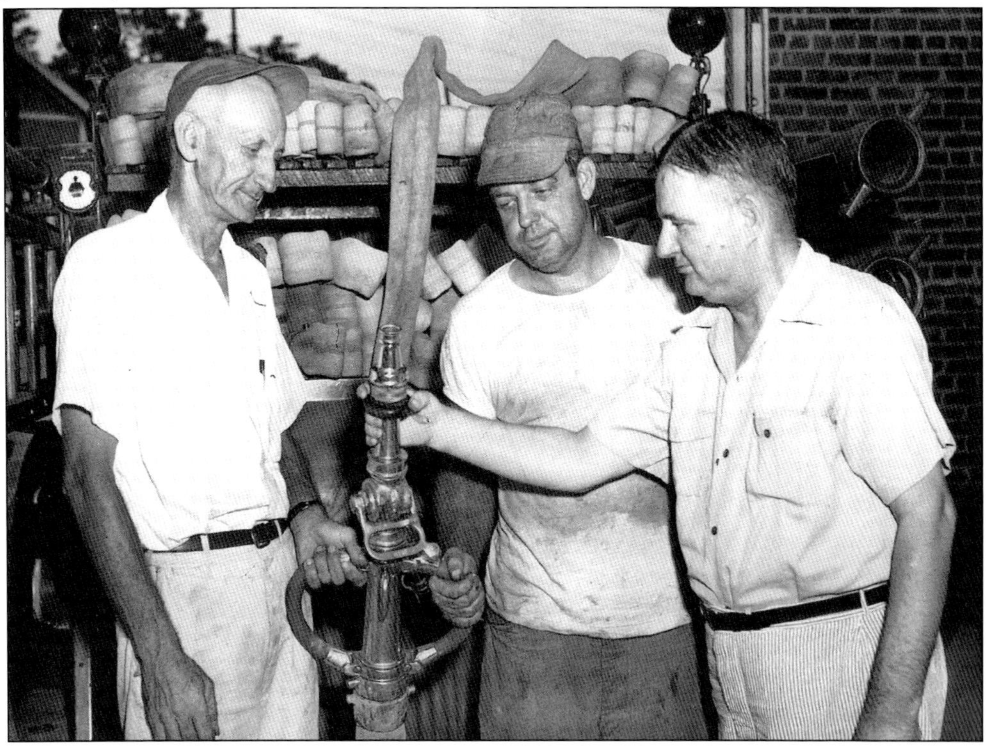

Jack Barry, left, was the mayor of Germantown for more than 46 years. This photograph was taken in the fire station in the early 1950s. Shown with Mayor Barry is C. C. Burford (center), the city's first manager. He served from 1939 until 1954. On the right is Stanley Law, who served as alderman.

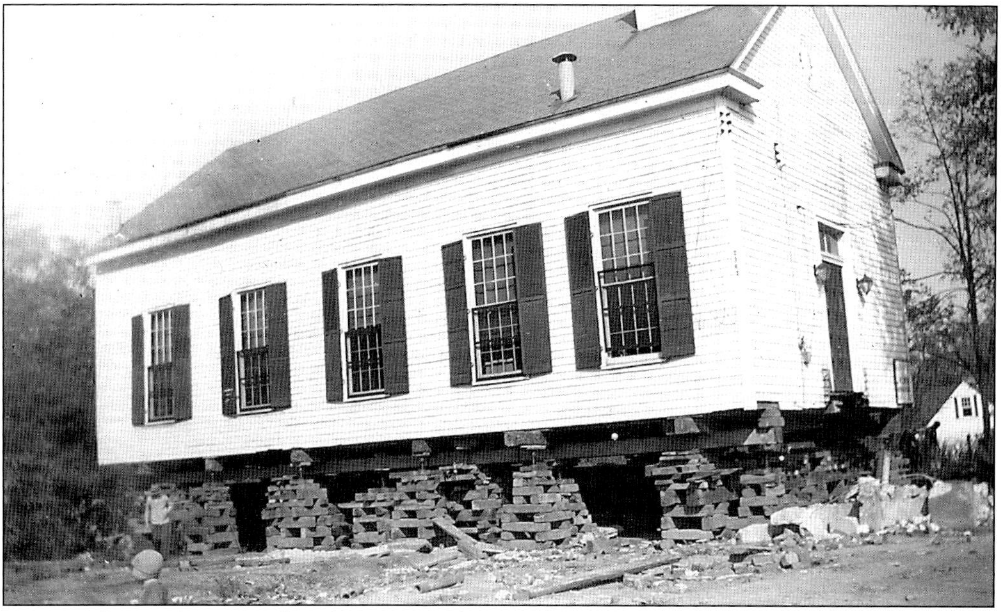

In 1959, the Presbyterian church was moved so as to face the east. The structure was placed on large timbers and slowly rotated from a north-south orientation to an east-west view.

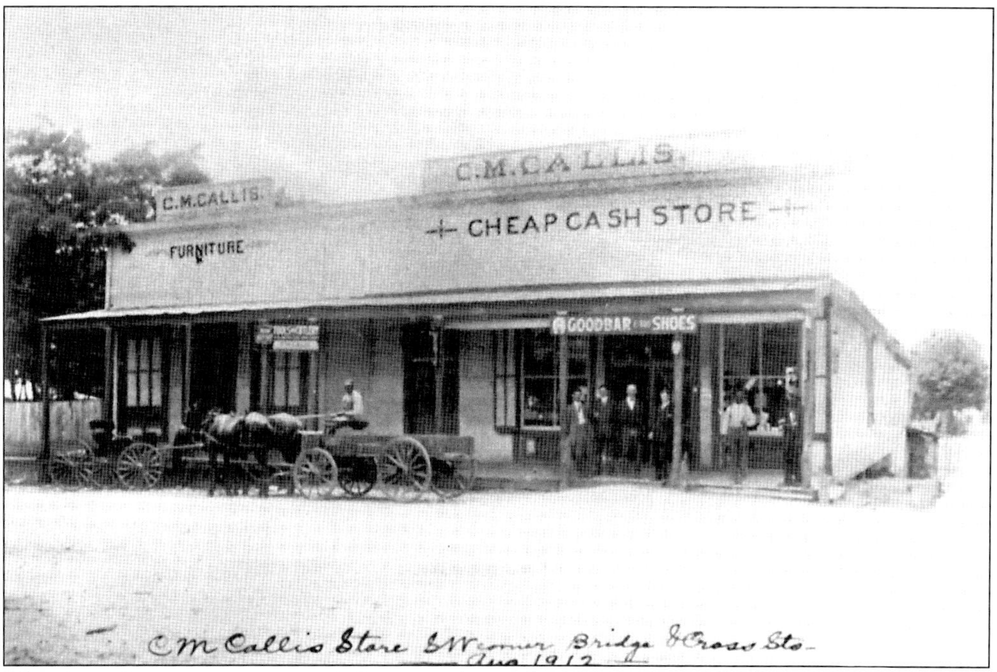

The first Germantown Post Office was located in the C. M. Callis Store, shown here around 1912.

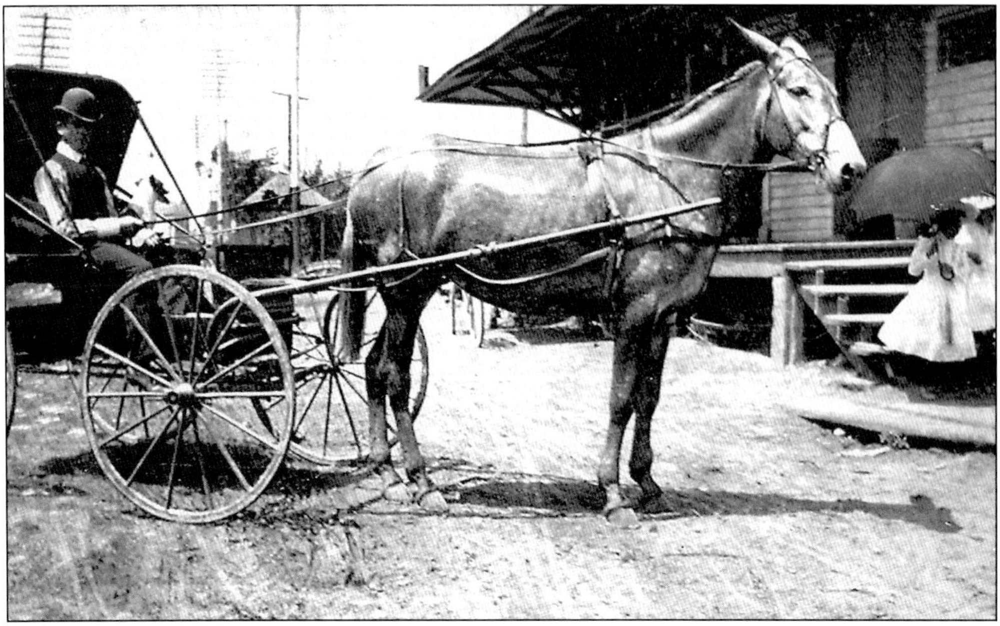

This 1912 photograph shows saloon owner James Turner outside the Germantown Depot.

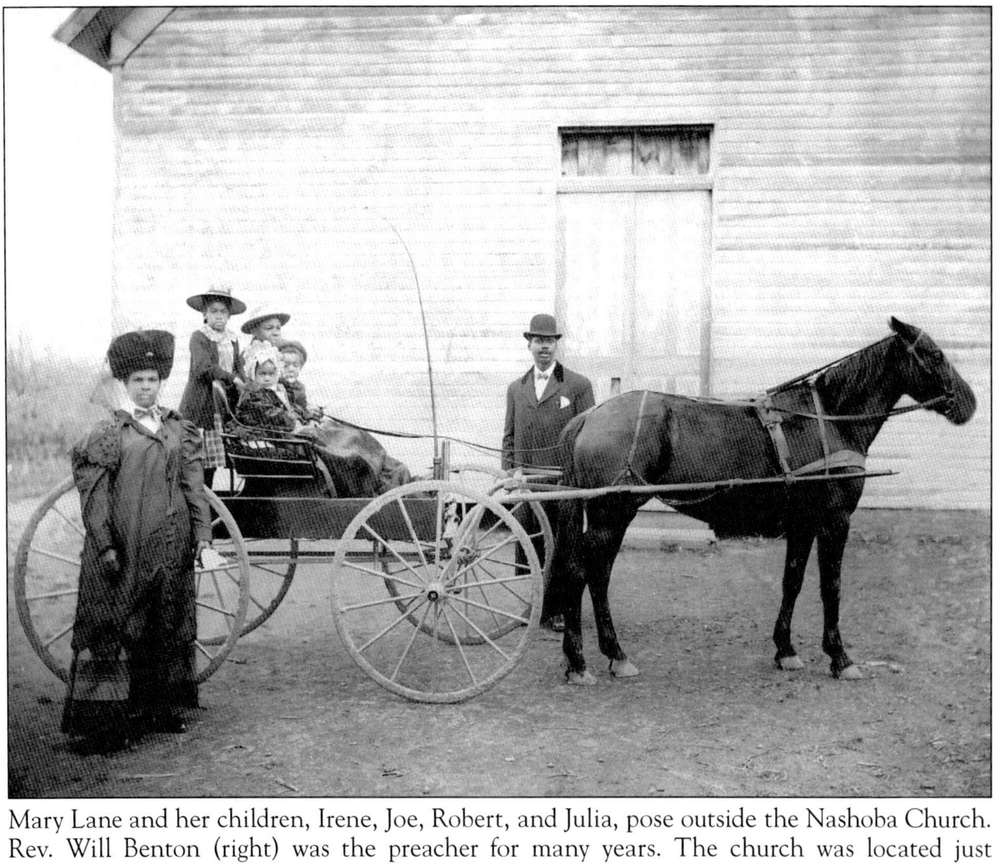

Mary Lane and her children, Irene, Joe, Robert, and Julia, pose outside the Nashoba Church. Rev. Will Benton (right) was the preacher for many years. The church was located just outside Germantown.

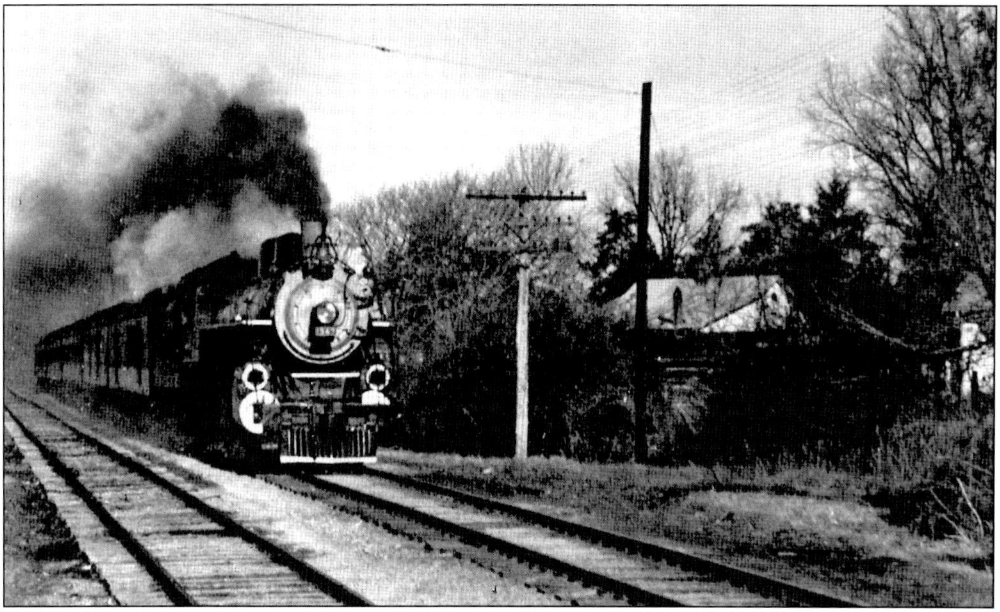

Engine #36 travels on its regular run from Memphis to Germantown and Collierville in 1942 along the Memphis-to-Charleston line. The rail line was originally laid in the 1850s and is the oldest in Shelby County.

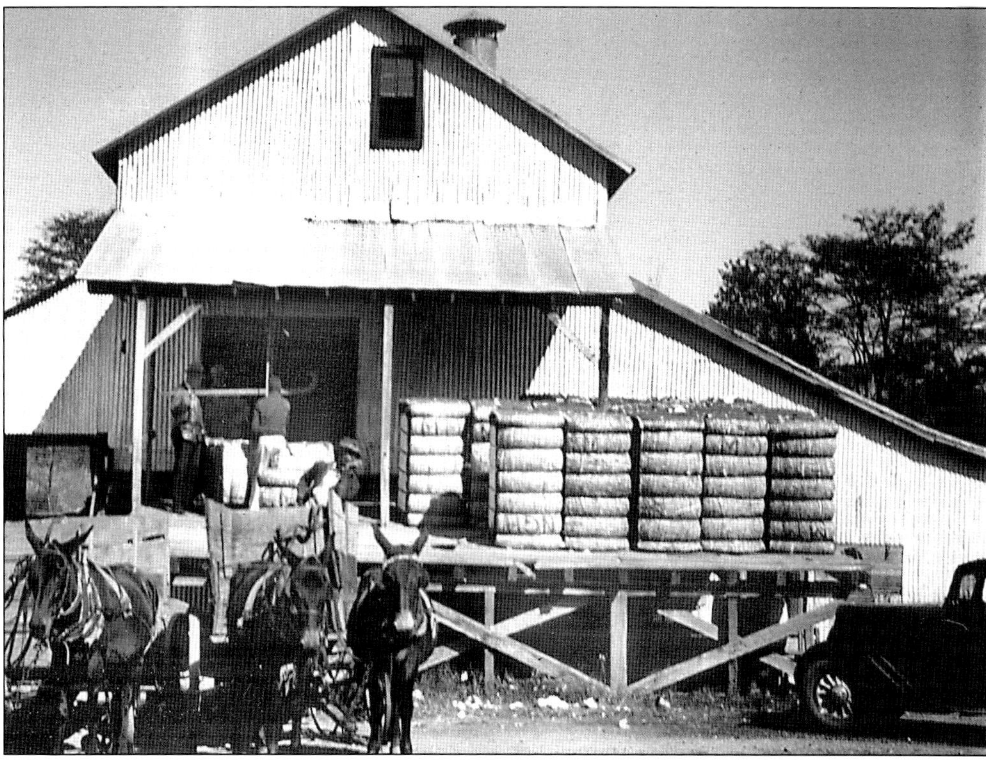

Built by C. M. Callis in 1912, the A. P. Foster Gin and Coal Company was located behind the Masonic lodge on Germantown Road. Farmers would bring their loose cotton for the gin to bale. Until the gin was closed in 1965, 900 to 1200 bales were produced each year.

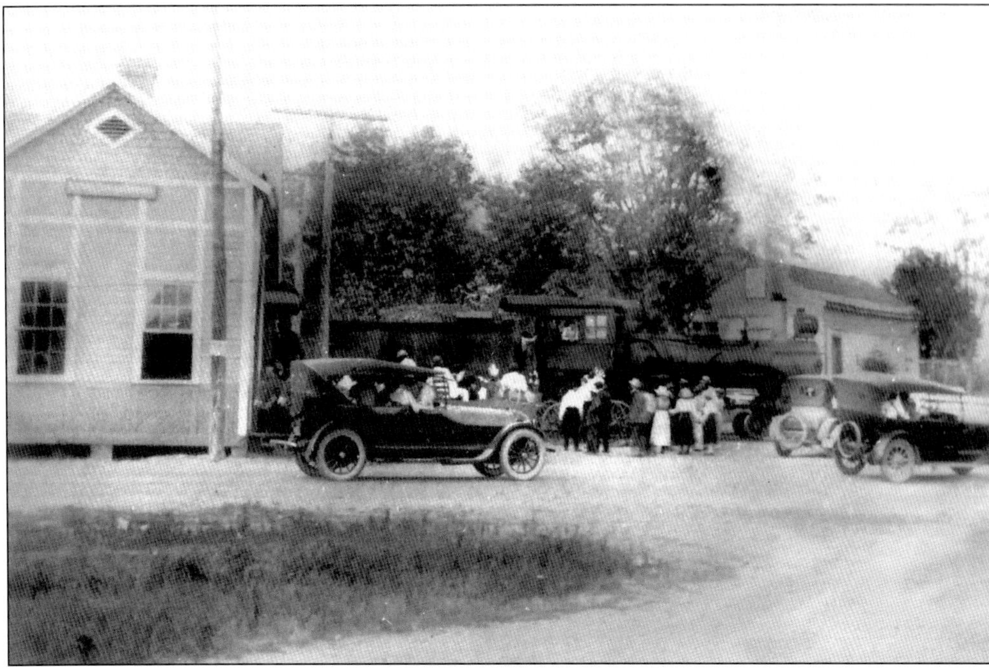

The Germantown depot, shown here around 1925, was a gathering place for the city. Commuters who worked in Memphis would travel by the passenger train called the *Somerville Accommodation*. The train conductor, Mike Brady, worked on the Memphis and Charleston line for over 50 years. He is seen here talking to passengers before they board the train.

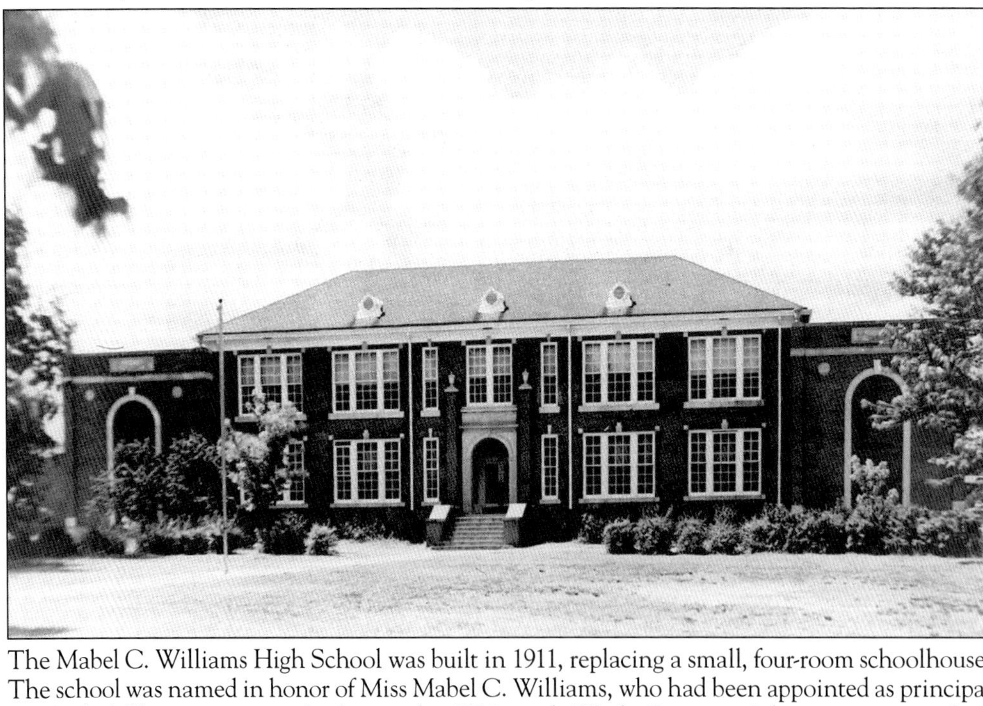

The Mabel C. Williams High School was built in 1911, replacing a small, four-room schoolhouse. The school was named in honor of Miss Mabel C. Williams, who had been appointed as principal in 1905. Additions were made during the 1930s with Works Progress Administration workers from Memphis. The school was torn down in 1973 to make way for a more modern high school.

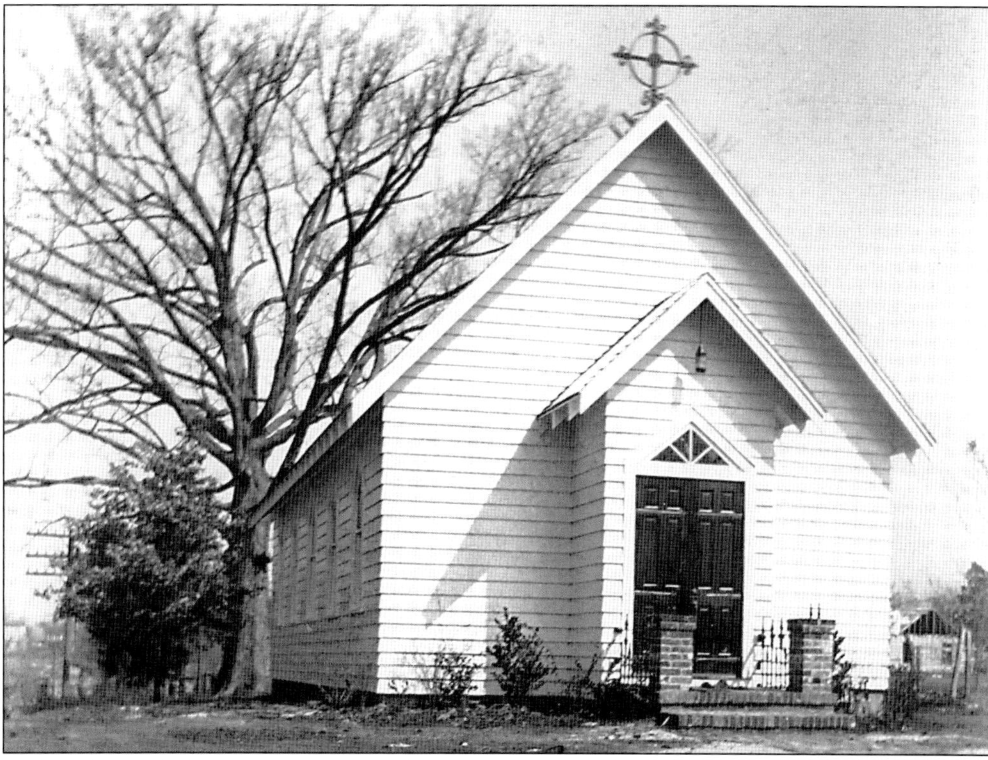

Built in 1934, St. George's Episcopal Church was dedicated on Easter Sunday 1937. In the early 1800s, members met in private homes; later services were held in the Presbyterian church and the Masonic lodge. Today the structure is used as a chapel at the church's current location on Poplar Avenue.

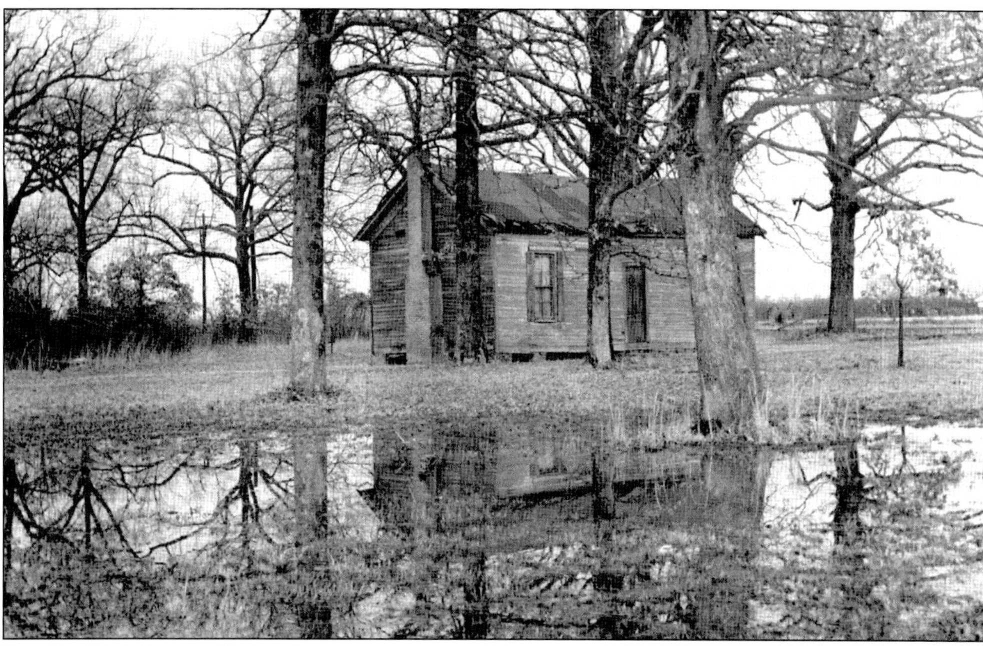

The Bedford farm at Bailey Station was located between Germantown and Collierville.

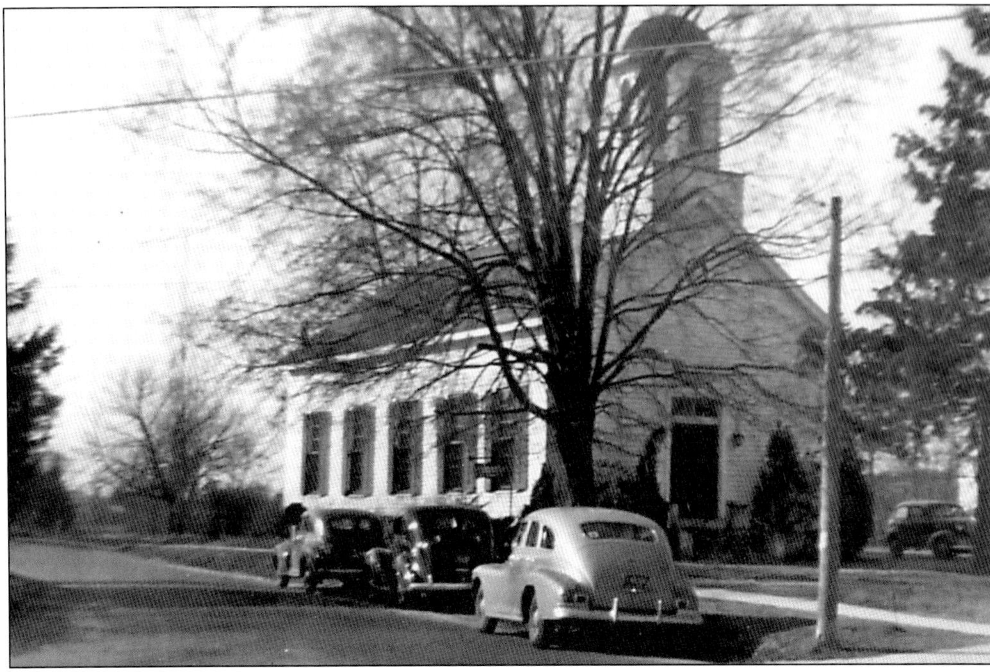

The Germantown Presbyterian Church dates back to 1838. The congregation built the sanctuary seen above in 1851, with a bell tower being added just after the Civil War. The church was saved from destruction during the war because the Union commander and the minister were both Masons. The Masonic lodge was also spared. In 1950, the church was moved from facing the north to facing the east.

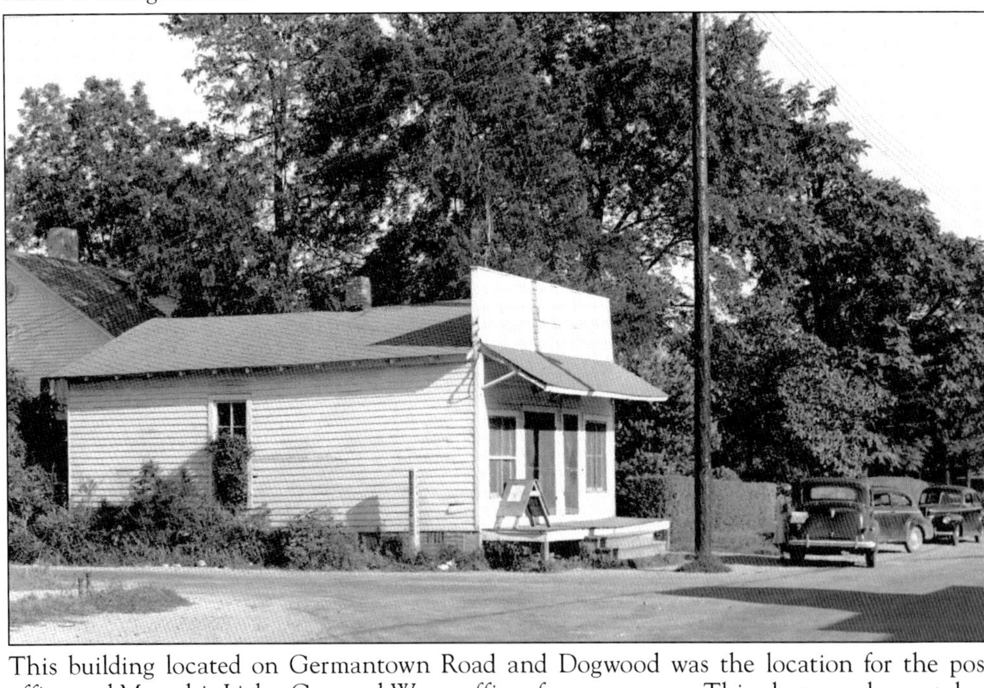

This building located on Germantown Road and Dogwood was the location for the post office and Memphis Light, Gas, and Water offices for many years. This photograph was taken around 1940.

Six

Collierville

Originally known as Oak Grove, the town of Collierville has a long and dramatic history. Situated on an old Native American trail that eventually became Poplar Avenue, Collierville's earliest settlers arrived in the 1820s and soon laid out the city we have today. William A. Tharp was awarded a grant from the state of Tennessee for 640 acres. On October 29, 1836, the first lots for the town of Collierville were sold by Jesse Collier and H. G. Barbee. Lots could be purchased for $10 to $15 per acre. The first post office moved from State Line Road in 1837 to Collierville with John W. Koen as postmaster. Its location between the Wolf River to the north and Nonconnah Creek to the south was a natural draw for homesteaders. Collierville was incorporated on February 7, 1850, with a total of 320 acres and 250 residents. Richard W. Ramsey was elected the first mayor.

A major boost to the young town was the laying of the Memphis and LaGrange Railroad in 1842. The line was finally finished in 1852 and purchased by the Memphis and Charleston Railway Company. A large barbecue was held on July 25, 1852, at the plantation of Eppy White to celebrate the completion of the line. Trains left from Beale Street daily and cost 50¢. A depot was built on land donated by Peter Adams. This structure was burned during the Civil War, and it was not until the 1880s that a modern facility was constructed at a cost of $4,299. Lighting was installed in 1916, and telephone service was added in 1927. A new depot was imported in 1944. Because building materials were scarce during World War II, it was decided to move the LaGrange depot to Collierville. The structure was cut in half and transported to Collierville. Its new location would be about 300 feet east of the old depot. In 1975, Mrs. James M. Russell wrote to the officials of the Southern Railway asking for the depot to be donated to the city of Collierville for the purpose of a museum. In 1976, the Southern Railway Company donated the depot, which today serves as the building for Main Street Collierville, a visitor and tourist information center.

By 1860, the city had doubled in size to 500 citizens with six stores, a flour mill, and one hotel. The city was self-supporting with doctors, dentists, lawyers, shoe repairers, blacksmiths, and carpenters. Eighty men volunteered for the Southern cause under the name Wigfall Grays, after a Texas senator who had given an impassioned speech supporting secession. They fought in some of the fieriest battles of the Civil War, including Shiloh, Atlanta, Missionary Ridge, and

Chickamauga. On October 11, 1863, William Tecumseh Sherman was traveling from Memphis to Corinth, Mississippi, by rail with 600 troops. As they approached Collierville, a Confederate force of 3,000 men under Gen. James R. Chalmers attacked the rail cars. The Confederates quickly overtook the rail cars and actually had time to eat Sherman's food and drink his wine. They also took his prize horse and a uniform with a sword. Before leaving the train, Sherman had telegraphed to Germantown that they needed reinforcements. Soon the train was recaptured by the Northern army and Collierville was restored to Union hands. The Memphis and Charleston Railroad was important as it supplied Corinth, Mississippi, a valuable city for the Union to hold. There were many other smaller battles in the Collierville area throughout the war, but October 11, 1863, was a day about which locals talked for years.

One of Collierville's unique features is its beautiful town square. Its central park was designed in 1867 and was originally enclosed with a white picket fence. A bandstand was added in the late 1870s. It was from this bandstand that W. C. Handy performed his "Memphis Blues," revivals were held, and numerous community functions took place. The structure was destroyed in 1955 by a tornado and was rebuilt in 1965. Although Collierville was incorporated in 1857, the war had caused government to cease so Collierville was re-incorporated in 1870, with J. B. Abington as mayor. Like many towns in Shelby County, Collierville was affected by yellow fever. One of the worst years was 1878: despite being quarantined, the city suffered 135 cases of the fever. Like many towns, cotton was king. In the late 1920s, dairies began to overtake cotton as a means of farming. Mostly due to the infestation of the boll weevil and the introduction of government crop subsidies, dairies became more profitable. Collierville today has a population of just over 40,000.

James B. Abington was elected mayor of Collierville in 1870. He became the first mayor after the town was re-incorporated. Collierville was originally incorporated in 1850 with Richard W. Ramsey as mayor, but it lost its charter during the Civil War. Collierville has been incorporated longer than any city in Shelby County including Memphis, which lost its charter in 1879 during the yellow fever epidemic.

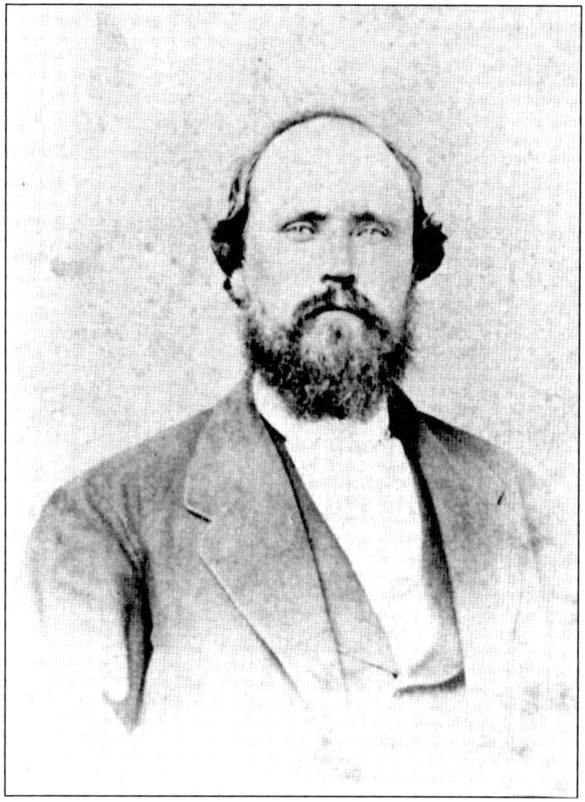

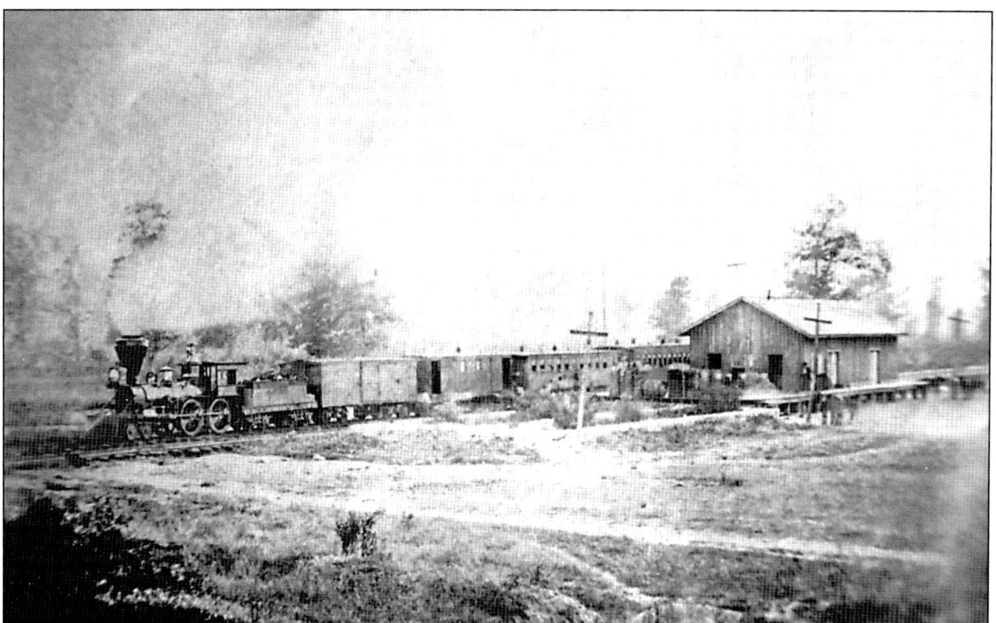

The Collierville depot, shown here around 1890, was built just after the Civil War. This was the second of four depots built in Collierville.

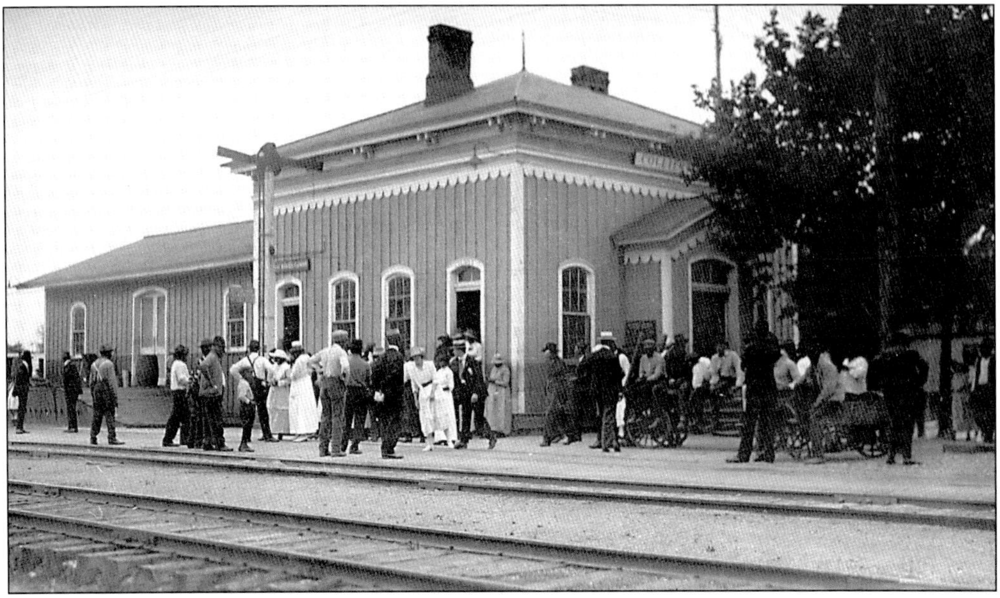

The Collierville depot was constructed in 1885 and was located west of the present-day structure. A large cotton platform adjoined the depot on the east side, with an ice house on the west side. For many years, a commuter train called the *Somerville Accommodation* transported passengers to and from Memphis. The train ran from 1856 until 1930. The train, operated for many years by engineer Mike Brady, arrived each morning at 7:00 a.m. Brady retired in 1930 after 50 years of service on the *Somerville Accommodation*. A round-trip ticket to Memphis cost around 20¢ in the 1920s.

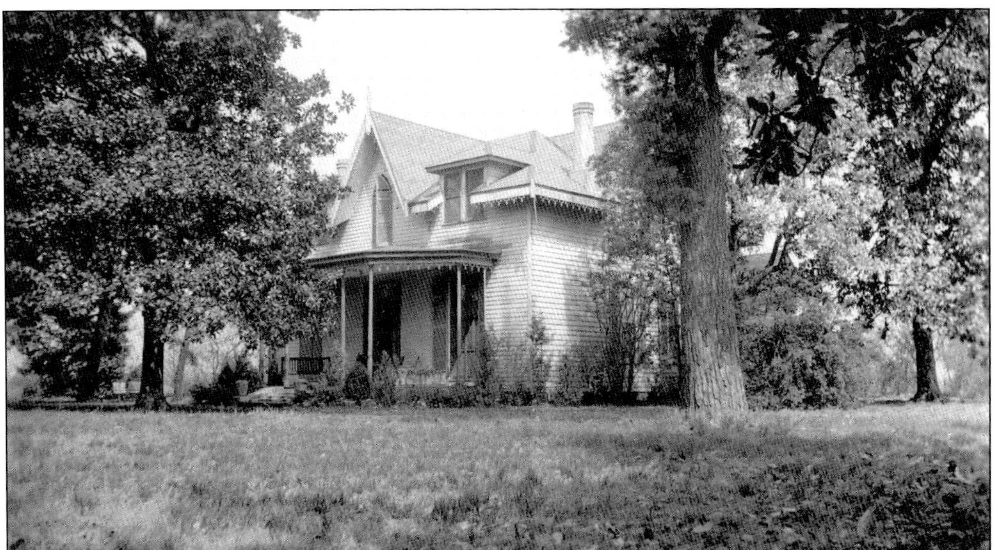

Built in the 1840s by Thomas Hill Peters, this two-story frame house was located on Poplar Avenue, west of Collierville. General Grant visited the owner, Josiah DeLoach, there during the Civil War on his way to Memphis. This visit was recorded by Grant in his diary, dated June 23, 1862. The house was torn down to make way for Baptist Hospital and is now a vacant lot.

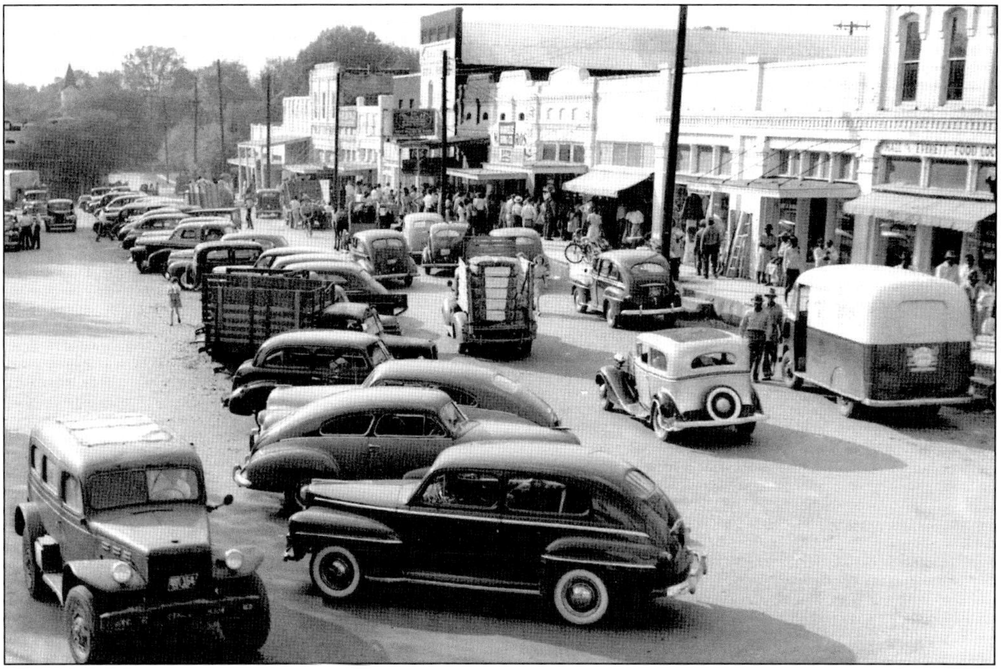

The Collierville town square, shown here in the 1940s, was unusual in that most towns with a central square had a courthouse in the center. The photographer, Paul Madison Wilson, documented the life and times in Collierville during the 1940s and 1950s.

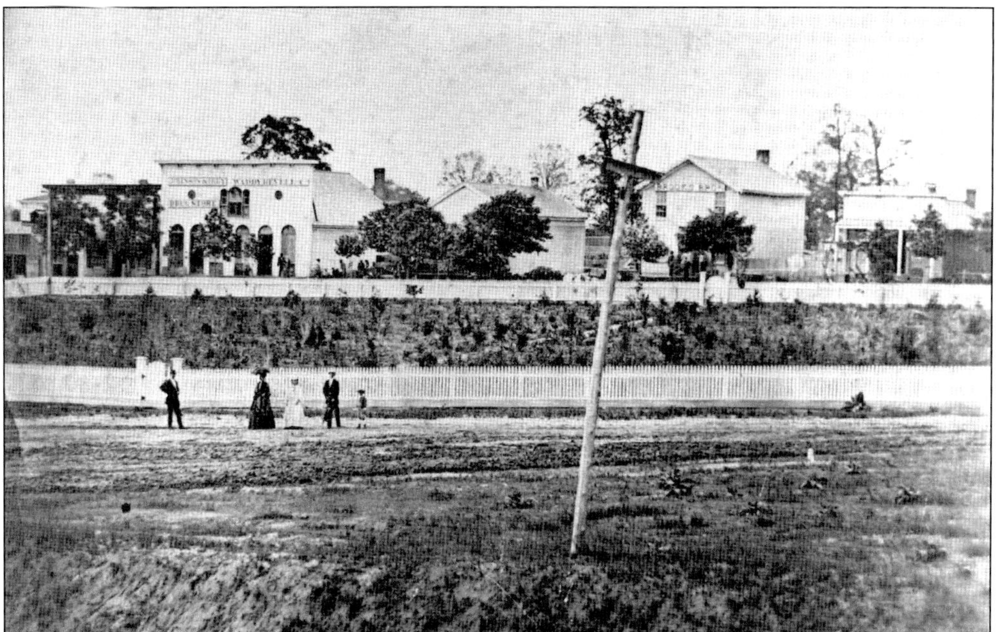

The tree-lined park in Collierville's town square was laid out in 1866. It was originally named Confederate Park and contained peacocks and a deer. The entire area was enclosed with a white picket fence. The two-story bandstand was constructed in 1876 and survived until 1955, when it was destroyed by a tornado.

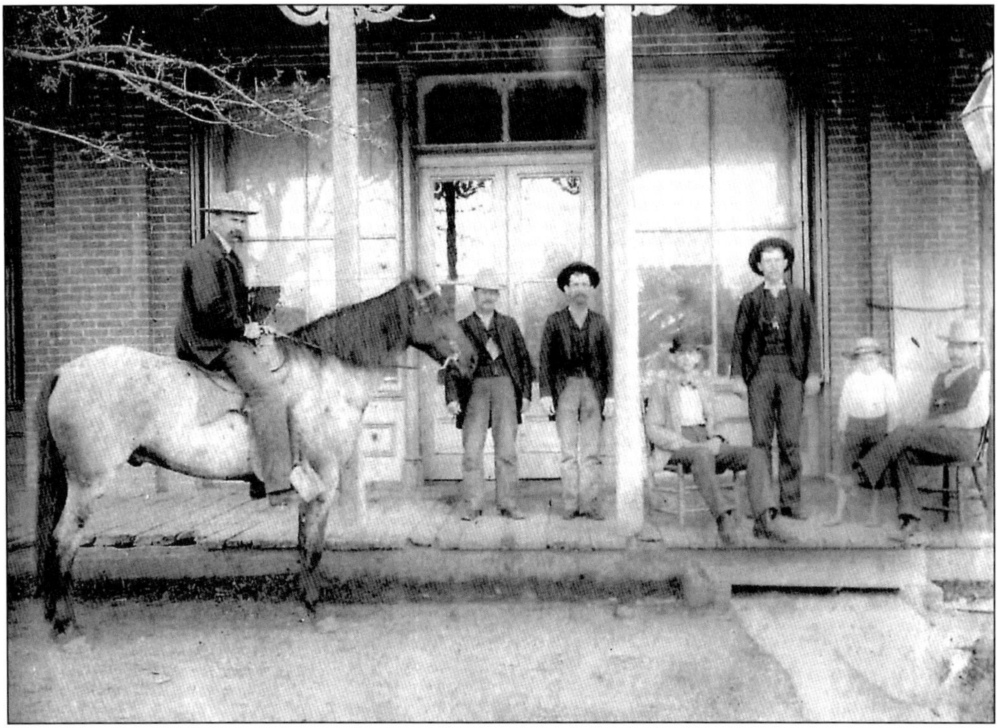

A dry goods and notions store was located at the corner of Center and Mulberry in the early 1900s. The man third from the right is James M. Northcross Jr. In 1897, the Collierville town square had 14 dry goods and grocery stores.

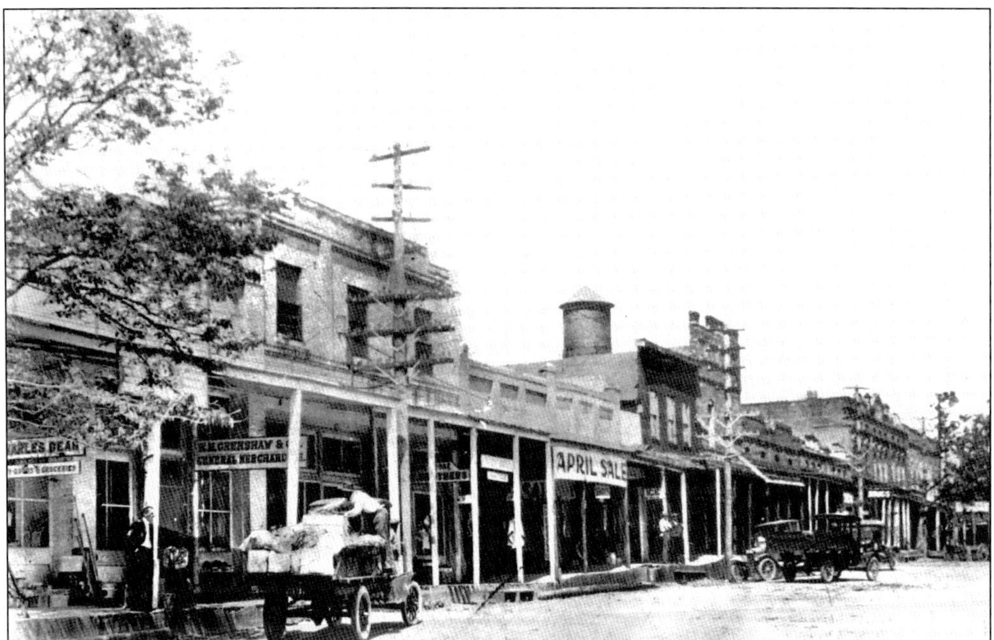

Stores located on the north side of the town square in 1900 included Charles Dean Groceries and H. H. Crenshaw General Merchandise. The city water tower can be seen in the distance.

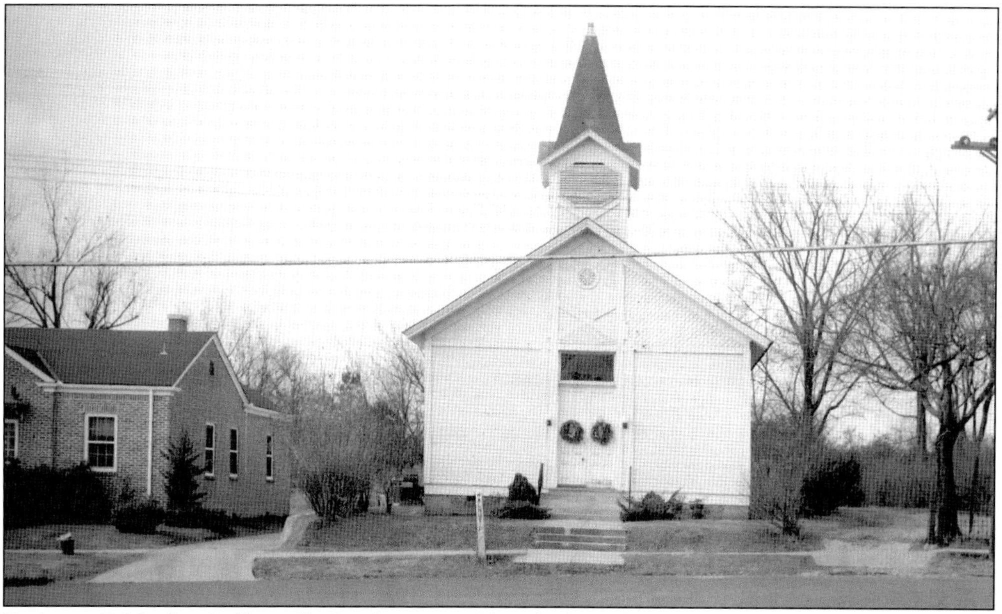

Built in 1886, the Collierville Presbyterian Church dates back to 1844, when a congregation was established called Salem. The church was chartered with 17 members and was located at Holmes and Byhalia Roads. From 1871 to 1886, it held services at the Collierville Methodist Church. The lot for the new church was purchased in 1885 from Mrs. Dora A. Clark for $100. Congregants continued to worship at this location until 1965.

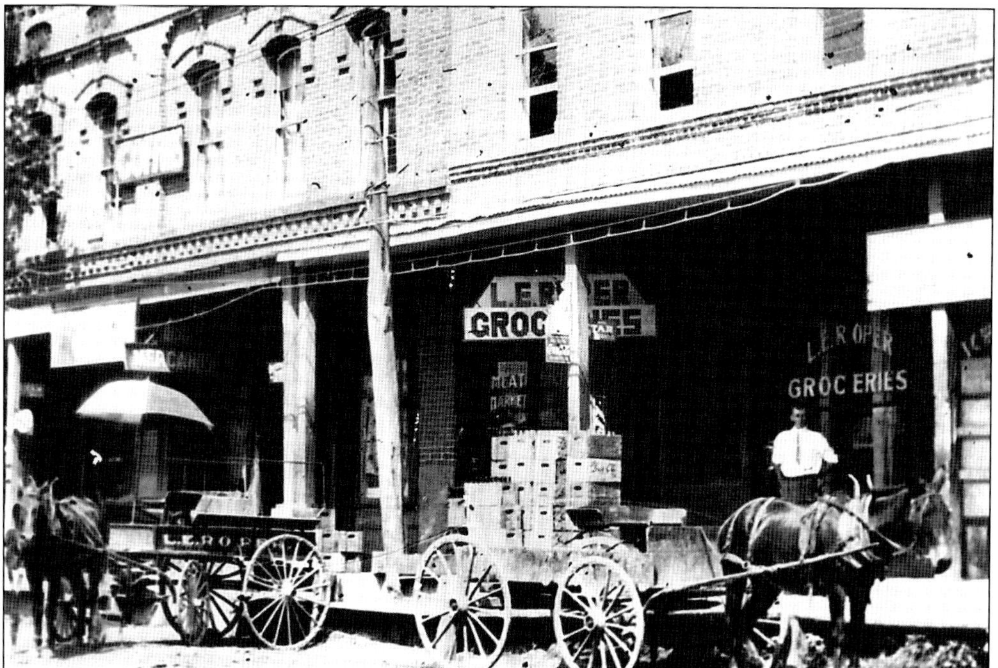

Collierville in 1890 had a population of over 1,200 citizens. The north side of the town square, shown above in 1892, included an undertaker, millinery shop, theater, druggists, and numerous general stores.

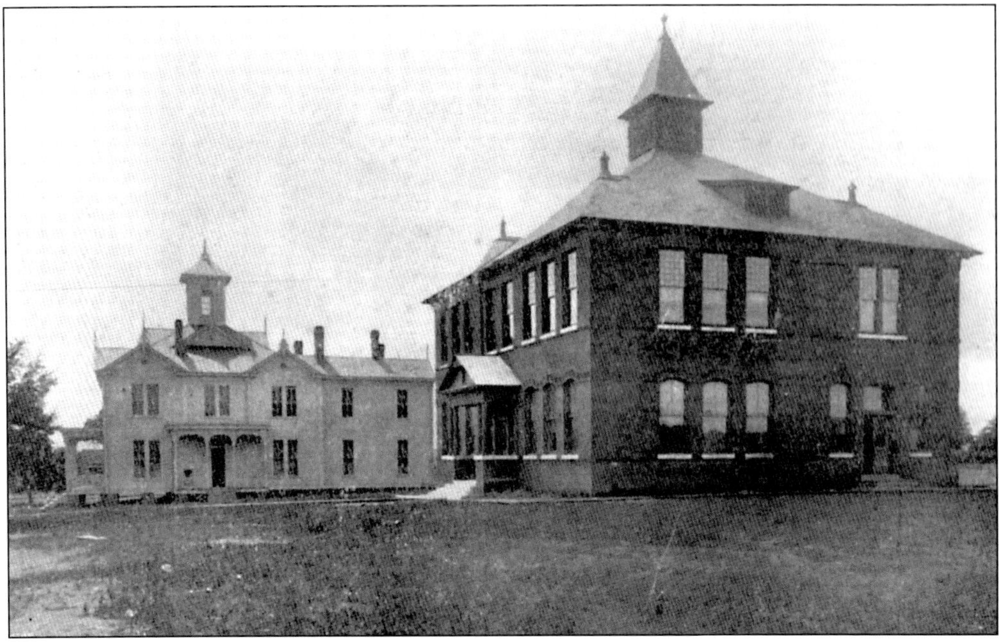

The Bellevue Female College was founded in 1872 and located on College Street, north of the town square. The school, on the right, was built in 1873; the boarding house is seen in the background. High school tuition was $3 per month, with an additional $13.50 for boarding. The school operated until 1904.

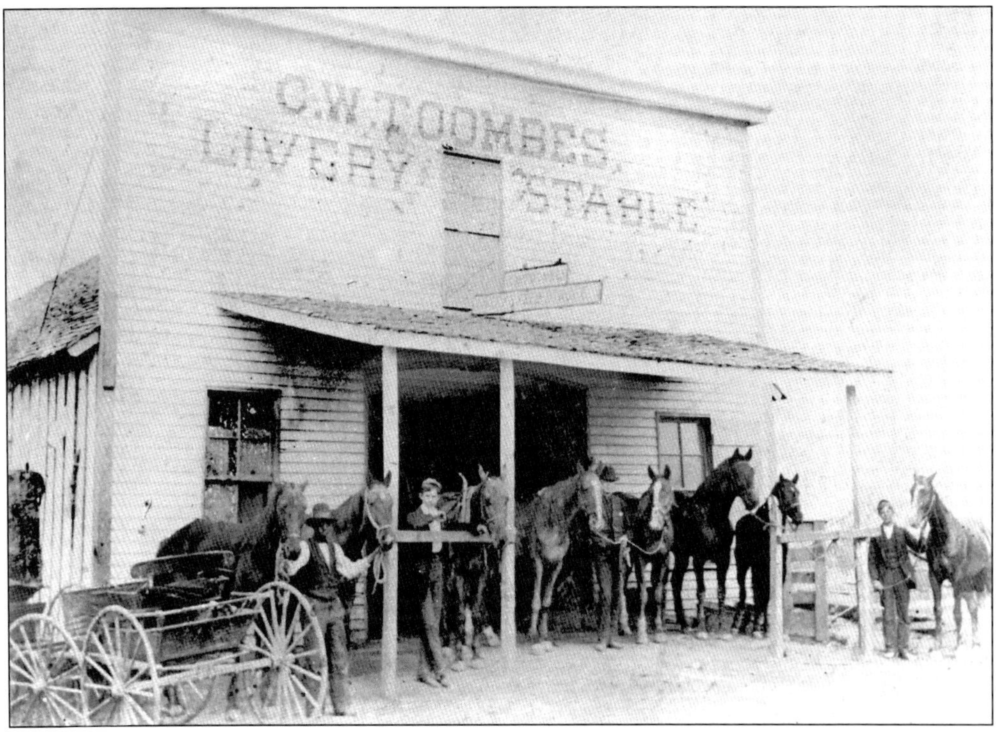

The C. W. Toombes Livery Stable was located on Main Street, north of the town square. Livery stables boarded horses as well as repaired wagons and buggies.

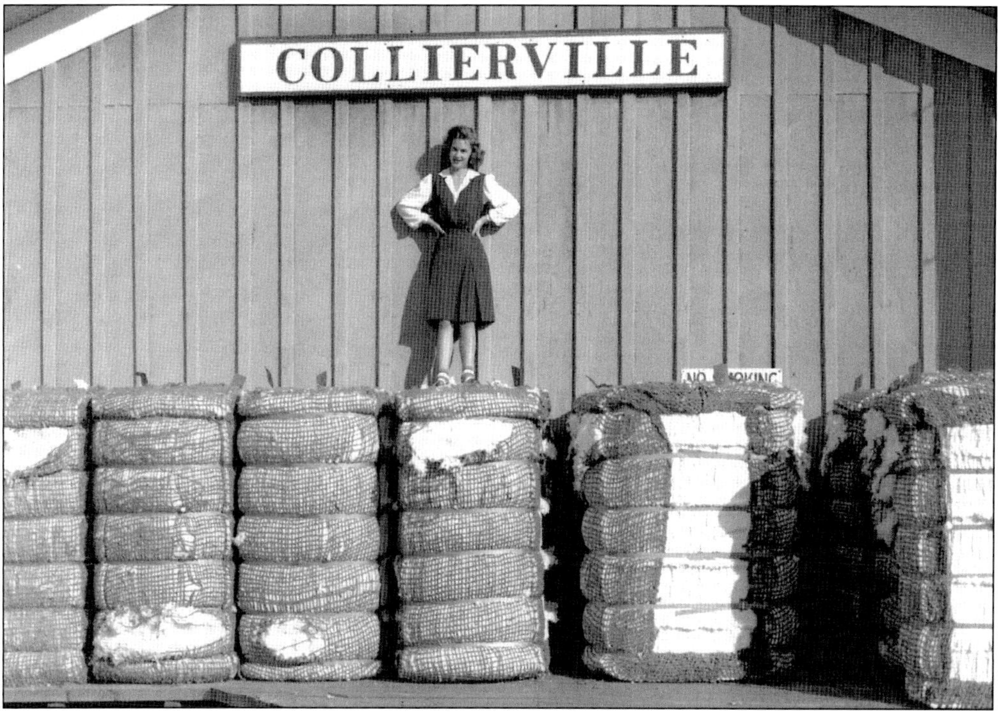

Dorothy Ann Wilson stands on cotton bales waiting for delivery at the Collierville depot in the 1940s. Collierville was a central market for farmers in Shelby, Fayette, and Desoto Counties. From here, they purchased supplies, had equipment repaired, and at harvest time sold their crops or transported them by train to larger markets.

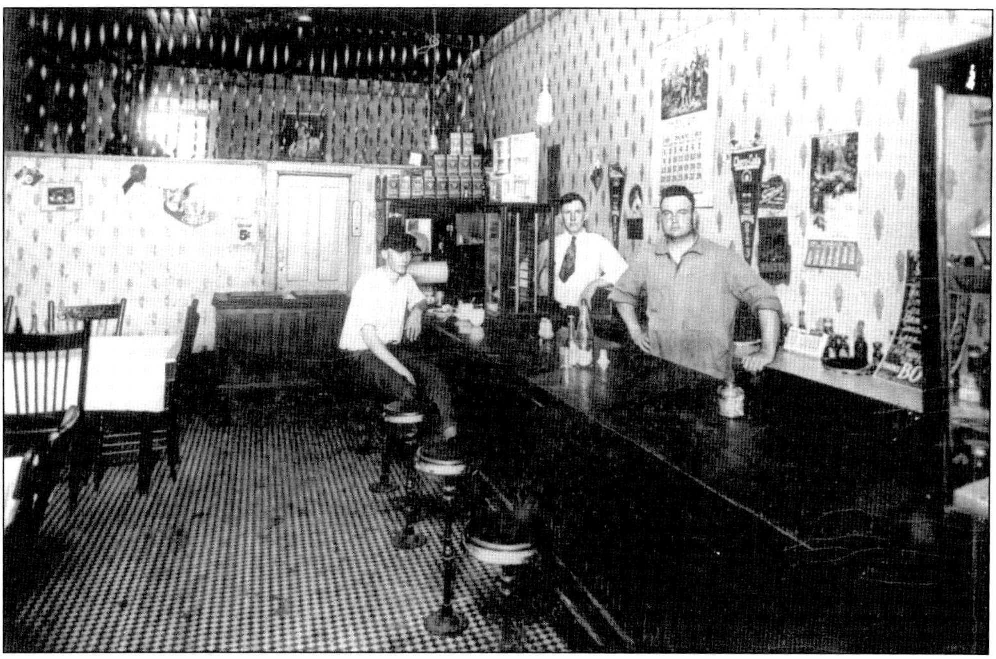

The White Café, shown here in 1922, was located on Main Street, south of Washington. Henry Scrader was the owner.

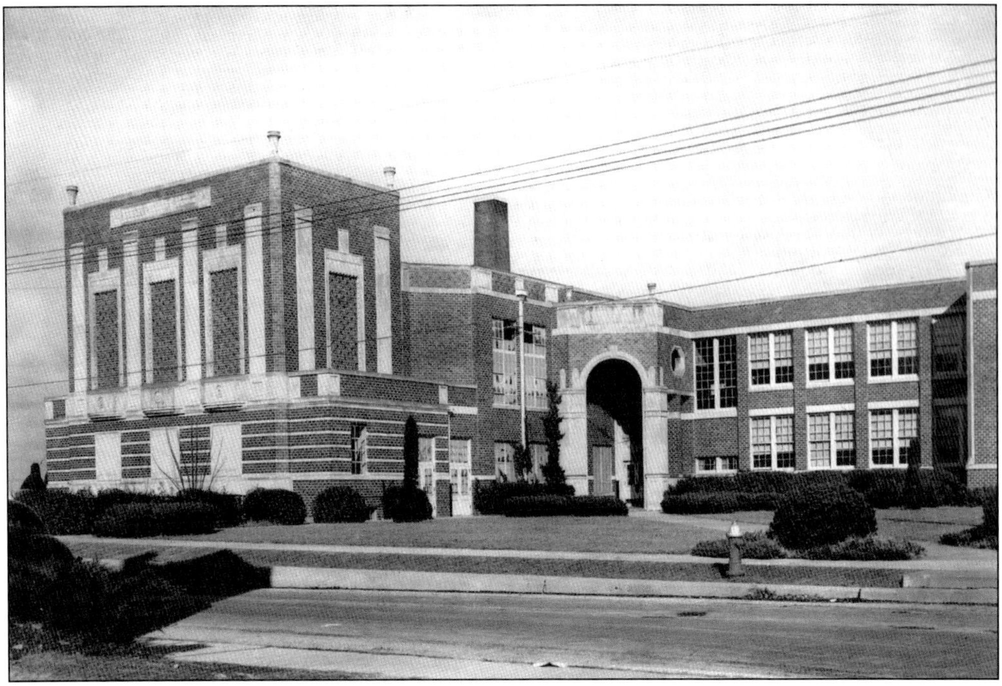

Collierville High School is situated on the same property that held the Bellevue Female College from 1872 to 1904. The high school was built in the early 1900s with additions made in 1911 and 1924. A large gymnasium was added in 1926. A teacher's salary averaged $40 per month during the 1910s. In the 1930s, Collierville High School became one the first buildings in Tennessee to be built by the Civilian Conservation Corps. An auditorium, library, and study hall were added over the years with hundreds of workers bused in from Memphis.

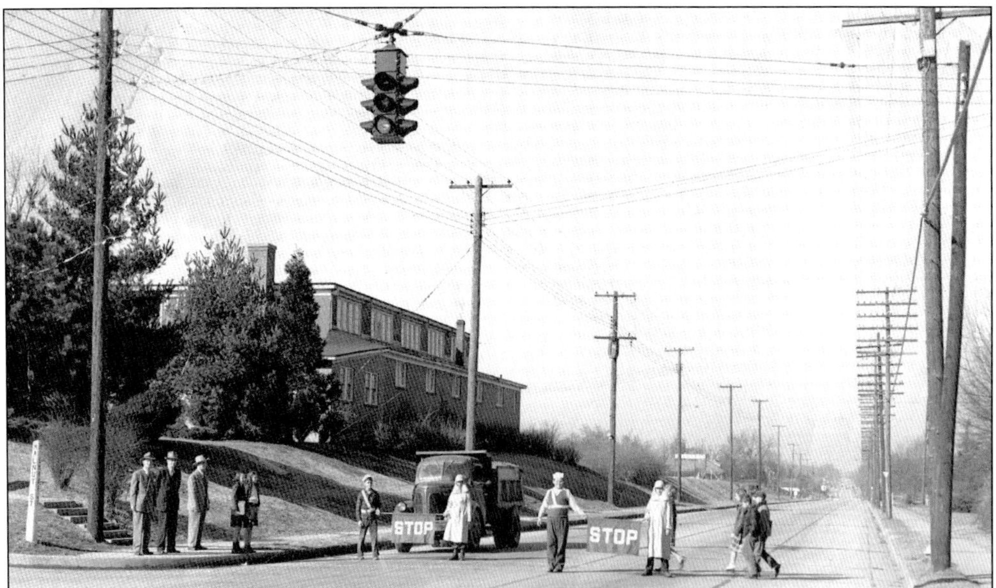

School crossing guards watch as students cross a deserted Highway 57 (present-day Poplar Avenue) in the 1940s.

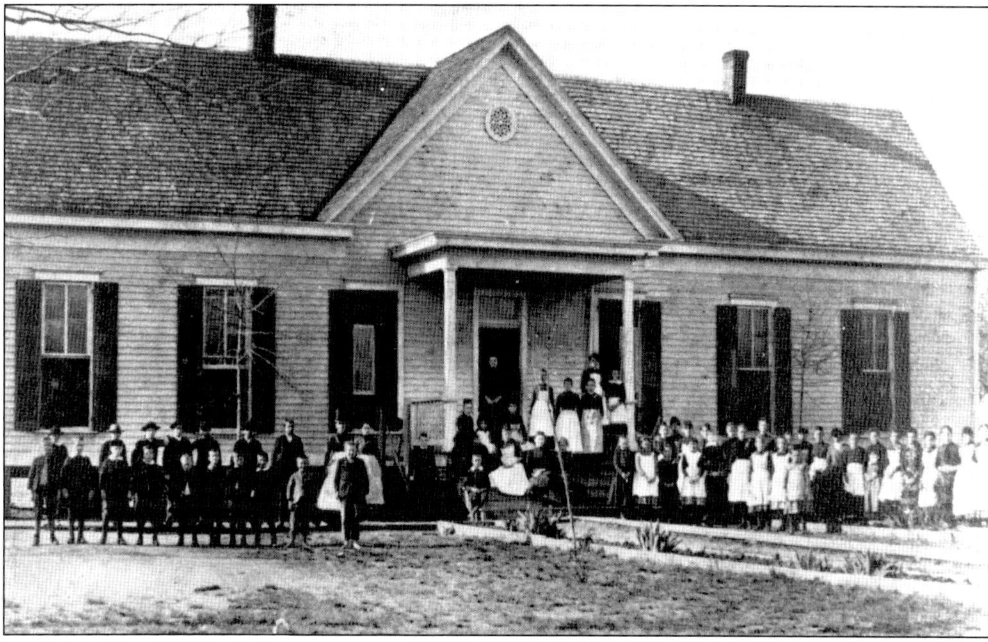

In 1881, Miss Holden's Seminary opened in Collierville on present-day Rowlett Street. The school, which was open to both boys and girls, was considered ahead of its time. Miss Anna Holden had graduated in 1859 from the LaGrange Institute and, with the help of her two brothers, established her school in Collierville. In 1893, it was purchased by the board of education.

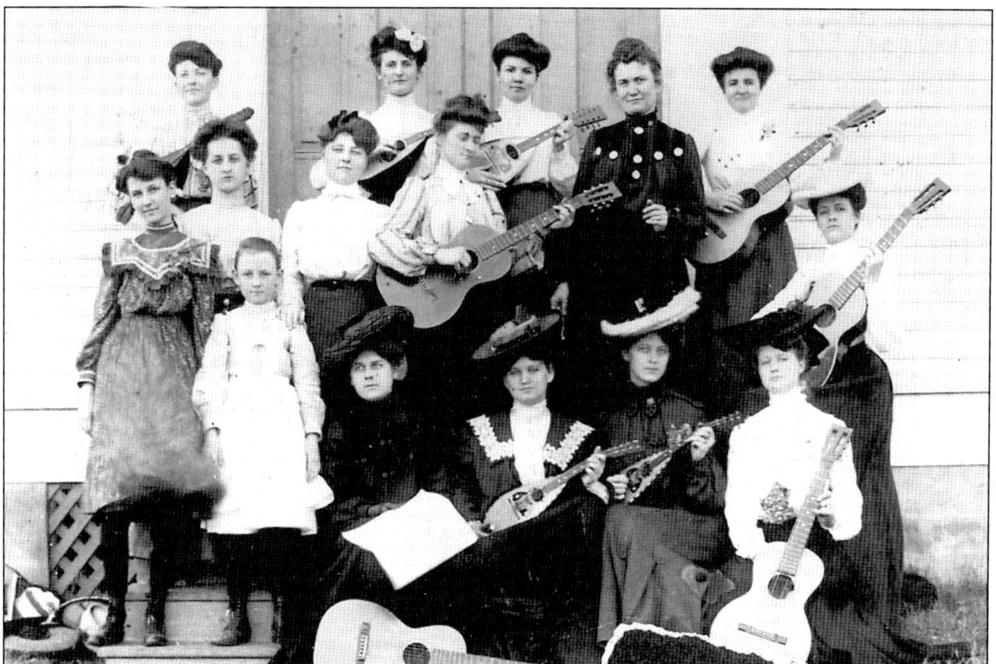

Music classes were held at Miss Holden's Seminary and conducted by Mrs. J. A. Holden. Students were charged an additional $4 per year, and a recital was held at the year's end. Students often entertained at local churches and festivals.

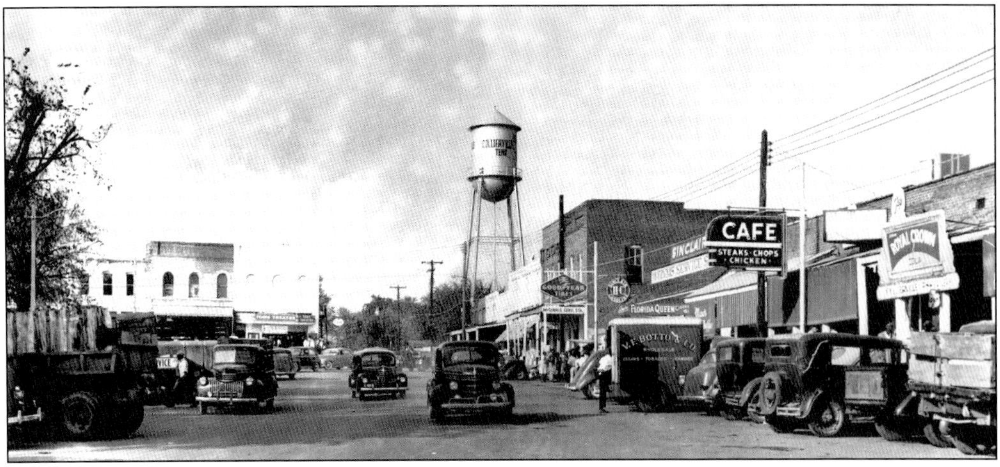

Located on the east side of the Collierville square, shown here in 1940, were a movie theater, Treadwell groceries and meats, McGinnis service station, city hall, and the Collierville cash grocery.

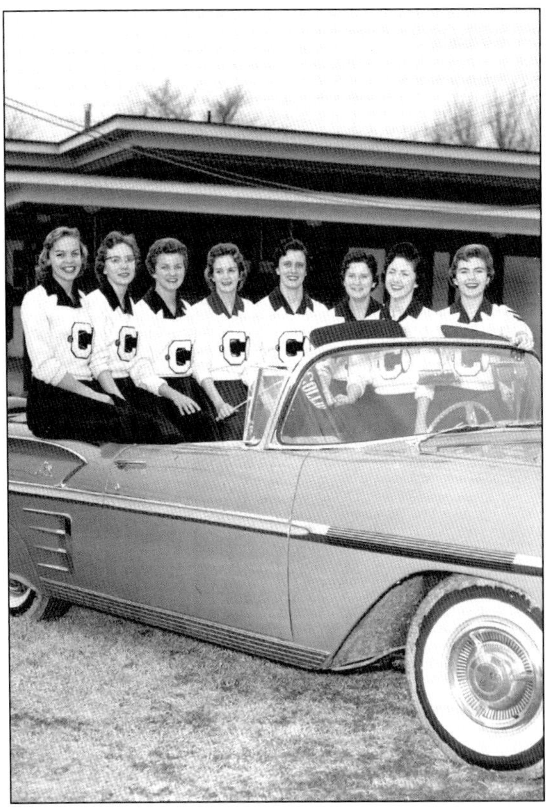

Collierville High School saw tremendous growth during the 1940s and 1950s. The school's athletic programs were always near the top in football and basketball. Collierville cheerleaders pose on a convertible in the 1950s.

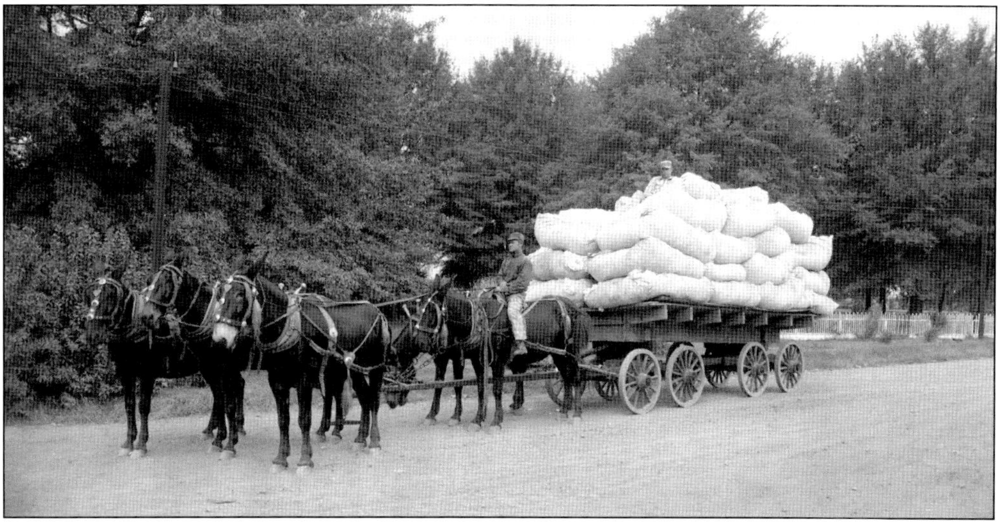

Cotton would be transported to the train station by mule-drawn wagons. Before the railroad, the trip could take days to reach the Memphis market. Rows of cotton bales sitting on the Collierville depot were a common sight as late as the 1950s.

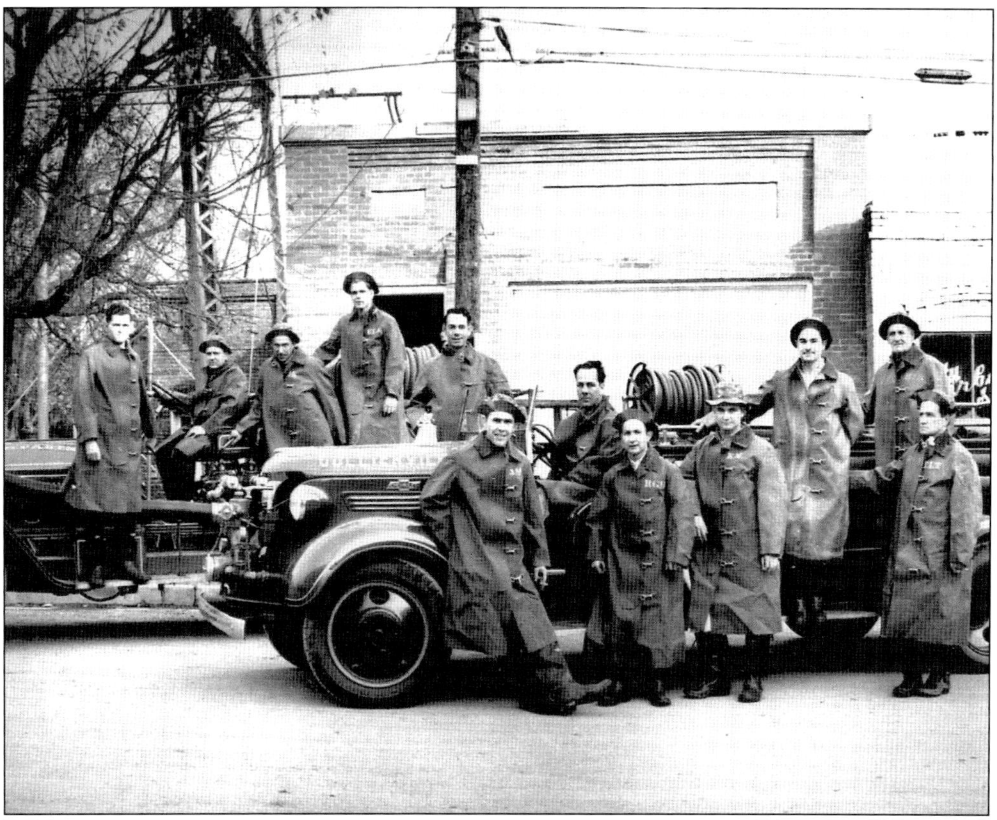

The 1946 Collierville volunteer fire department consisted of, from left to right, Lin Kelsey, Willard Ewing, Joe Ridgeway, Tommy Shepherd, Edgar Morton, Curtis Cox, Fred Hart, Garner Rutledge, Howard Jamison, Earl Parker, H. L. Sigrest, and O. C. Dean.

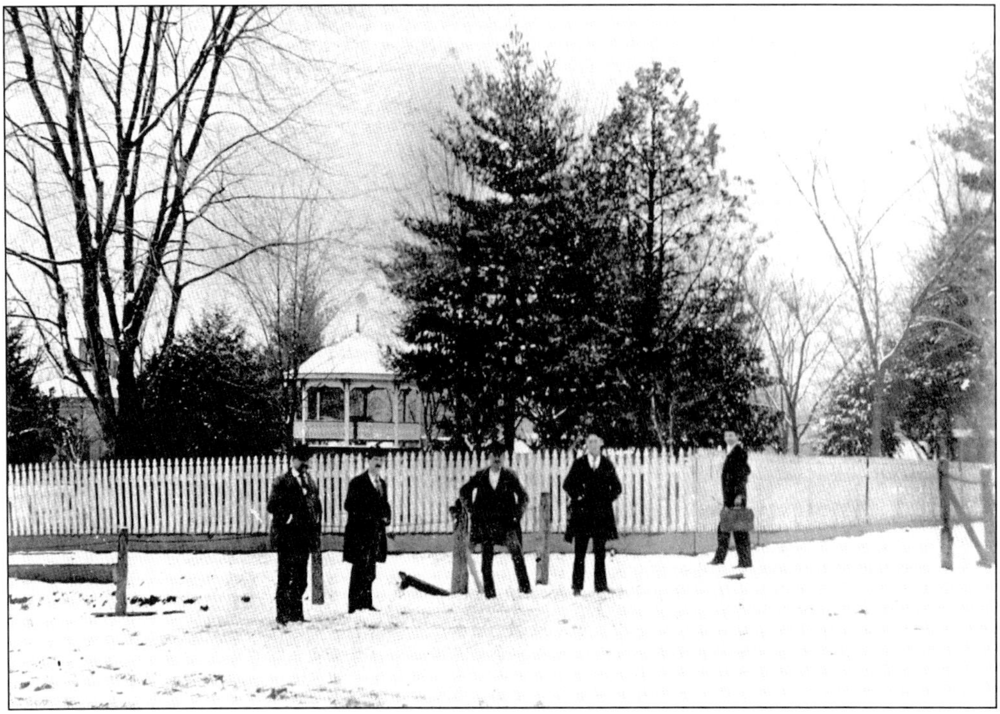

Confederate Park, seen here in the snow, has long been a gathering place for old and young alike. This photo, taken in 1900, shows, from left to right, Dudley Jones, unidentified, James Powell, W. H. Borun, and unidentified.

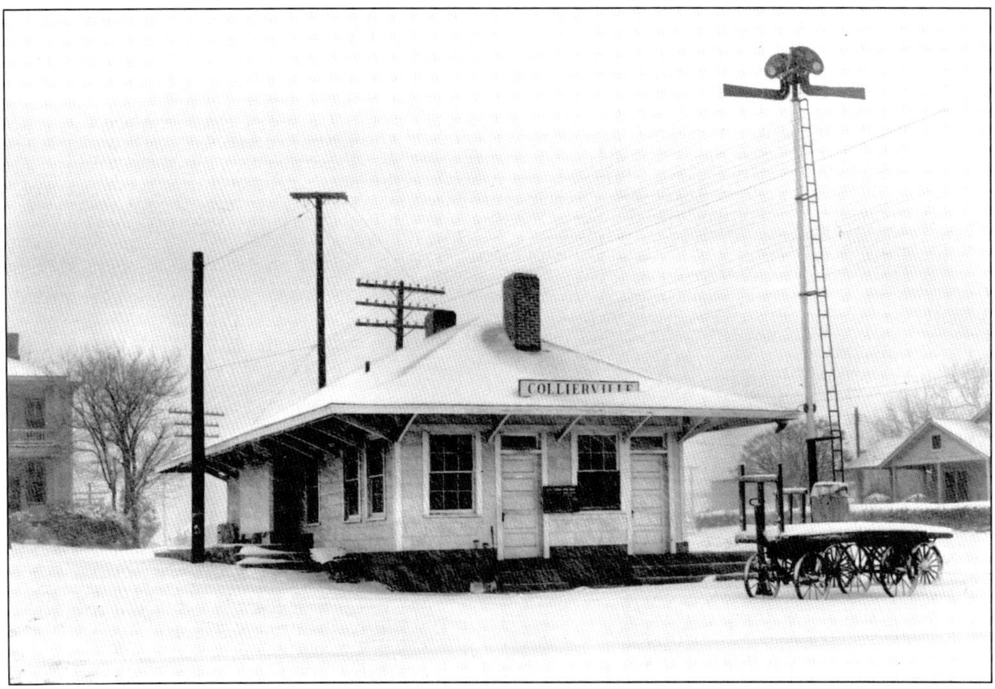

The Collierville depot, shown here in 1947, was originally the LaGrange depot and was transported to Collierville in two pieces by train.